1 MONTH of
FREE
READING

at
www.ForgottenBooks.com

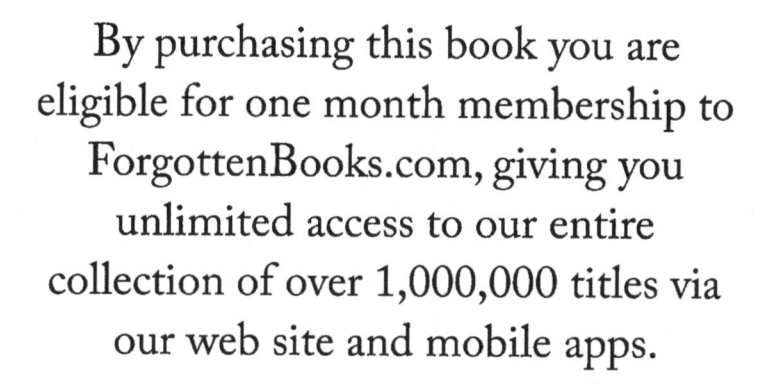

By purchasing this book you are eligible for one month membership to ForgottenBooks.com, giving you unlimited access to our entire collection of over 1,000,000 titles via our web site and mobile apps.

To claim your free month visit: www.forgottenbooks.com/free216926

* Offer is valid for 45 days from date of purchase. Terms and conditions apply.

English
Français
Deutsche
Italiano
Español
Português

www.forgottenbooks.com

Mythology Photography **Fiction**
Fishing Christianity **Art** Cooking
Essays **Buddhism** Freemasonry
Medicine **Biology** Music **Ancient Egypt** Evolution Carpentry Physics
Dance Geology **Mathematics** Fitness
Shakespeare **Folklore** Yoga Marketing
Confidence Immortality Biographies
Poetry **Psychology** Witchcraft
Electronics Chemistry History **Law**
Accounting **Philosophy** Anthropology
Alchemy Drama Quantum Mechanics
Atheism Sexual Health **Ancient History**
Entrepreneurship Languages Sport
Paleontology Needlework Islam
Metaphysics Investment Archaeology
Parenting Statistics Criminology
Motivational

1,000,000 Books

are available to read at

Forgotten Books

www.ForgottenBooks.com

Read online
Download PDF
Purchase in print

ISBN 978-1-331-64299-2
PIBN 10216926

This book is a reproduction of an important historical work. Forgotten Books uses state-of-the-art technology to digitally reconstruct the work, preserving the original format whilst repairing imperfections present in the aged copy. In rare cases, an imperfection in the original, such as a blemish or missing page, may be replicated in our edition. We do, however, repair the vast majority of imperfections successfully; any imperfections that remain are intentionally left to preserve the state of such historical works.

Forgotten Books is a registered trademark of FB &c Ltd.
Copyright © 2018 FB &c Ltd.
FB &c Ltd, Dalton House, 60 Windsor Avenue, London, SW19 2RR.
Company number 08720141. Registered in England and Wales.

For support please visit www.forgottenbooks.com

C. Tiebout Sc.

REV.D JOHN WESLEY A.M.

Engraved for his Life,
Published by John Hagerty, George Dobbin & T. Murphy.
Baltimore.

THE LIFE

OF THE

REV. JOHN WESLEY, A. M.

WITH

MEMOIRS OF THE WESLEY FAMILY.

TO WHICH ARE SUBJOINED,

Dr. WHITEHEAD'S FUNERAL SERMON,

AND

A COMPREHENSIVE HISTORY

OF

AMERICAN METHODISM.

BY GEORGE BOURNE.

In sermone, conversatione, charitate, spiritu, fide, et in castitate, fidelium exemplar.

BALTIMORE:

PRINTED BY GEORGE DOBBIN AND MURPHY,
FOR THEMSELVES,
JOHN HAGERTY AND ABNER NEAL.

1807.

Copy-Right Secured.

TO THE

Ministers and Members

OF THE

METHODIST CHURCH;

AND

TO ALL THOSE WHO LOVE

OUR LORD JESUS CHRIST,

IN SINCERITY:

THIS VOLUME

IS

Respectfully and affectionately inscribed

BY

THE AUTHOR.

PREFACE.

THIS volume however deficient in other respects, has the most powerful recommendation, novelty. *Even to the numerous members of the church which in this country has been formed by the ministers in connection with the late Mr.* WESLEY, *the events of his life are very imperfectly known ; and the Christian professors of other sects hold opinions of the founder and nature of Methodism, so inaccurate, that this history has been ardently desired,—to impart information to the Societies, and to correct illiberal mistakes.*

The Christian feels a peculiar interest in the portrait of those men and gospel ministers, whose piety " *like a city set upon a hill, could not be hid ;*" *whose example so luminously shone among men* " *that others seeing their good works, glorified their Father who is in heaven ;*" *whose zeal for the Redeemer animated them to surmount every difficulty to propagate that heavenly doctrine,* " *which is a faithful saying and worthy of all acceptation, that Jesus Christ came into the world to save even the chief of sinners ;*" *and whose perseverance and efforts, aided by the Spirit of God, were crowned with unusual success ;* " *numberless sinners being converted from darkness to light,*

I make no apology for the manner in which this work is executed. It required no colouring, it demanded no painting and artificial dress to recommend it: its own intrinsic value and excellence will introduce it where the gospel is beloved, and where Christian ministers are esteemed.

The Life of Mr. Wesley will, I hope, expand the hearts of all those who may study it, and the brilliancy of his example stimulate them to "follow him as he followed Christ." If it confirm the resolution of one drooping Christian, and if it convince one soul only who is now a stranger to the blessed Redeemer; the best of all objects will be promoted:—and if the Author's defects be concealed by the strength of faith, hope, joy, humility and penitence, which it is calculated to excite—much benefit will be derived from this display of the real character of Mr. Wesley, and the genuine nature of Methodism.

Baltimore, June 13, 1807.

OF THE

REV. JOHN WESLEY, A. M.

THE WESLEY FAMILY.

Mr. John Wesley, Senior.

MR. WESLEY's grandfather John Wesley was a nonconformist minister, and one of the worthies ejected by the act of uniformity from his living in Dorsetshire. After having encountered numberless difficulties and trials, a gentleman who owned a house at Preston, gave him the use of it free of any charge for rent; and there he continued until he was released from this vale of tears to dwell where Jesus reigns in glory. His residence in that village led to the formation of a connection with a society of Christians as their Pastor at Poole, in which relation he ministered to them until the day of his death: and although he shewed all possible prudence in the management of his meetings—he was often disturbed, several times apprehended, and four times imprisoned. He died about the year 1670, previous to his father's dissolution, who had also been expelled from his pastoral functions, and who was so much affected with the loss of his son, that he did not long survive him.

Dr. Annesley.

Dr. Annesley, the father of Mr. Wesley's mother, one of the ejected Non-conformist ministers, was a remarkable instance of the directing Providence of God, through the whole of his life. He had in his infancy conceived a desire for the ministerial work; and not long after the death of his father, which event occurred when he was four years of age only, he began the practice of reading twenty chapters in the holy scriptures daily, which he afterwards continued. Whilst very young, but after he had formed his resolution concerning the ministry, he dreamt that he was a clergyman, and that he was summoned to attend the Bishop of London to be burnt as a martyr. At the age of fifteen he entered Oxford, and took his degrees according to the usual course. In 1644, he was ordained chaplain of the ship Globe, at that time commanded by the admiral. He made a voyage with the fleet; but having no fondness for a maritime life, he speedily retired from it, and was settled at Cliff, where he was at first most violently opposed—but his piety, forbearance, fortitude and perseverance surmounted every obstacle, and those who had threatened to stone him, separated from him upon his removal to London with tears and much affection.

He was invited to London in 1652, was unanimously chosen to the parish of John the Apostle, became lecturer of St. Pauls—and in 1658 was called to Cripplegate. Subsequent to his ejectment, he suffered much for his non-conformity, but he continued stedfast: the Providence of God signally and frequently interposing for him; and one person was summoned to Heaven's dread tribunal, whilst signing the warrant to apprehend him. After a most exemplary life, he died as he had lived, in the full enjoyment of the favour of God, and in 1696 resigned his soul to his heavenly Father, leaving us a memorial "how to live and how to die."

Mr. Samuel Wesley, senior.

Mr. Samuel Wesley, the son of Mr. John Wesley, was not more than nine years of age at the time of his father's dissolution. He imbibed his prejudices against the dissenters at a very early age, and entered Exeter college Oxford, without having consulted any of his relations. At this time his fortune consisted of two pounds sixteen shillings; but by assisting the younger students—and instructing those who applied to him, he supported himself until he took his Bachelor's degree:—as soon as he had procured this testimonial he removed to London, his property having increased to ten pounds fifteen shillings. Here he was ordained Deacon, supplied a curacy during one year, and afterwards accepted of an appointment as chaplain in the fleet. He officiated on board twelve months, and then returned to London, where he obtained a curacy for two years, married, and was presented to a small living in the country, as a reward for some publications which had raised him into notice, and rendered him popular. Being a man of high church principles, and having been known by some publications against the dissenters which manifested much intolerance, he was requested by the friends of James II. to support the declaration in favour of popery, with promises of preferment: but this he absolutely refused, and preached a bold sermon against the King's measures from the example of the children in the fiery furnace. Mr. Wesley was one of the first writers in defence of the revolution of 1688; he dedicated his work to Queen Mary, who soon after gave him the living of Epworth, Lincolnshire, to which was added in 1723 that of Wroote. He would have attained to some rank in the church through the influence of the Duke of Marlborough, had he not so virulently opposed the whigs at the beginning of Queen Anne's reign; but from this period it appears, that he perceived the evil tendency of his want of christian love, and applied himself entirely to his pastoral duties, and the studies immediately connected with them. This gentleman possessed considerable genius and erudition: he was the author of a Latin commentary on the book of Job—the history of the Bible—the life of Christ, and some smaller pieces in verse. His piety was sterling and influential, and after a long and useful life, he died at Epworth in April, 1735. Mr. Charles Wesley related that event to his brother Samuel in a letter which merits insertion :——

Dear Brother,

After all your desire of seeing my father alive, you are at last assured you must see his face no more till he is raised in incorruption. You have reason to envy us who could attend him in the last stage of his illness. The few words he could utter I saved, and hope never to forget. Some of them were, " Nothing is too much to suffer for heaven. The weaker I am in body, the stronger and more sensible support I feel from God. There is but a step between me and death ; to-morrow I would see you all with me round this table, that we may once more drink of the cup of blessing, before we drink it new in the kingdom of God. With desire have I desired to eat this passover with you before I die." The morning he was to communicate, he was so exceedingly weak and full of pain, that he could not without the utmost difficulty receive the elements, often repeating, " Thou shakest me, thou shakest me ;" but immediately after receiving, there followed the most visible alteration. He appeared full of faith and peace, which extended even to his body ; for he was so much better, that we almost hoped he would have recovered. The fear of death he entirely conquered, and at last gave up his latest human desires of finishing Job, paying his debts, and seeing you. He often laid his hand upon my head, and said, " Be steady! The christian faith will surely revive in this kingdom; you shall see it, though I shall not." To my sister *Emily* he said, " Do not be concerned at my death, God will then begin to manifest himself to my family." When we were met about him, his usual expression was, " Now let me hear you talk of heaven." On my asking him whether he did not find himself worse, he replied, " O my *Charles*, I feel a great deal; God chastens me with great pain, but I praise him for it, I thank him for it, I love him for it." On the 25th his voice failed him, and nature seemed completely spent, when on my brother's asking, whether he was not near heaven, he answered distinctly, and with the most of hope and triumph that could be expressed in sounds, " Yes I am." He spoke once more, just after my brother had used the commendatory prayer; his last words were, " Now you have done all!" This was about half an hour after six, from which time till sun-set, he made signs of offering up himself, till my brother again having used the commendatory prayer, the very moment on which it was finished, he expired. His passage was so smooth and sensible, that notwithstanding the stopping of his pulse, and the ceasing of all signs of life and motion, we continued over him a considerable time, in doubt whether the soul was departed or not. My mother, who for several days before he died, hardly ever went into his chamber but she was carried out again in a fit, was far less shocked at the news than we expected, and told us that now she was heard, in his having so easy a death, and her being so strengthened to bear it."

Mrs. Wesley.

Mrs. Wesley, the mother of Mr. John Wesley, was the daughter of Dr. Annesley, and some years younger than her husband. She enjoyed the privilege of a pious education, and early imbibed a reverence for religion;

before she was thirteen years of age, she had examined the controversy between the Dissenters and the Episcopacy—and immediately subsequent to that scrutiny, studied the evidences of natural and revealed religion with sedulous care. Although she always employed one hour in the morning and one in the evening in devotional exercises, unless prevented by sickness, or any insuperable engagement, no woman was more diligent or more attentive in her domestic duties. She had nineteen children, ten of whom grew up to be educated: this duty fell upon her, and it was impossible for the children to have had a better instructor: she had acquired some knowledge of the Latin and Greek languages in her youth, had read much, thought deeply, and in general very accurately on every part of natural and revealed religion, and on the common affairs of life: she had studied human nature well, and knew how to adapt her discourse either to youth or age; she had commenced in life with a determination to think and judge for herself, and not to be influenced by custom in matters of importance, unless when custom appeared to be founded in reason and truth. This principle governed her in the education of her children; disapproving of the common modes of governing and instructing youth, she adopted those methods which appeared to her to be the most rational and proper. Their rising, dressing, eating, exercise, and every thing which related to them was managed by rule, unless when sickness hindered. They were very early taught obedience to their parents, and to wait their decision in every thing which they were to have or to do. As soon as they could speak, they learnt the Lord's prayer, and were made to repeat it at rising and bed time constantly: and as they grew bigger, they recited a short prayer for their parents, and some collects, a short catechism, and some portions of scripture, as their memories could bear them. They were early made to distinguish the sabbath from other days; and were soon instructed to be quiet at family prayers, and to ask a blessing immediately before meals, which they used to do by signs before they could kneel or speak. Her method of teaching them to read is detailed in a letter to Mr. John Wesley. " None of them were taught to read till five years old, except Kezzy, in whose case I was over-ruled; and she was more years in learning than any of the rest had been months. The way of teaching was this: the day before a child began to learn, the house was set in order, every one's work appointed them, and a charge given that none should come into the room from nine till twelve, or from two till five, which were our school-hours. One day was allowed the child wherein to learn its letters, and each of them did in that time know all its letters, great and small, except Molly and Nancy, who were a day and a half before they knew them perfectly; for which I then thought them very dull; but the reason why I thought them so was, because the rest learned them so readily, and your brother Samuel, who was the first child I ever taught, learnt the alphabet in a few hours. He was five years old on the tenth of February; the next day he began to learn, and as soon as he knew the letters began at the first chapter of Genesis. He was taught to spell the first verse, then to read it over and over, till he could read it at once without any hesitation; so on to the second, &c. till he took ten verses for a lesson, which he quickly did. Easter fell low that year, and by Whitsuntide he could read a chapter very well; for he read continually, and had such a prodigious memory, that I cannot remember ever to have told him the same word twice. What was yet more strange, any word he had learnt in his lesson, he knew wherever he saw it, either in his bible or any other book, by which means he learnt very soon to read an English author well.

"The same method was observed with them all. As soon as they knew the letters they were first put to spell and read one line, then a verse, never leaving till perfect in their lesson, were it shorter or longer. So one or other continued reading at school time without any intermission; and before we left school, each child read what he had learnt that morning; and ere we parted in the afternoon, what they had learned that day."

Mr. Wesley usually attended the sittings of convocation; during his absence in the year 1712, Mrs. Wesley formed a little meeting at her house on the Sabbath day evenings, when she read a sermon, prayed and conversed with the people who came for this purpose. She acquainted her husband of their meeting, who, on account of the newness and singularity of the thing, made some objections against it. Her answer is dated the 6th of February, 1712, in which she says, " I heartily thank you for dealing so plainly and faithfully with me in a matter of no common concern. The main of your objections against our Sunday evening meetings, are, first, that it will look particular; secondly, my sex; and, lastly, your being at present in a public station and character; to all which I shall answer briefly.

" As to its looking particular, I grant it does, and so does almost every thing that is serious, or that may any way advance the glory of God, or the salvation of souls, if it be performed out of a pulpit or in the way of common conversation; because, in our corrupt age, the utmost care and diligence have been used to banish all discourse of God or spiritual concerns out of society; as if religion were never to appear out of the closet, and we were to be ashamed of nothing so much as of professing ourselves to be christians.

" To your second I reply, that as I am a woman, so I am also mistress of a large family. And though the superiour charge of the souls contained in it lies upon you as head of the family, and as their minister; yet in your absence I cannot but look upon every soul you leave under my care, as a talent committed to me under a trust by the great Lord of all the families of heaven and of earth; and if I am unfaithful to him or to you, in neglecting to improve these talents, how shall I answer unto him, when he shall command me to render an account of my stewardship.

"As these, and other such like thoughts, made me at first take a more than ordinary care of the souls of my children and servants; so, knowing that our most holy religion requires a strict observance of the Lord's day, and not thinking that we fully answer the end of the institution by going to church only; but that likewise we are obliged to fill up the intermediate spaces of that sacred time by other acts of piety and devotion, I thought it my duty to spend some part of the day in reading to, and instructing my family; especially in your absence, when having no afternoon service, we have so much leisure for such exercises; and such time I esteem spent in a way more acceptable to God than if I had retired to my own private devotions.

"This was the beginning of my present practice: other people's coming in and joining with us was purely accidental. Our lad told his parents; they first desired to be admitted; then others who heard of it begged leave also; so our company increased to about thirty, and seldom exceeded forty last winter; and why it increased since, I leave you to judge after you have read what follows.

"Soon after you went to London, Emily found in your study the account of the Danish Missionaries; which, having never seen, I ordered her to read to me. I was never, I think, more affected with any thing than with the relation of their travels; and was exceedingly pleased with the noble design in which they were engaged. Their labours refreshed my soul beyond measure, and I could not forbear spending a good part of that evening in praising and adoring the Divine Goodness for inspiring those good men with such an ardent zeal for his glory, that they were willing to hazard their lives and all that is esteemed dear to men in this world, to advance the honour of their Master Jesus! For several days I could think or speak of little else. At last it came into my mind; though I am not a man, nor a minister of the gospel, and so cannot be engaged in such a worthy employment as they were; yet, if my heart were sincerely devoted to God, and if I were inspired with a true zeal for his glory, and did really desire the salvation of souls, I might do somewhat more than I do. I thought I might live in a more exemplary *manner in some things;* I might pray more for *the people,* and speak with more warmth to those with whom I have an opportunity of conversing. However, I resolved to begin with my own children; and accordingly I proposed and observed the following method. I take such a proportion of time as I can best spare every night, to discourse with each child by himself, on something that relates to his principal concerns. On Monday I talk with Molly; on Tuesday with Hetty; Wednesday with Nancy; Thursday with Jacky; Friday with Patty; Saturday with Charles; and with Emily and Suky together on Sunday.

" With those few neighbours who then came to me, I discoursed more freely and affectionately *than before;* I chose the best and most awakening sermons which we had, and I spent more time with them in such exercises. Since this our company has increased every night; for I dare to deny none who ask admittance. Last Sunday I believe we had above 200, and yet many went away for want of room.

"But I never dared positively to presume to hope that God would make use of me as an instrument in doing good; the farthest I ever expected was, it may be, who can tell? With God all things are possible; I will resign myself to him: Or, as Herbert better expresses it,

"Only, since God doth often make
Of lowly matter, for high uses meet,
I throw me at his feet;
There will I lie, until my Maker seek
For some mean stuff, whereon to shew his skill,
Then is my time——"

And thus I rested, without passing any reflection on myself, or forming any judgment about the success or event of this undertaking.

"Your third objection I leave to be answered by your own judgment. We meet not upon any worldly design. We banish all temporal concerns from our society; none is suffered to mingle any discourse about them with our reading or singing; we keep close to the business of the day, and as soon as it is over they all go home. And where is the harm of this? If I and my children went a visiting on Sunday nights, or if we admitted of impertinent visits, as too many do who think themselves good christians, perhaps it would be thought no scandalous practice, though in truth it would be so; therefore, why any should reflect upon you, let your station be what it will, because your wife endeavours to draw people to church, and to restrain them, by reading and other persuasions, from their profanation of God's most holy day, I cannot conceive. But if any should be so mad as to do it, I wish you would not regard it. For my part, I value no censure on this account: I have long since shook hands with the world, and I heartily wish I had never given them more reason to speak against me.

"As for your proposal of letting some other person read, alas! you do not consider what a people these are.

I do not think one man among them could read a sermon, without spelling a good part of it; and would that edify the rest? Nor has any of our family a voice strong enough to be heard by such a number of people.

"But there is one thing about which I am much dissatisfied; that is, their being present at family prayers. I do not speak of any concern I am under, barely because so many are present. For those who have the honour of speaking to the great and holy God, need not be ashamed to speak before the whole world, but because of my sex. I doubt, if it be proper for *me* to present the prayers of the people to God. Last Sunday I would fain have dismissed them before prayers; but they begged so earnestly to stay, I dared not to deny them."

Mrs. Wesley, although satisfied of the propriety of her own conduct, determined to abide by her husband's decision. Inman the curate and some others highly disapproved of it, and complained to Mr. Wesley of this conventicle; and the representations which were made, induced him to write to her in terms of strong disapprobation. Her answer is dated February 25th.

"Some few days since," says she, "I received a letter from you, I suppose dated the 16th instant, which I made no great haste to answer; because I judged it necessary for both of us to take some time to consider, before you determine in a matter of such great importance. I shall not inquire how it was possible that you should be prevailed on, by the senseless clamours of two or three of the worst of your parish, to condemn what you so lately approved: but I shall tell you my thoughts in as few words as possible. I do not hear of more than three or four persons who are against our meeting, of whom Inman is the chief. He and Whitely, I believe, may call it a conventicle; but we hear no outcry here, nor has any one said a word against it to me. And what does their calling it a conventicle signify? does it alter the nature of the thing? or do you think that what they say is a sufficient reason to forbear a thing that has already done much good, and by the blessing of God may do much more? If its being called a conventicle by those who know in their conscience that they misrepresent it, did really make it one, what you say would be somewhat to the purpose: but it is plain in fact, that this one thing has brought more people to church than ever any thing did in so short a time. We used not to have above twenty or twenty-five at evening service, whereas now we have between two and three hundred; which are more than ever came before to hear Inman in the morning.

"Besides the constant attendance on the public worship of God, our meeting has wonderfully conciliated the minds of this people towards us, so that we now live in the greatest amity imaginable; and what is still better, they are very much reformed in their behaviour on the Lord's day; and those who used to be playing in the streets, now come to hear a good sermon read, which is surely more acceptable to Almighty God.

"Another reason for what I do, is, that I have no other way of conversing with this people, and therefore have no other way of doing them good; but by this I have an opportunity of exercising the greatest and noblest charity, that is, charity to their souls.

"Some families who seldom went to church, now go constantly; and one person who has not been there for seven years, is now prevailed upon to go with the rest.

"There are many other good consequences of this meeting, which I have not time to mention. Now I beseech you to weigh all things in an impartial balance: on the one side, the honour of Almighty God, the doing much good to many souls, and the friendship of the best among whom we live; on the other, if folly, impiety, and vanity may abide in the scale against so ponderous a weight, the senseless objections of a few scandalous persons, laughing at us, and censuring us as precise and hypocritical: and when you have duly considered all things, let me know your positive determination.

"I need not tell you the consequences, if you determine to put an end to our meeting. You may easily foresee what prejudices it may raise in the minds of these people against Inman especially, who has had so little wit as to speak publickly against it. I can now keep them to the church, but if it be laid aside, I doubt they will never go to hear him more, at least those who come from the lower end of the town; but if this be continued till you return, which now will not be long, it may please God that their hearts may be so changed by that time, that they may love and delight in his public worship so as never to neglect it more.

"If you do, after all, think fit to dissolve this assembly, do not tell me that you desire me to do it, for that will not satisfy my conscience: but send me your *positive command*, in such full and express terms, as may absolve me from all guilt and punishment for neglecting this opportunity of doing good, when you and I shall appear before the great and awful tribunal of our Lord Jesus Christ."

The meeting was continued until Mr. Wesley returned to Epworth.

Mrs. Wesley appears in the most amiable light in her behaviour to her sons while at Oxford—After the death of her husband, she divided her time between her children, until 1739, when she removed to London and resided chiefly in that city.

Mr. Wesley gives the following account of his mother's death: "I left Bristol in the evening of Sunday the 18th July 1742, and on Tuesday came to London. I found my mother on the borders of eternity. But she had no doubt or fear; nor any desire, but as soon as God should call, *to depart and to be with Christ.*

"Friday the 23rd, about three in the afternoon, I went to my mother, and found her change was near. She was in her last conflict; unable to speak, but I believe quite sensible. Her look was calm and serene, and her eyes fixt upward, while we commended her soul to God. From three to four the silver cord was loosing, and the wheel breaking at the cistern: and then, without any struggle or sigh or groan, her soul was set at liberty! We stood round the bed, and fulfilled her last request, uttered a little before she lost her speech; " Children, as soon as I am released, sing a psalm of praise to God."

"Sunday, August 1st. Almost an innumerable company of people being gathered together, about five in the afternoon, I committed to the earth the body of my mother, to sleep with her fathers. The portion of scripture from which I afterwards spoke, was, *I saw a great white throne and him that sat on it; from whose face the earth and the heaven fled away, and there was found no place for them. And I saw the dead small and great, standing before God, and the books were opened— And the dead were judged out of those things which were written in the books, according to their works.* It was one of the most solemn assemblies I ever saw, or expect to see, on this side of eternity.

"We set up a plain stone at the head of her grave, inscribed with the following words;

"Here lies the body of Mrs. *Susannah Wesley*, the youngest and last surviving daughter of Dr. *Samuel Annesley*.

> "In sure and stedfast hope to rise,
> And claim her mansion in the skies,
> A Christian here her flesh laid down,
> The cross exchanging for a crown.
>
> True daughter of affliction she
> Inur'd to pain and misery,
> Mourn'd a long night of griefs and fears,
> A legal night of seventy years.
>
> The Father then reveal'd his son,
> Him in the broken bread made known.
> She knew and felt her sins forgiv'n
> And found the earnest of her heav'n.
>
> Meet for the fellowship above,
> She heard the call, "arise, my love;"
> "I come" her dying looks replied,
> And lamb like, as her Lord, she died."

Mr. Samuel Wesley, junior.

Samuel Wesley, the eldest son, was born about 1692, a year or two before his father removed to Epworth. Until he entered upon his fifth year, he never spoke, which produced a fear that he was deficient in his understanding: but his answer to a question which had been proposed to another person concerning him in his presence, very much surprized all his auditors, and he found no difficulty from that time. He received his education at Westminster, thence removed to Christ Church Oxford, and in both institutions was reputed to be an excellent classical scholar. Having taken his Master's degree he was called to officiate as usher of Westminster; and not long after, under the patronage of Atterbury appeared in orders proving, himself to be an able preacher, and a judicious divine. He was a man of great honour and integrity; humane and charitable in a high degree, being indefatigable in the service of the indigent: to him the Westminster infirmary is much indebted for his industrious charity. With Oxford, Pope, and other literary characters of the first rank he was acquainted, and maintained a friendly correspondence—but his attachment to Atterbury lost him the favour of Walpole, then prime minister, who in consequence of this intimacy, determined against Mr. Wesley's preferment at Westminster; he therefore retired from his situation—and removed to Tiverton, presiding in the free grammar school there until his death; which event occurred on the sixth of November 1739—in the forty-ninth year of his age: and as he had lived much esteemed, his departure was long regretted. The following letter was written to Mr. Charles Wesley, informing him of the flight of his brother from this pilgrimage state:

" TIVERTON, Nov. 14, 1739.

" *Reverend and dear Sir,*

" Your brother and my dear friend, for so you are sensible he was to me, on Monday the fifth of November went to bed, as he thought, as well as he had been for some time before; he was seized about three o'clock in the morning very ill, when your sister immediately sent for Mr. Norman, and ordered the servant to call me. Mr. Norman came as quick as he possibly could, but said, as soon as he saw him, that he could not get over it, but would die in a few hours. He was not able to take any thing, nor able to speak to us, only yes or no to a question asked him, and that did not last half an hour. I never went from his bed-side till he expired, which was about seven the same morning. With great difficulty we persuaded your dear sister to leave the room before he died—I trembled to think how she would bear it, knowing the sincere affection and love she had for him—But blessed be God, he hath heard and answered prayer on her behalf, and in a great measure calmed her spirit, though she has not yet been out of her chamber. Your brother was buried on Monday last in the afternoon—and is gone to reap the fruit of his labours—I pray God we may imitate him in all his virtues and be prepared to follow. I should enlarge much more, but have not time; for which reason I hope you will excuse him who is under the greatest obligations to be, and really is, with the greatest sincerity, yours in all things.

AMOS MATTHEWS."

He was a man of very considerable learning—in 1736 he published a quarto volume of poems, many of which possess much excellence; the tales are admirable and highly entertaining, the satire pointed, and the moral instructive: the volume abounds with much knowledge of mankind, profound erudition, and evinces a lively and vigorous imagination—but his energy is superior to his correctness—though the poems are masculine and nervous in the highest degree, they are deficient in that harmony which with a little more attention might have been infused into them—His modesty and diffidence were uncommon: in his preface to the edition of the poems published by himself he declares, " that it was not any opinion of excellence in the verses themselves, which occasioned their present collection and publication, but merely the profit proposed by the subscription:" notwithstanding this unfavourable report the subscription list was so large as to provide a very considerable part of a decent competency which he bequeathed for the support of his widow and daughter.

Mr. Charles Wesley.

Mr. Charles Wesley was born December 18th 1708 several weeks before his time, at Epworth: he appeared upon his entrance into our world dead rather than alive; he did not cry, nor open his eyes, and was kept wrapt up in soft wool until the time when he would have been born according to nature's course—and not until then did he open his eyes and cry.

His mother imparted to him the first rudiments of learning. In 1716 he was sent to Westminster school under the care of his brother Samuel; here he manifested a sprightly, active mind, with a considerable facility in receiving instruction.

When he had been some years at school, Mr. R. Wesley, a gentleman of large fortune in Ireland, wrote to his father, and asked if he had any son named Charles, if so, he would make him his heir. Accordingly a gentleman in London brought money for his education several years. But one year another gentleman called, probably Mr. Wesley himself, talked largely with him, and asked if he was willing to go with him to Ireland. Mr. Charles desired to write to his father, who answered immediately, and referred it to his own choice. He chose to stay in England. Mr. W. then found and adopted another Charles Wesley, who was the late Earl of Mornington.

In 1721 he was admitted a scholar of St. Peter's Westminster, from which he was removed to Christ Church Oxford in 1726, his brother John being Fellow of Lincoln. He thus narrates his mode of life at Oxford.

" My first year at College I lost in diversions: the next I set myself to study. Diligence led me into serious thinking: I went to the weekly sacrament, and persuaded two or three young students to accompany me, and to observe the method of study prescribed by the statutes of the university. This gained me the harmless name of *Methodist*. In half a year after this, my brother left his curacy at Epworth, and came to our assistance. We then proceeded regularly in our studies, and in doing what good we could to the bodies and souls of men."

In the course of the following summer he became more serious, and diligent both in the means of grace, and in his studies; his zeal for God was already kindled, and manifested itself in considerable exertions to animate his fellow students with the spirit and temper of Christianity—in a short time he was sucessful:——upon this occasion he wrote to his brother dated May, 1729.

" Providence has at present put it into my power to do some good. I have a modest, humble, well disposed youth lives next me, and have been, thank God, somewhat instrumental in keeping him so. He was got into vile hands, and is now broken loose. I assisted in setting him free, and will do my utmost to hinder him from getting in with them again. He was of opinion that passive goodness was sufficient ; and would fain have kept in with his acquaintance and God at the same time. He durst not receive the sacrament, but at the usual times, for fear of being laughed at. By convincing him of the duty of frequent communicating, I have prevailed on both of us to receive once a week.

" I earnestly long for, and desire the blessing which God is about to send me in you. I am sensible this is my day of grace ; and that upon my employing the time before our meeting and next parting, will in a great measure depend my condition for eternity."

Mr. John Wesley having returned to Oxford from Epworth where he had been assisting his Father; a regular society was formed, that the members might fortify each other in their pious design and duties: and not long after, Mr. Charles Wesley assumed the character of a preceptor. He became M. A. in the usual course ; and at that time intended to devote his whole life to the instruction of students at Oxford ; but the God of Providence who " makes all things work together for good," had otherwise designed; for he accepted of the office of Secretary to Mr. Oglethorpe the governor of Georgia, and of the Indian affairs, and in this character accompanied his brother to that state having been ordained both Deacon and Priest previous to his departure.

They sailed from Gravesend on the 22nd of October 1735, but were detained at Cowes until December the 10th, here Mr. Wesley preached on several occasions to large congregations. The vessel arrived in Savannah river on February 5th, 1736. He was appointed to Frederica; whilst his brother received the charge of Savannah; on the ninth of March he landed on Simon's island, and on the same day commenced his ministerial labours—in the evening he read prayers in the open air, Mr. Oglethorpe being one of his auditors. The accommodations for the colony were at this time very insufficient. They had no house for public worship, so that Mr. Wesley, although there was a heavy storm of rain, was obliged to lead the devotions of the people before Mr. Oglethorpe's tent.

A division existed between some of the women which caused much uneasiness to the governor, and excited considerable animosity in the colony. Mr. Wesley's deportment, and reproof of their improper conduct, united the contending parties in a rooted dislike to him—which ended in a plan, to eradicate Mr. Oglethorpe's affecton for him, or if that should appear to be impracticable, to remove him by violence: hence his situation became very alarming, his usefulness was destroyed, and his personal safety precarious. Some persons treated him with great indecency, whilst Mr. Oglethorpe's behaviour evinced that he had imbibed disadvantagous impressions respecting him; although of his accusers, and of the subject of accusation he was equally ignorant. On the 10th of March, he had retired to his myrtle grove, and whilst he was repeating, " I will thank thee for thou hast heard me, and art become my salvation," a gun was discharged from the opposite side of the bushes. Providentially he had the moment before turned from that end of the walk where the shot entered, yet he heard it pass close by him.

A circumstance occurred on the third day after this event which forced Mr. Oglethorpe to an explanation : he had ordered that no man should shoot on the Lord's day; nevertheless in the midst of sermon, on Sunday the 21st, a gun was fired : the constable ran out, found it was the Doctor, and told him that it was contrary to orders, and that he must go with him to the officer. The Doctor's passion kindled; "What," said he, "don't you know that I am not to be looked upon as a common fellow?" The constable not knowing what to do, went back, and after consulting with Hermsdorff, returned with two centinels, and took him to the guard-room. His wife then charged and fired a gun, and ran thither like a mad woman, and said she had shot, and would be confined too. She curst and swore in the utmost transport of rage, threatening to kill the first man who should come near her; but at last was persuaded to go away. In the afternoon she assailed Mr. Wesley in the street with the greatest bitterness and scurrility; asserting he was the cause of her husband's confinement, but she would be revenged, &c. &c. He replied, that he pitied her, but defied all that she or the devil could do; and that he hoped she would soon be of a better mind.

Mr. Oglethorpe being immediately expected to return from his excursion with the Indians ; the violence of the party against Mr. Wesley was so great, that the Doctor sent his wife to arm herself from among his instruments to force her escape, that she first might speak to the governor on his landing, and even to wound any person who should oppose her.

Mr. Charles Wesley thus relates his interview with Mr. Oglethorpe. " When notice was given us of Mr. Oglethorpe's landing, Mr. H. Mr. Ingham, and I were sent for. We found him in his tent, with the people round it, and Mr. and Mrs. H. within. After a short hearing the officers were reprimanded, and the prisoners dismissed. At going out Mrs. H. modestly told me, that she had something more to say against me, but she would take another opportunity—I only answered, you know, Madam, it is impossible for me to fear you. When they were gone, Mr. Oglethorpe said, he was convinced and glad that I had no hand in all this—I told him that I had something to impart of the last importance, when he was at leisure. He took no notice, but read his letters, and I walked away. At half past seven, Mr. Oglethorpe called me out of my hut; I looked up to God and went. He charged me with mutiny and sedition; and with stirring up the people to leave the colony. Accordingly he said, they had a meeting last night, and sent to him this morning, desiring leave to go—That their speaker had informed against them, and me the spring of all—That the men were such as constantly came to prayers, therefore I must have instigated them—That he should not scruple to shoot half a dozen of them at once, but that he had, out of kindness, first spoken to me. My answer was, I desire, Sir, that you would have no regard to my friends, or to the love you have had for me, if any thing of this charge be made out against me—I know nothing of their meeting or designs. Of those you have mentioned, not one comes to prayers or sacrament—I never invited any one to leave the colony—I desire to answer my accusers face to face. He said my accuser was Mr. Lawley, whom he would bring, if I would wait here—I added, Mr. Lawley is a man who has declared, that he knows no reason for keeping fair with any one, but a design to get all he can by him ; but there was nothing to be got by the poor Parson.

" When Mr. Oglethorpe returned with Lawley, he observed the place was too public—I offered to take him to my usual walk in the woods—In the way, it came into my mind to say to Mr. Oglethorpe, shew the least disinclination only to find me guilty, and you will see what a turn it will give to the accusation. He took the hint, and insisted on Lawley to make good his charge. He began with the quarrel in general, but did not shew himself angry with me, or desirous to find me blame. Lawley, who appeared full of guilt and fear, upon this dropt his accusation, or rather shrunk it into my forcing the people to prayers. I replied, the people themselves would acquit me of that; and as to the quarrel of the officers, I appealed to the officers themselves for the truth of my assertion, that I had no hand at all in it. I professed my desire and resolution of promoting peace and obedience—Here Mr. Oglethorpe spoke of reconciling matters: bade Lawley tell the people that he would not so much as ask who they were, if they were but quiet for the future. I hope, added he, they will be so; and Mr. Wesley here, hopes so too. Yes, says Lawley, I really believe it of Mr. Wesley: I had always a great respect for him. I turned and said to Mr. Oglethorpe, did I not tell you it would be so? He replied to Lawley, yes, you had always a very great respect for Mr. Wesley; you told me he was a stirrer up of sedition, and at the bottom of all this disturbance. With this gentle reproof he dismissed him; and I thanked Mr. Oglethorpe for having first spoken to me of the things of which I was accused, begging he would always do so, which he promised."

On the 10th of April Mr. John Wesley and Mr. Delamotte arrived from Savannah to visit Mr. C. Wesley, who was considerably reduced from his labours, privations and exercises of mind—after a few days stay in which they animated him with all possible encouragement they returned to Savannah: On the 24th he was requested to attend Mr. Oglethorpe. Thier meeting is thus described by him. "When I entered he addressed me, Mr. Wesley, you know what has passed between us. I took some pains to satisfy your brother about the reports concerning me, but in vain ; he here renews his suspicions in writing. I did desire to convince him, because I have an esteem for him ; and he is just as considerable to me as my esteem makes him. I could clear up all, but it matters not; you will soon see the reason of my actions. I am now going to death, you will see me no more. Take this ring, and carry it from me to Mr. V,—if there be a friend to be depended on, he is: his interest is next to Sir Robert's ; whatever you ask, within his power, he will do for you, your brother and family. I have expected death for some days. These letters shew that the Spaniards have long been seducing our Allies, and intend to cut us off at a blow. I fall by my friends, on whom I depended to send their promised succours. But death is nothing to me ; I will pursue all my designs, and to Him I recommend them and you." He then gave me a diamond ring I took it, and said, "If, *postremum fato quod te alloquor hoc est*, hear what you will quickly know to be a truth as soon as you are entered on a separate state ; this ring I shall never make any use of for myself: I have no worldly hopes, I have renounced the world—life is bitterness to me—I came hither to lay it down—You have been deceived as well as I—I protest my innocence of the crimes I am charged with, and think myself now at liberty to tell you what I thought never to have uttered." It is probable that he unfolded to Mr. Oglethorpe the whole plot, as Mrs. W. had discovered it to him.

"When I had finished this relation he seemed entirely changed ; full of his old love and confidence in me. After some expressions of kindness, I asked him, are you now satisfied? He replied, "Yes, entirely." Why then Sir, I desire nothing more on earth, and care not how soon I follow you. He added, how much he desired the conversion of the heathen, and believed my brother intended for it. But I believe, said I, it will never be under your patronage; for then men would account for it, without taking God into the account. He replied, I believe so too—then embraced and kissed me with the most cordial affection."

On the 29th of April Mr. Oglethorpe returned from his expedition: three large ships and four others had been off the mouth of the river during the three weeks previous, but the wind being boisterous and contrary, they could not make a descent, and circumstances obliged them to depart. The governor now evinced his former kindness and respect for Mr. Wesley, which he ever after retained. In May the Indian traders met him at Savannah to procure their licences, upon which Mr. John Wesley visited Frederica. In July, Mr. Oglethorpe and the two brothers were at Savannah: on the 21st of that month, it was intimated to Mr. Charles Wesley that he must prepare to sail for England in a few days, as the bearer of dispatches from Mr. Oglethorpe to the Board of Trustees, to the Board of trade, and to the Government. The two brothers arrived at Charleston on the 31st of July; and whilst they resided there, Mr. C. Wesley's disorders increased—but he was determined to sail in the first vessel, and notwithstanding the dissuasions of his friends, the very leaky condition of the vessel, and the brutality of the Captain, he persisted. He accordingly engaged his passage on board the London Galley which left that port on the 16th of August:— but it was soon discovered that they could not weather the passage: for on the 26th, in addition to the quantity of water which entered the vessel, they were reduced to short allowance, and after immense difficulty and danger they reached Boston on the 24th of September.

Mr. Wesley was much esteemed whilst in Boston, and the hospitality which was shewn to him received his warmest acknowledgements—he left that port on the 25th of October :—on the evening of the 28th they encountered a most violent storm, which raged with so much fury, and the ship filled so fast with water, that it became necessary to cut away the mizen-mast ; the gale abated on the 30th, and after a common passage for that season of the year, they arrived opposite Deal on the 3d of December, and he immediately landed. When he arrived in London, he was received with much joy as one returned from the dead, it having been reported that the vessel in which he had sailed, was drowned : and one lady was reading an account of his death when he visited her. He found letters, and a journal of all the proceedings in Georgia from the time of his departure, which his brother had forwarded. Before he finally quitted America, Mr. Charles Wesley had written to his brother, freely expressing his sentiments of some persons—but had cautiously inserted their names in Greek : this letter the latter dropt, and it was in the possession of his enemies, to whom he was so candid as to explain who were designated ; the writer had escaped from those them, therefore the enmity raged with increased violence, and the receiver was obliged to bear all its fury.

Most of the Trustees for Georgia were Dissenters ; and they must have possessed unbounded liberality of sentiment, to approve of the Messrs. Wesleys as preachers of the gospel in their colony ; they being men of high church principles. On the 7th of December one of them called upon Mr. C. W. "We had much discourse of Georgia", says Mr. W. " and of my brother's persecution among that stiff-necked people. He seems a truly pious humble christian ; full of zeal for God, and love to man." Mr. Oglethorpe arrived in London on the seventh of January 1737, and prevailed upon Mr. Wesley to retain his office as Secretary and to return to Georgia. He expected to have sailed in October, but the appointment was delayed—and on the third of April 1738 he resigned his office, in consequence of his Physician's opinion, who peremptorily forbade his voyage, and the advice of his friends who solicited him to stay at Oxford; Mr. Oglethorpe offered him a deputy until his health permitted him to enter upon his duties, but he altogether relinquished his intention of revisiting Georgia.

Early in 1737, Count Zinzendorff arrived in England; the principal object of his journey was to unite the English and Moravian churches in Georgia, and to procure the sanction of them as such in England. The Count had been informed of the piety and zeal of the two brothers, and on the nineteenth, a few days after his arrival, he sent for Mr. Charles Wesley. He went, and the Count saluted him with all possible affection, and made him promise to call every day. He was acquainted with the object of the Count's voyage to England. From him he went to the Bishop of Oxford, who received him with equal kindness, and desired him to call as soon as he could, without ceremony or further invitation. They had much talk of the state of religion among the Moravians, and of the object of the Count's visit. Mr. Wesley spent this year in attending on the Trustees and the Board of Trade; in visiting his friends in London, Oxford, and different parts of the country; and his brother and mother in the West of England. He preached occasionally at the places in which he rested and was every where zealous for God, and remarkably useful to a great number of persons by his religious conversation.

In August he was requested to carry up the Address from the University of Oxford to his Majesty. Accordingly, on the 26th, he waited on the King with the Address, at Hampton-Court, accompanied by a few friends.

Peter Bohler visited England about the time of Mr. John Wesley's return from Georgia, February 1738; his acquaintance with the two brothers soon commenced, and Mr. C. Wesley consented to assist him in acquiring the English language. Immediately after this Mr. C. W. was attacked by the pleurisy. On the 24th, the pain became so violent as to threaten sudden death. Whilst he was in this state, Peter Bohler came to his bed side. " I "asked him," adds Mr. Wesley," to pray for me. He " seemed unwilling at first; but beginning faintly, he " raised his voice by degrees, and prayed for my re- " covery with strange confidence. Then he took me " by the hand and calmly said you will not die now. " I thought within myself, I cannot hold out in this " pain till morning—He said, " Do you hope to be " saved?" I answered, yes. " For what reason do " you hope to be saved?" Because I have used my best endeavours to serve God. He shook his head and said no more."

On May the 17th, Mr. Wesley first saw Luther on the Galatians, which Mr. Holland had accidentally procured. They immediately began to read him; " And my " friend," adds Mr. Wesley, " was so affected in hearing " him read, that he breathed sighs and groans unutter- " able. I marvelled that we were so soon and entirely " removed from him that called us into the grace of " Christ, unto another gospel. Who would believe " that our Church had been founded on this important " article of justification by faith alone? I am astonished " that I should ever think this a new doctrine; especial- " ly while our Articles and Homilies stand unrepealed, " and the key of knowledge is not yet taken away. " From this time I endeavoured to ground as many of " our friends as came to see me, in this fundamental " truth.—Salvation by faith alone—not an idle dead " faith, but a faith which works by love, and is inces- " santly productive of all good works and all holiness."

" Behold the Saviour of mankind,
    Nail'd to the shameful tree;
  How vast the love which him inclin'd,
    To bleed and die for thee."

" It was one of the most triumphant hours which I have
" ever known. Yet on July 19th I rose very heavy and
" backward to visit them for the last time. At six in the
" morning, I prayed and sung with them altogether.
" The Ordinary would read prayers, and he preached
" most miserably." Mr. Sparks and Mr. Broughton were
present; the latter of whom administered the sacrament,
and then prayed; Mr. Wesley prayed after him. At
half past nine o'clock, their irons were knocked off,
their hands tied, and they prepared for the solemn journey and the fatal hour. The Clergymen went in a
coach, and about eleven the criminals arrived at Tyburn.
Mr. Wesley, Mr. Sparks, and Mr. Broughton got upon
the cart with them: the Ordinary endeavoured to follow; but the poor prisoners begged that he would not,
and the mob kept him down. They were all cheerful;
full of comfort, peace and triumph; firmly persuaded
that Christ had died for them, had taken away their sins,
and waited to receive them into paradise.—They shewed
no natural terror of death; no fear, no crying, no tear.
" I never saw," says Mr. Wesley, " such calm triumph,
" such incredible indifference to dying. We sang se-
" veral hymns; particularly,

    A guilty, weak and helpless worm,
      Into thy hands I fall;
    Be thou my life, my righteousness,
      My Jesus and my all.

" I took leave of each in particular. Mr. Broughton
" bid them not to be surprised when the cart should
" draw away. They cheerfully replied, they should
" not. We left them, going to meet their Lord. They
" were turned off exactly at twelve o'clock; not one
" struggled for life. I spoke a few suitable words to the

" crowd, and returned full of peace and confidence in
" our friends happiness."

He consented on the 20th to take charge of Mr. Stonehouse's parish at Islington, as Curate; in which church he officiated daily; and was incessantly employed in the Redeemer's service, either in reading prayers, preaching in the churches, or in holding meetings in private houses to pray and expound the Scriptures; and the number of persons converted to God was very great.

During the month of October the two brothers waited upon the Bishop of London to answer to some complaints which had been made concerning them: and on November 14th Mr. Charles Wesley alone conversed with him—at both these interviews the Bishop exhibited that candour and liberality for which he was so highly distinguished.

Immediately after this last conference with the Bishop, Mr. Charles Wesley met Mr. Whitefield in Oxford, who urged him to accept of a college living—and his brother with all his other friends strenuously argued in favour of his settlement at Oxford; which clearly demonstrates that the plan of itinerant preaching had not then been agitated.

Having judged it prudent to remove any incorrect opinion which the heads of the Church might have formed from the variety of false reports that had been propagated with regard to their ministerial labours, Messrs. John and Charles Wesley stated in person to the Archbishop of Canterbury their doctrines, object and success: the prelate behaved to them with much affection, and assenting to their doctrines, merely cautioned them against giving unnecessary offence, and against the use of exceptionable phrases.

Mr. Whitefield whilst staying in Bristol, frequently preached in the open air in the early part of the spring

of 1739, which probably led to the second interview between the Archbishop and Mr. C. Wesley, as the two gentlemen were known to be particularly intimate: the Archbishop was very severe, and talked of excommunication, not on account of the doctrines which Mr. Wesley and his fellow-labourers preached, but because of their irregularity. He bore the reproof with great firmness while in his presence; but after leaving him, he fell into much heaviness, and for several days suffered a severe inward conflict. He perceived that it arose from the fear of man. Mr. Whitefield urged him to preach in the fields the next Lord's day: by this step he would break down the bridge, render his retreat difficult or impossible, and be forced to fight his way forward in the work of the Ministry. This advice he followed. June 24th, " I prayed, says he, and went forth,
" in the *Name of Jesus Christ*. I found near a thousand
" helpless sinners, waiting for the word in Moorfields.
" I invited them in my Master's words, as well as name;
" *Come unto me, all ye that labour and are heavy laden,*
" *and I will give you rest.* The Lord was with me, even
" me, the meanest of his messengers, according to his
" promise. At St Paul's, the Psalms, Lessons, &c. for
" the day, put new life into me: and so did the sacra-
" ment. My load was gone, and all my doubts and
" scruples. God shone on my path, and I knew this
" was his will concerning me.—I walked to Kenning-
" ton-Common, and cried to multitudes upon multi-
" tudes, *Repent ye and believe the Gospel.*"

After a journey to Oxford which occupied him but three or four days, although he preached before the University on Justification, and was engaged with the Vice Chancellor in endeavouring to exculpate the Methodists from the stigma which was attached to them, he returned to London, and on the 8th of July in Moorfields addressed a congregation which was computed to include ten thousand auditors—and on the same day another at Kennington-Common; from this period his labours daily increased, and his success through the mercy of God was proportionate.

It is impracticable and it would be unprofitable, to detail the various towns and villages through which Mr. Wesley travelled after he had determined upon itinerancy. The selections which have been made, contain the striking events only in which he was concerned.

He commenced itinerant on the 16th of August 1739, and on the following day was hindered altogether from preaching at Wickham; passing through Oxford, he arrived at Evesham, where some good was done in the name of the Lord. Thence he proceeded to Gloucester, and upon his arrival sent to borrow the church: the clergyman returned a civil message, " that he should be happy to drink a glass of wine with Mr. Wesley, but that he durst not lend him the pulpit." Mr. Whitefield, his friend's brother, lent him his field which suited the emergency, and was equally profitable to all engaged in the service. He continued his tour to Painswick, and dispensed the Gospel to a large assembly in the street: this town he visited again, and the church being too small to contain the people who had collected, he stood in one of the windows of the church which had been opened for the purpose, and by this mean, those within and those without who alone were supposed to amount to two thousand people, were able to understand him. He now hastened to Bristol—and throughout his whole journey, received every mark of Christian esteem and fellowship from every sect of the Dissenters. In Bristol, Kingswood, or the neighbouring villages, he generally preached twice or thrice each day to large congregations, many of whom acknowledged that the " Gospel was the power of God to their salvation." Bradford, Glouces-

ter, Bengeworth, Westcot, Idbury, Oxford, Evesham, and the surrounding country were included in the circle through which he travelled at the commencement of the year 1740: but in August his labours were interrupted by a fever which endangered his life so much, as to admit of the publication of a report that he had been called to his heavenly home. He recovered in September, and quelled a mob of Colliers who were hastening to Bristol in a tumult on account of the high price of corn.—Soon after this he visited Wales—and in one instance was exposed to some danger from a strong opposition which had been excited against his ministerial work. During the Sermon on Sunday, while Mr. Wesley was describing the state of the Pharisee, a Physician of the place found himself hurt, rose from his seat and walked out of the church. On the Tuesday following, being unusually heated with wine, and urged on by a company of Players determined on mischief, he came to the house where the people were assembled, to demand satisfaction for the injury he supposed that he had received. He struck Mr. Wesley and several of the women with his cane, and raged like a madman, till the men forced him out of the room, and shut the door. Soon after, it was broken open by a Justice of the Peace, and the Bailiff or head Magistrate. " The latter began expostulating with me," says Mr. Wesley, " upon the affront offered to the Doc-
" tor. He said, as it was a public injury, I ought to make
" him a public satisfaction. I answered, Mr. Bailiff, I
" honour you for your office sake ; but were you, or his
" Majesty King George among my hearers, I should tell
" you both, that you are by nature sinners, *or, children*
" *of wrath even as others*. In the church while preach-
" ing I have no superior but God, and shall not ask man
" leave to tell him of his sins. As a Ruler it is your du-
" ty to be a terror to evil doers, but a praise to them
" that do well. Upon thus speaking to him, he became

"exceedingly civil, assured me of his good will, that
"he had come to prevent me from being insulted, and
"that no one should touch a hair of my head."

"While we were talking, the Doctor made another
"attempt to break in and get at me, but the two Jus-
"tices and others, with much trouble sent him away;
"and we continued our triumph in the name of the
"Lord our God. The shout of a King was among us.
"We sang unconcerned, though the Players had beset
"the house, were armed, and threatened to burn it.
"The ground of their quarrel with me was, that the
"preaching of the Gospel had starved them. We pray-
"ed and sang with great tranquility till one in the morn-
"ing: then I lay down till three. I rose again, and was
"scarcely got into the room when they discovered a play-
"er, who had stolen in unobserved. They seized him,
"and F. Farley wrested the sword from him. There
"was no need of drawing it, for the point and blade
"were stript of the scabbard about an hand's breadth.
"Great was our rejoicing within, and the uproar of the
"Players without. My female advisers were by no
"means for my venturing out, but wished me to defer
"my journey. I preferred Mr. Wells' advice, to go
"with him through the midst of our enemies. We called
"on the poor creature whom they had secured. On sight
"of me he cried out, " Indeed Mr. Wesley, I did not
"intend to do you any harm." That, I answered, was
"best known to God and his own heart; but told him
"that my principle was to return good for evil, and
"therefore desired that he might be released. I assured
"him of my good wishes, and with Mr. Wells walked to
"the water side, no man forbidding me."

Until the middle of July 1741, Mr. Wesley's labours were confined principally to London and Bristol and their vicinity:—at that time he travelled in Wales, and was employed with great success in various parts of the kingdom until May 1743 :—in which month he reached Sheffield, and having arrived at the meeting, he says, " As soon as I was in the desk with David Taylor, the floods began to lift up their voice. An Officer in the Army contradicted and blasphemed. I took no notice of him, but sang on. The stones flew thick, striking the desk and the people. To save them, and the house from being pulled down, I gave out, that I should preach in the street and look them in the face. The whole army of the alien Chaldeans followed me. The Captain laid hold on me, and began rioting: I gave him for answer, *A word in season, or advice to a Soldier.* I then prayed, particularly for his majesty king George, and preached the gospel with much contention. The stones often struck me in the face. I prayed for sinners, as servants of their master the devil; upon which the captain ran at me, threatening revenge for abusing, as he called it, " the king his master." He forced his way through the brethren, drew his sword, and presented it to my breast. I immediately opened my breast, and fixing my eye on his, and smiling in his face, calmly said, " I fear God and honour the king." His countenance fell in a moment, he fetched a deep sigh, and putting up his sword, quietly left the place. He had said to one of the company who afterwards informed me, " You shall see if I do but hold my sword to his breast, he will faint away." His course led him to Thorpe; of his treatment there he thus informs us: " David Taylor told me, that the people of Thorpe, through which we should pass, were exceedingly mad against us. So we found them as we approached the place, and were turning down the lane to Barley-Hall. The ambush rose, and assaulted us with stones, eggs, and dirt. My horse flew from side to side, till he found his way through them. They wounded D. Taylor in the forehead, and the wound bled much. I turned back, and asked, what was the reason a clergyman could not pass without such treatment? At first the rioters scattered,' but their captain rallying them, answered with horrible imprecations and stones. My horse took fright, and turned away with me down a steep hill. The enemy pursued me from afar, and followed shouting. Blessed be God, I received no hurt, only from the eggs and dirt. My clothes indeed abhorred me, and my arm pained me a little from a blow which I received at Sheffield." Passing through Newcastle, and preaching there to great profit, he rode to Shields, "where," says he, " I went to church, and the people flocked in crowds after me. The minister spake so low that he could not be heard reading prayers; but I heard him loud enough afterwards, calling to the church-wardens to quiet the disturbance, which none but himself had raised. I fancy he thought I should preach in the church where I stood like some of the first Quakers. The clerk came to me bawling out, " it was consecrated ground, and I had no business to preach on it. That I was no minister," &c. When he had cried himself out of breath, I whispered in his ear that I had no intention to preach there. He stumbled on a good saying, " if you have any word of exhortation to the people, speak to them without." I did so, to an huge multitude waiting in the church-yard: many of them very fierce, threatening to drown me, and what not! I walked through the midst of them, and discoursed in strong awakening words on the Jailor's question, *What must I do to be saved?* The Church-Wardens and others laboured in vain to interrupt me, by throwing dirt, and even money among the people. Having delivered my message, I rode to the Ferry, crossed it, and met as rough friends on the other side. The mob of North Shields waited to salute me, with the Minister at their head. He had got a man with a horn instead of a trumpet, bade him to blow, and his companions to shout. Others were almost as violent in their approbation. We went through honour and dishonour; but neither of them hurt us, and by six o'clock with God's blessing we came safe to Newcastle."

He now visited Epworth, Wednesbury, Birmingham, Oxford, London, Bristol, and through Devonshire to St. Ives—whilst he was preaching at the latter place he observes;—" All was quiet, the Mayor having declared his resolution to swear twenty more constables, and to suppress the rioters by force of arms. Their drum he had seized. All the time I was preaching he stood at a little distance to awe the rioters. He has set the whole town against him, by not giving us up to their fury. But he plainly told Mr. Hoblin, that fire and faggot Minister, that he would not be perjured to gratify any man's malice. He informed us, that he had often heard Mr. Hoblin say, they ought to drive us away by blows, not by arguments."

In February 1744 he returned to Wednesbury, and found the people in great commotion, having been inflamed by the Clergyman to oppose the Methodists in their attempts to evangelize the town:—not many days after his arrival, the rioters gave notice that they would come on the Tuesday following, and pull down the houses and destroy the goods of the Methodists. " One would think," says Mr. Wesley, " there was no king in Israel. There is certainly no Magistrate, who will put them to shame in any thing. Mr. Constable offered to make oath that their lives were in danger, but the Justice refused it, saying that he could do nothing. Other of our complaining bretheren met with the same redress, being driven away with revilings. The Magistrates do not themselves tear off their clothes and beat them, they only stand by and see others do it. One of them told Mr. Jones, it was the best thing the mob ever did, so to treat the Methodists; and he himself would give five pounds to drive them out of the country. Another, when our brother Ward begged his protection, delivered him up to the mercy of the mob, who had half-murdered him before, and throwing his hat round his head, cried, huzza boys, well done, stand up for the church."

Mr. Wesley during the remainder of this year, travelled and preached the Gospel, with great zeal, diligence and success, through the whole of the kingdom from Newcastle to the Land's End.

In 1745 he was confined chiefly to London, Bristol and Wales. The following year was consumed in a tour throughout the kingdom. In January 1747, he arrived at Grimsby, where he was saluted with a shouting mob. In the evening he attempted to preach at the Room, but the mob was so violent that he could not proceed. At length one of the rioters aimed a severe blow at Mr. Wesley, which a friend who stood near him received. Another of them cried out, "What you dog, do you strike a clergyman?" and assailed his comrade. Immediately every man's hand was against his fellow: they began fighting and beating one another, till, in a few minutes, the room was cleared of all disturbers, when Mr. Wesley preached for half an hour, without further molestation. On the 24th of February, he reached the Devizes in his way to Bristol, in company with Mr. Minton. They soon perceived that the enemies of religion had taken the alarm, and were mustering their forces for battle. They began ringing the bells backward, and running to and fro in the streets, as lions roaring for their prey. The curate's mob went in search of Mr. Wesley to several places, particularly to Mr. Philips', where it was expected that he would preach. They broke open, and ransacked the house; but not finding him there, they hastened to Mr. Rogers,' where he and several others being met together, were praying and exhorting one another to continue steadfast in the faith, and through much tribulation, to enter the kingdom. The zealous curate Mr. Innys, stood with them in the street dancing for joy. "This," says Mr. Wesley, " is he, who declared in the pulpit, as well as from house to house, ' that he himself heard me preach blasphemy before the University, and tell them, if you do not receive the Holy Ghost while I breathe upon you, ye are all damned.' He had been about the town during several days, stirring up the people, and canvassing the gentry for their vote and interest; but could not raise a mob while my brother was here: the hour of darkness was not fully come." Mr. Innys, by assiduity, and falsehood boldly asserted as truth, at length engaged the gentlemen of the town in his party, and prevailed with them to encourage the mob. While they beset the house where Mr. Wesley and the company with him were assembled, he often heard his own name mentioned, with, " Bring him out, bring him out." He observes, " The little flock were less afraid than I expected; only one of our sisters fainted away."—It being now dark, the besiegers blocked up the door with a waggon, and set up lights lest Mr. Wesley should escape. One of the company however, retired unobserved, and with much intreaty prevailed on the mayor to come down. He came with two constables, and threatened the rioters; but so gently that no one regarded him. Having tore down the shutters of the shop, and broken the windows, it is wonderful they did not enter the house: but a secret hand seemed to restrain them. After some time they hurried away to the inn where the horses were put up, broke open the stable door, and turned out the beasts. " In the mean time," says Mr. Wesley, " we were at a loss what to do; when God put it into the heart of our next door neighbour, a Baptist, to take us through a passage into his own house, to offer us his bed, and to engage for our secu-

rity. We accepted his kindness, and slept in peace."
February 25. " A day never to be forgotten. At seven o'clock, I walked quietly to Mrs. Philips' and began preaching a little before the time appointed. For three quarters of an hour, I invited a few listening sinners to Christ. Soon after Satan's whole army assaulted the house. We sat in a little ground room, and ordered all the doors to be thrown open. They brought a hand engine and began to play into the house. We kept our seats, and they rushed into the passage: just then, Mr. Borough the Constable came, and seizing the spout of the engine carried it away. They swore if he did not deliver it, they would pull down the house. At that time they might have taken us prisoners; we were close to them, and none to interpose: but they hurried out to fetch the larger engine. In the mean time we were advised to send for the Mayor; but Mr. Mayor was gone out of town in the sight of the people, which gave great encouragement to those who were already wrought up to a proper pitch by the Curate, and the Gentlemen of the town; particularly Mr. Sutton and Mr. Willy. Mr. Sutton, frequently came out to the mob, to animate their exertions. He sent to Mrs. Philips to say, that if she did not turn that fellow out to the mob, he would send them to drag him out. Mr. Willy passed by again and again, assuring the rioters, that he would stand by them and secure them from the law, do what they would."

The rioters " now began playing the larger engine; which broke the windows, flooded the rooms, and spoiled the goods. We were withdrawn to a small upper room in the back part of the house; seeing no way to escape their violence, as they seemed under the full power of the old murderer. The first laid hold on the man who kept the Society-house, dragged him away, and threw him into the horse-pond; and it was said, broke his back.—We gave ourselves unto prayer, believing that the Lord would deliver us; how, or when, we saw not; nor any possible way of escaping: we therefore stood still to see the salvation of God—Every now and then, some or other of our friends would venture to us; but rather weakened our hands, so that we were forced to stop our ears, and look up. Among the rest, the Mayor's maid came, and told us her mistress was in tears about me; and begged me to disguise myself in women's clothes, and try to make my escape. Her heart had been turned towards us by the conversion of her son, just on the brink of ruin. God laid his hand on the poor prodigal, and instead of running to sea, he entered the society.—The rioters without, continued playing their engine, which diverted them for some time; but their number and fierceness still increased; and the gentlemen supplied them with pitchers of ale, as much as they would drink. They were now on the point of breaking in, when Mr. Borough thought of reading the proclamation: he did so at the hazard of his life. In less than an hour, of above a thousand wild beasts, none were left, but the guard. Our constable had applied to Mr. Street, the only justice in town; who would not act. We found there was no help in man, which drove us closer to the Lord; and we prayed, with little intermission, the whole day.

"Our enemies at their return, made their main assault at the back door, swearing horribly they would have me if it cost them their lives. Many seeming accidents concurred to prevent their breaking in. The man of the house came home, and instead of turning me out as they expected, took part with us, and stemmed the tide for some time. They now got a notion, that I had made my escape; and ran down to the inn, and played the engine there. They forced the inn-keeper to turn out our horses, which he immediately sent to Mr. Clark's; which drew the rabble and their engine thither. But the resolute old man charged, and presented his gun, till they retreated.—Upon their revisiting us, we stood in jeopardy every moment. Such threatenings, curses and blasphemies I have never heard. They seemed kept out by a continual miracle. We were preserved from all hurry and discomposure of spirits, by a Divine Power resting upon us. We prayed and conversed as freely as if we had been in the midst of our brethren; and had great confidence that the Lord would either deliver us from the danger, or in it. In the height of the storm, just when we were falling into the hands of the drunken, enraged multitude, Mr. Minton was so little disturbed that he fell fast asleep.

" They were now close to us on every side, and over our heads untiling the roof. A ruffian cried out, " Here they are, behind the curtain.'" At this time we fully expected their appearance, and retired to the furthermost corner of the room; and I said, *this is the crisis.* In that moment, Jesus rebuked the winds and the sea, and there was a great *calm.* We heard not a breath without, and wondered what was become of them. The silence lasted for three quarters of an hour, before any one came near us; and we continued in mutual exhortation and prayer, looking for deliverance. I often told my companions, now God is at work for us: he is contriving our escape: he can turn these leopards into lambs: can command the heathen to bring his children on their shoulders, and make our fiercest enemies the instruments of our deliverance. About three o'clock Mr. Clark knocked at the door, and brought with him the persecuting constable. He said, " Sir, if you will promise never to preach here again, the gentlemen and I will engage to bring you safe out of town." My answer was, I shall promise no such thing—setting aside my office, I will not give up my birth-right as an Englishman of visiting what place I please of his majesty's dominiops. "Sir," said the constable, "we expect no such promise, that you will never come here again: only tell me that it is not your *present* intention, that I may tell the gentlemen, who will then secure your quiet departure." I answered I cannot come again at this time, because I must return to London a week hence. But, observe, I make no promise of not preaching here, when the door is opened; and do not you say that I do.

"He went away with this answer, and we betook ourselves to prayer and thanksgiving. We perceived it was the Lord's doing, and it was marvellous in our eyes. The hearts of our adversaries were turned. Whether pity for us, or fear for themselves, wrought strongest, God knoweth; probably the latter; for the mob were wrought up to such a pitch of fury, that their masters dreaded the consequence, and therefore went about appeasing the multitude, and charging them not to touch us in our departure:

"While the constable was gathering his posse, we got our things from Mr. Clark's, and prepared to go forth. The whole multitude were without expecting us, and saluted us with a general shout. The man Mrs. Naylor had hired to ride before her was, as we now perceived, one of the rioters. This hopeful guide was to conduct us out of the reach of his fellows. Mr. Minton and I took horse in the face of our enemies, who began clamouring against us: the gentlemen were dispersed among the mob, to bridle them. We rode a slow pace up the street, the whole multitude pouring along on both sides, and attending us with loud acclamations—such fierceness and diabolical malice I have not before seen in human faces. They ran up to our horses as if they would swallow us, but did not know which was Wesley. We felt great acquiescence in the honour done to us, while the whole town were spectators of our march. When out of sight, we mended our pace, and about se-ten o'clock came to Wraxall. The news of our danger arrived thither before us; but we brought the welcome tidings of our deliverance. We joined in hearty prayer to our Deliverer, singing the hymn,

"Worship, and thanks, and blessing," &c.

February 26, I preached at Bath, and we rejoiced like men who take the spoil. We continued our triumph at Bristol, and reaped the fruit of our labours and sufferings."

In August, Mr. Wesley sailed for Ireland accompanied by Mr. Charles Perronet—he experienced much opposition in Dublin, and numberless inconveniences. Having determined to make an excursion into the country, he left Dublin on the 11th of February 1748, accompanied by six of his friends, and proceeded towards Athlone, where notice had been given of their coming. On the road some persons overtook them, running in great haste, and one horseman riding in full speed. It soon appeared that the Papists had laid a plan to do them some violent mischief, if not to murder them, at the instigation of their priest Father Terrill, who had sounded the alarm on the preceding Lord's day They spoke of their designs with so much freedom, that a report of them reached Athlone, and a party of dragoons being quartered there, were ordered out to meet Mr. Wesley and his friends on the road, and to conduct them safe to town. But of this they were ignorant; and being earlier than was expected, the Papists were not assembled in full force, nor did the dragoons meet them at that distance from the town which was intended. They rode on, suspecting nothing, until within about half a mile of Athlone, when, rising up a hill, several persons appeared at the top of it, and bid them turn back. "We thought them in jest," says Mr. Wesley, "till the stones flew," one of which knocked J. Healy from his horse, and laid him senseless on the ground; and it was with great difficulty the Papists were hindered from murdering him. The number of these barbarians was soon greatly increased, and though the Protestants began to rise upon them, they kept their ground till the dragoons appeared, when they immediately fled. Mr. Wesley and his little company, their wounded friend having recovered his senses, were now conducted in safety to Athlone, where the soldiers flocked about them with much affection, and the whole town expressed the greatest indignation at the treatment which they had received: J. Healy was put under the care of a surgeon, and at length recovered of his wounds.

Mr. Wesley returned to London in April, and having made a journey into Wales, he landed again at Dublin, in August, and during this second tour visited Cork, Kinsale, Bandon, &c. He departed from Ireland in October, and was providentially preserved from a watery grave—he related the scene to one of his friends : " On Saturday evening, at half past eight, I entered that small boat, and were two hours in getting to the vessel. There was not then water to cross the bar; so we took our rest till eleven on Sunday morning. Then God sent us a fair wind, and we sailed smoothly before it five hours and a half. Towards evening the wind freshened, it became extremely dark, and no small tempest lay upon us. The captain had ordered in all the sails. I kept mostly on deck till half past eight, when upon inquiry, he told me, that he expected to be in the harbour by nine : I answered, we would compound for ten. While we were talking, the mainsail probably got loose; at the same time the small boat, for want of fastening, fell out of its place. The master called all hands on deck, and thrust me down into the cabin; when, in a minute, we heard a cry above, " We have lost the mast!" A passenger ran up, and brought us worse news, that it was not the mast, but the poor master himself, whom I had scarcely left, when the boat, as they supposed, struck him and knocked him overboard. From that moment he was seen and heard no more. My soul was bowed before the Lord. I kneeled down, and commended the departing spirit to his mercy in Christ Jesus. I adored his distinguishing goodness. *The one shall be taken, and the other left.* I thought of those lines of Young: " No warning given! unceremonious death! a sudden rush from life's meridian joys; a plunge opaque beyond conjecture." The sailors were so confounded they knew not what they did. The decks were strewed with sails; the wind shifting about the compass; we just on the shore, and the vessel driving where or how they knew not. One of our cabin passengers ran to the helm, and gave orders as captain, until they had righted the ship. But I ascribe it to our invisible Pilot, that we got safe to shore soon after ten. The storm was so high, that we doubted whether boats would venture to fetch us. At last one answered and came. I thought it safer to lie in the vessel; but one calling, Mr. Wesley you must come, I followed; and by eleven o'clock found out my old lodgings at Robert Griffiths'." From this period until his marriage, he was engaged chiefly in London, Bristol, and their neighbourhood. On the ninth of April 1749, he was married by his brother John to Miss Sarah Gwynne, at Garth, in Wales.

February 8th, 1750, there was an earthquake in London. " This morning," Mr. Wesley remarks, " March 8th, a quarter after five, we had another shock of an earthquake, far more violent than that of February 8th. I was just repeating my text, when it shook the Foundery so violently, that we all expected it to fall on our heads. A great cry followed from the women and children. I immediately cried out, *Therefore we will not fear, though the earth be moved and the hills be carried into the midst of the sea; for the Lord of Hosts is with us; the God of Jacob is our refuge.* He filled

H

my heart with faith, and my mouth with words, shaking their souls as well as their bodies. The earth moved Westward, then East, then Westward again, through all London and Westminster. It was a strong and jarring motion, attended with a rumbling noise like that of thunder. Many houses were much shaken, and some chimnies thrown down, but without any further hurt."

April 4th, " Fear filled our chapel, occasioned by a prophecy of the return of the earthquake this night. I preached my written sermon on the subject, with great effect. It was a glorious night for the disciples of *Jesus*. April 5, I rose at four o'clock, after a night of sound sleep, while my neighbours watched. I sent an account to M. G. as follows:—The late earthquake has found me work. Yesterday I saw the Westminster end of the town full of coaches, and crowds flying out of the reach of Divine Justice, with astonishing precipitation. Their panick was caused by a poor madman's prophecy. Last night they were all to be swallowed up. The vulgar were in almost as great consternation as their betters. Most of them watched all night; multitudes in the fields and open places; several in their coaches: many removed their goods. London looked like a sacked city. A lady just stepping into her coach to escape, dropped down dead. Many came all night knocking at the Foundery door, and begging admittance for God's sake."

Mr. W. Briggs, in a letter to Mr. John Wesley, says, " This great city has been, for some days past, under terrible apprehensions of another earthquake. Yesterday, thousands fled out of town, it having been confidently asserted by a dragoon, that he had a revelation, that great part of London and Westminster especially, would be destroyed by an earthquake on the 4th instant, between twelve and one at night. The whole city was under direful apprehensions. Places of worship were crowded with frightened sinners, especially our two chapels, and the Tabernacle where Mr. Whitefield preached.

"Though crowds left the town on Wednesday night, yet crowds were left behind; multitudes of whom, for fear of being suddenly overwhelmed, left their houses, and repaired to the fields, and open places in the city. Tower-Hill, Moorfields, but above all, Hyde-Park, were filled best part of the night, with men, women, and children lamenting. Some, with stronger imaginations than others, mostly women, ran crying in the streets, an earthquake! an earthquake! Mr. Whitefield preached at midnight in Hyde-Park."

In the year 1751 Mr. Wesley visited the Methodist societies throughout the kingdom, correcting mistakes, destroying irregularities, and superintending the general interests of the body—he relates a trial which had not long before excited general attention, and as it is of importance to know how the Gospel has been opposed of late years, it is extracted: "At Whitecoat-Hill, three miles from Leeds, a few weeks since, as our Brother Maskew was preaching, a Mob arose, broke the windows and doors, and struck the Constable Jacob Hawley, one of the Society. On this we indicted them for an assault; and the ringleader of the Mob John Hellingworth, indicted our Brother the Constable, and got persons to swear the Constable struck him. The Grand Jury threw out our indictment, and found their's against us; so we stood trial with them, on Monday July 15th, 1751. The Recorder, Richard Wilson, Esq. gave it in our favour, with the rest of the Court. But the Foreman of the Jury, Matthew Prestley, with two others, Richard Cloudesly, and Jabez Bunnel, would not agree with the rest, being our avowed enemies. The Foreman was Mr. Murgatroyd's great friend and champion against the Methodists. However the Recorder gave strict orders to a guard of Constables, to watch the Jury, that they should have neither meat, drink, candles, nor tobacco, till they were agreed in their verdict. They were kept prisoners all that night and the next day till five in the afternoon, when one of the Jury said, he would die before he would give it against us. Then he spake closely to the Foreman concerning his prejudices against the Methodists, till at last he condescended to refer it to one man. Him the other charged to speak as he would answer it to God in the day of judgment. The man turned pale, trembled, and desired that another might decide it. Another, John Hardwick, being called upon, immediately decided it in favour of the Methodists. After the trial, Sir Henry Ibeson one of the Justices, called a Brother and said, you see God never forsakes a righteous man, take care you never forsake him."

Mr. Wesley continued his usual mode of life from this period until November 1756, always present whereever he appeared to be necessary—exciting the societies to that harmony and love which are indispensably requisite in a large body of people. After the year 1756 it does not appear that he travelled to any great distance—his labours were principally confined between London and Bristol, and he preached until within a short time previous to his dissolution.

Mr. Wesley's body was weak, and his health precarious during the greater part of his life: his intense application to study and abstinence from food, if not the causes, certainly increased the unpleasantness of his sensations in a very considerable degree. His constant equestrian exercise strengthened him much, and probably protracted his life to its great age. It is related of him, that he was always subject to an instinctive fear of death, arising from an anticipation of which he could never divest himself, that in his last moments, his sufferings would be exquisite. This operated very powerfully upon his mind—his body was reduced to the utmost weakness in his last illness, and during his affliction it was his constant desire expressed to his visitants, that they would pray to God to vouchsafe him patience and ease in death. The Father of mercies did not permit his fears to be realized, he possessed that frame of soul which in others had always been pleasing to him—unaffected humility, holy resignation to the will of God, solid hope and unshaken confidence in Christ : these kept him in perfect peace ; and his frame being decayed, he resigned his soul into the hands of the redeemer with Christian sincerity, on the 29th of March 1788, in his eightieth year, and by his own directions, his remains were interred in Marybone church yard. The circumstances of his death are related by his daughter in a letter to Mr. John Wesley.

Dear and honoured Uncle,

" We were all present, when my dear respected father departed this life. His end was what he particularly desired it might be, Peace !

" For some months past he seemed totally detached from earth ; he spoke very little, nor wished to hear any thing read, but the Scriptures. He took a solemn leave of all his friends. I once asked, if he had any presages that he should die? he said, " No : but his weakness was such, that he thought it impossible he should live through March." He kindly bade me remember him ; and seemed to have no doubt, but I should meet him in heaven.

" All his prayer was, " Patience and an easy death!" He bade every one who visited him, to supplicate for these, often repeating, " an easy death !"

" He told my mother, the week before he departed, that no fiend was permitted to approach him ; and said to us all, " I have a good hope !"

" When we asked if he wanted any thing, he frequently answered, " Nothing but Christ." Some person observed, that the valley of the shadow of death was hard to be passed; " Not with Christ," replied he.

" On March the 27th, after a most uneasy night, he prayed as in an agony, that he might not have many such nights. " O my God," said he, " not many !" It was with great difficulty he seemed to speak. About ten days before, on my brother Samuel's entering the room, he took hold of his hand, and pronounced, with a voice of faith, " I shall bless God to all eternity, that ever you were born: I am persuaded I shall !"

" My brother Charles also seemed much upon his mind: " That dear boy," said he, " God bless him !" He spoke less to me than to the rest, which has since given me some pain. However, he bade me trust in God and never forsake him, and then, he assured me, he never would forsake me !

" The 28th my mother asked if he had any thing to say to us; raising his eyes, he said, " Only thanks! Love! Blessing !"

" Tuesday and Wednesday he was not entirely sensible. He slept much, without refreshment, and had the restlessness of death for I think the whole week.

" He was eager to depart; and if we moved him, or spoke to him, he answered, " Let me die! let me die!"

" A fortnight before, he prayed with many tears for his enemies; naming Miss ———. " I beseech thee, O Lord, by thine agony and bloody sweat," said he, " that she may never feel the pangs of eternal death !"

" When your kind letter to my brother came, in which you affectionately tell him, that you will be a father to him and to my brother Samuel, I read it to our father; " He will be kind to you," said he, " when I am gone: I am certain, your uncle will be kind to all of you."

"The last morning which was the 29th of March, being unable to speak, my mother intreated him to press her hand if he knew her, which he feebly did.

"His last words which I could hear, were "Lord—my heart—my God!" He then drew his breath short, and the last so gently, that we knew not exactly the moment in which his happy spirit fled.

"His dear hand was in mine for five minutes before, and at the awful period of his dissolution.

"It often had been his desire that we should attend him to the grave; and though he did not mention it again, as he did the place of his burial, during his illness, we all mean to fulfil his wish. Trusting we shall be supported, as we have been hitherto, in our afflicting situations, I am, your afflicted and dutiful Niece,

S. WESLEY."

The following lines which were written by himself upon the death of one of his friends, were engraven on his tombstone:—

> "With poverty of spirit bless'd,
> Rest happy saint, in Jesus rest;
> A sinner sav'd, through grace forgiv'n,
> Redeem'd from earth to reign in heav'n!
> Thy labours of unwearied love,
> By thee forgot, are crown'd above;
> Crown'd through the mercy of thy Lord,
> With a free, full, immense reward!"

Dr. Whitehead thus describes Mr. C. Wesley: "He was of a warm and lively disposition; of great frankness and integrity, generous and steady in his friendships. He was an excellent scholar, and his poetical genius and taste were very considerable. In conversation he was pleasing, instructive, and cheerful; and his observations were often seasoned with wit and humour. His religion was genuine and unaffected. As a Minister, he was familiarly acquainted with every part of divinity; and his mind was furnished with an uncommon knowledge of the Scriptures. His discourses from the pulpit were not dry and systematick, but flowed from the present views and feelings of his own mind. He had a remarkable talent of expressing the most important truths with simplicity and energy; his sermons were sometimes truly apostolick, forcing conviction on the hearers, in spite of the most determined opposition: and whether we view him as a husband, a divine, a father, or a friend, his character was peculiarly amiable."

THE LIFE

OF THE

REV. JOHN WESLEY, A. M.

From his birth until his departure for America in 1735.

MR. JOHN WESLEY, second son of Samuel and Susannah Wesley, was born at Epworth, Lincolnshire, June 17th, 1703. A domestick affliction nearly deprived him of life ere he attained six years of age. The parsonage house was entirely destroyed by fire. His escape is recorded in one of his early portraits: under the likeness, is represented a house in flames with this motto: " *Is not this a brand plucked out of the burning ?*" Mrs. Wesley's relation of that interesting event is contained in a letter to Mr. Hoole, dated August 24th, 1709.

" *Reverend Sir*,

" My master is much concerned that he was so unhappy as to miss of seeing you at Epworth; and he is not a little troubled that the great hurry of business about building his house will not afford him leisure to write. He has therefore ordered me to satisfy your desire as well as I can, which I shall do by a simple relation of matters of fact; though I cannot at this distance of time recollect every calamitous circumstance that attended our strange reverse of fortune. On Wednesday night, February the 9th, between the hours of eleven and twelve, our house took fire, by what accident God only knows. It was discovered by some sparks falling from the roof upon a bed where one of the children Hetty lay, and burnt her feet. She immediately ran to the chamber and called us; but I believe no one heard her; for Mr. Wesley was alarmed by a cry of fire in the street, upon which he rose, little imagining that his own house was on fire; but, on opening his door, he found it was full of smoke, and that the roof was already burnt through. He immediately came to my room, as I was very ill he lay in a separate room from me, and bid me and my two eldest daughters rise quickly and shift for our lives, the house being all on fire. Then he ran and burst open the nursery door, and called to the maid to bring out the children. The two little ones lay in the bed with her; the three others in another bed. She snatched up the youngest, and bid the rest follow, which they did, except Jacky. When we were got into the hall, and saw ourselves surrounded with flames, and that the roof was on the point of falling, we concluded ourselves inevitably lost, as Mr. Wesley in his fright had forgotten the keys of the doors above stairs. But he ventured up stairs once more, and recovered them, a minute before the stair-case took fire. When we opened the street door, the strong north-east wind drove the flames in with such violence, that none could stand against them: Mr. Wesley only, had such presence of mind as to think of the garden-door, out of which he helped some of the children; the rest got through the windows. I was not in a condition to climb up to the windows; nor could I get to the garden-door. I endeavoured three times to force my passage through the street-door, but was as often beaten back by the fury of the flames. In this distress I besought our blessed Saviour to preserve me, if it were his will, from that death, and then waded through the fire, naked as I was, which did me no farther harm than a little scorching my hands and face.

"While Mr. Wesley was carrying the children into the garden, he heard the child in the nursery cry out miserably for help, which extremely affected him; but his affliction was much increased, when he had several times attempted the stairs then on fire, and found they would not bear his weight. Finding it was impossible to get near him, he gave him up for lost, and kneeling down, he commended his soul to God, and left him, as he thought, perishing in the flames. But the boy seeing none come to his help, and being frightened, the chamber and the bed being on fire, he climbed up to the casement, where he was soon perceived by the men in the yard, who immediately got up and pulled him out, just in the moment of time that the roof fell in, and beat the chamber to the ground. Thus, by the infinite mercy of Almighty God, our lives were all preserved by little less than a miracle, for there passed but a few minutes between the first alarm of fire, and the falling of the house."

Mr. John Wesley's account of what happened to himself, varies a little from this relation given by his Mother. " I believe," says he, " it was just at that time when they thought they heard me cry, I waked : for I did not cry, as they imagined, unless it was afterwards. I remember all the circumstances as distinctly, as though it were but yesterday. Seeing the room was very light, I called to the maid to take me up; but none answering, I put my head out of the curtains, and saw streaks of fire on the top of the room. I got up and ran to the door, but could get no further, all the floor beyond it being in a blaze. I then climbed upon a chest which stood near the window : one in the yard saw me, and proposed running to fetch a ladder : another answered, there will not be time; but I have thought of another expedient. Here I will fix myself against the wall ; lift a light man, and set him on my shoulders. They did so, and he took me out of the window. Just then the roof fell ; but it fell inward, or we should all have been crushed at once. When they brought me into the house where my father was, he cried out, "Come neighbours! let us give thanks to God! He has given me all my eight children; let the house go, I am rich enough!"

"The next day, as he was walking in the garden, and surveying the ruins of the house, he picked up part of a leaf of his Polyglot Bible, on which just those words were legible. *Vade; vende omnia quæ habes, et attolle crucem, et sequere me.* Go; sell all that thou hast, and take up thy cross, and follow me."

He received the first rudiments of knowledge from his mother, whose qualifications and success in this part of her maternal duties, were eminently conspicuous. In April 1712, he was afflicted with the small-pox, which he bore with much fortitude. Two years after that event he was placed under Dr. Walker at the Charterhouse, for which establishment he ever retained a strong predilection—being accustomed annually to visit it when in London. In his seventeenth year he was elected to Christ-Church, and during his stay in that College was much respected. His studies he pursued with alacrity; and by the excellence with which his compositions were distinguished, was soon pronounced to be a man of talents. The gaiety of his disposition, the liberality of his sentiments, and his knowledge of the languages, and logic, procured him the reputation of being an acute and sensible collegian. At this period, his great fondness for the sophistry of the logical art, was much noticed—he first puzzled his opponents with his shrewdness, and then ridiculed them on account of his conquest. But Mr. Wesley asserts, that he never opposed his own opinions on any topic. "It has been my first care for many years, to see that my cause was good, and never either in jest or earnest, to defend the wrong side of the question. And shame on me, if I cannot defend the right, after so much practice; and having been so early accustomed to separate truth from falsehood, how artfully soever they were twisted together."

At Christ-Church, in conjunction with the more laborious studies, he cultivated his poetical talents, and in many of his compositions, which are animated and elegant, he manifested his classical taste: but they were considered by him as the effusions of a moment, hasty productions—and though it may be presumed that they never received a careful revision, they are highly creditable to his genius.

In the year 1724, he began to reflect upon the propriety of entering into orders:—the education which he had received and the good example exhibited by his parents, cherished his early disposition to a life of piety; but being dubious whether the motives which ought to influence a Christian minister were correctly fixed in his mind—he addressed his Father upon that subject—his answer is dated January 26th, 1725.

Dear Son,

" As to what you mention of entering into Holy Orders, it is indeed a great work. I am pleased to find you think it so: as well as that you do not admire a callous cleryman any more than I do. The principal spring and motive, to which all others should be only secondary, must undoubtedly be the glory of God, and the edification of our neighbours. And wo to him, who with any meaner leading view, attempts so sacred a work. For this he should take all the pains he possibly can to qualify himself with the advice of wiser and older men, especially imploring the direction and assistance of Almighty God, with all humility, sincerity, and intention of mind. The knowledge of the languages is a considerable help in this matter, which I thank God all my three sons have. But then this must be prosecuted to the thorough understanding the original text of the

Holy Scriptures, by conversing with them long and constantly. You ask me, " Which is the best comment on the Bible ?" I answer, the Bible itself. For the several paraphrases and translations of it in the polyglot, compared with the original, and with one another, are in my opinion, to an honest, devout, industrious, and humble man, infinitely preferable to any comment I ever saw. But Grotius is the best, for the most part: especially on the New Testament. By all this you see, I am not for your going too hastily into orders. When I am for your taking them, you shall know : and it is not impossible, I may then be with you, if God so long spare the life and health of your affectionate father,

Samuel Wesley.

P. S. Work and write while you can ! You see, Time has shaken me by the hand, and Death is but a little behind him. My eyes and heart are now almost all I have left ; and I bless God for them."

His mother repeated these sentiments in a letter written during the following month—upon which he soon commenced the study of Thomas á Kempis and Taylor's Rules of Holy Living and Dying. These authors strongly influenced his judgment and affections; and convinced him that the Christian religion operates upon the heart and life more extensively than he had before imagined. Being supported by his parents, and encouraged by a religious friend, he prepared to assume the ministerial character, and on the 19th of September 1725, was ordained Deacon by Dr. Potter, bishop of Oxford. He preached his first sermon at Southlye, in the vicinity of the university. A fellowship having become vacant in Lincoln college, his friends exerted all their influence to procure it for him, and after an arduous contest, he was elected Fellow on the 17th of March 1726.

He was employed in the summer of that year, to assist his Father in the discharge of his official duties :—

he preached twice on each Lord's day, and otherwise aided as circumstances demanded. He returned to Oxford in September, and resumed his studies. His literary character was now established, as he was chosen Greek Lecturer and Moderator of the classes on the 7th of November. Not having procured his Master's Degree, he was in some measure interrupted, and obliged to be attentive to the collegians. This interval was not however injurious to his religious impressions, which is evinced by the tenderness and piety of a letter to his mother, dated January, 1727.

" About a year and a half ago," says he, " I stole out of company at eight in the evening, with a young gentleman with whom I was intimate. As we took a turn in the aisle of St. Mary's Church, in expectation of a young lady's funeral, with whom we were both acquainted, I asked him if he really thought himself my friend? and if he did, why he would not do me all the good he could? He began to protest,—in which I cut him short, by desiring him to oblige me in an instance, which he could not deny to be in his own power: to let me have the pleasure of making him a whole Christian, to which I knew he was at least half persuaded already. That he could not do me a greater kindness, as both of us would be fully convinced when we came to follow that young woman."

" He turned exceedingly serious, and kept something of that disposition ever since. Yesterday was a fortnight he died of a consumption. I saw him three days before he died; and on the Sunday following, did him the last good office I could here, by preaching his funeral sermon; which was his desire when living."

He was advanced to the rank of A. M. on the 14th of February 1727, and his exercises added considerably to the reputation which he had already acquired. His mode of study was very regular, and from the plan upon which he determined he never deviated : the two first days of the week were devoted to the Greek and Roman Classics, Historians and Poets—Wednesday to Logic and Ethics—Thursday to Hebrew and Arabic—Friday to Metaphysics and Natural Philosophy—Saturday to Oratory and Poetry, chiefly composition—and the Lord's Day to Divinity. The time which was not included in this course, was dedicated to the French language and the perusal of modern authors in every department of literature. Mr. Wesley to oblige his Father, and to aid in the performance of his pastoral duties, quitted Oxford on the 4th of August 1727, and continued at Epworth and Wroote until July 1728 :—He proceeded to Oxford by London, and on the 22nd of September, was ordained Priest by Dr. Potter. On the 1st of October he left the University and resided with his Father until June 1729. At this time, his brother Charles, Mr. Morgan, &c. formed a little society to assist each other in their studies, and to consult on the most advantageous methods of employing their time. Whilst in Oxford Mr. John Wesley assembled with them constantly— but in August he revisited Wroote ; whence he was recalled by an ordinance of the university, which rendered his presence at the college adviseable; he arrived there in November.

Immediately after his return he became Tutor, and presided in the hall six times weekly, as Moderator in the disputations. In his former character, he evinced that discipline which was one of his excellencies ; whilst anxious to improve his pupils, he was scrupulous of their morals, and exacted the performance of the duties which he enjoined, with a strictness altogether unprecedented in the university.

Mr. Charles Wesley had been an indefatigable student during the whole time that his brother was absent ; and for some months whilst Mr. John Wesley supplied at

Wroote, in conjunction with two or three young collegians had received the Lord's Supper weekly. The regularity of all their studies and employments procured that body the name of *Methodists* before Mr. John Wesley was summoned from Lincolnshire: he states the circumstance thus: " The exact regularity of their lives as well as studies, occasioned a young gentleman of Christ-Church to say, here is a new set of Methodists sprung up; alluding to some ancient Physicians who were so called. The name was new and quaint; so it took immediately, and the Methodists were known all over the university." Their meetings however were reduced to no order and precision until Mr. Wesley's constant residence at the college: then his history commences: " In November 1729, four young gentlemen of Oxford, Mr. John Wesley, Fellow of Lincoln-College; Mr. Charles Wesley, Student of Christ-Church; Mr. Morgan, Commoner of Christ-Church; and Mr. Kirkman, of Merton-College, began to spend some evenings in a week together, in reading chiefly the Greek Testament. The next year two or three of Mr. John Wesley's pupils desired the liberty of meeting with them: and one of Mr. Charles Wesley's pupils.— It was in 1732, that Mr. Ingham of Queen's-College, and Mr. Broughton of Exeter were added to their number. To these in April, was joined Mr. Clayton of Brazen-Nose, with two or three of his pupils. About the same time, Mr. James Hervey was permitted to meet with them, and afterwards Mr. Whitefield."

The books before alluded to produced no slight alteration in Mr. Wesley. He says, " he began to alter the form of his conversation, and to set out in earnest upon a new life." The value of time was more apparent to him; the folly of trifling acquaintance, and the necessity of discarding it was clearly displayed; the propriety of a closer application to his studies was indisputable—his

K

watchfulness against actual sin was regular, and his advice to others to live according to the gospel model was affectionately given, at all times, and to all those who dwelt within the circle in which he moved. For this conduct he was reproached with fanaticism ; the Lord grant that all mankind may speedily become such fanatics!

The society to which he belonged—added to their unusual deportment—to their regularity of life, and to their frequent meetings, a more diffused usefulness.— This was commenced by Mr. Morgan, at that time the most active of the body—they visited the sick, and the prisoners in the castle ; raised a fund for the relief of the poor ; and evinced so much diligence in obeying the ordinances of Christ—and so much industry in following his example, by going about doing good, that the scoffers in the university soon distinguished them by the name of *the Godly Club.*

Mr. Wesley and his associates abridged themselves of every superfluity, and even of some of the necessaries of life—and being aided by some gentlemen to whom they proposed their charitable objects—their fund was increased to nearly eighty pounds per year. They observed the fasts of the ancient church, communicated weekly, and became more strictly attentive to the duties of religion, until their conduct was censured in the university—the young men ridiculing, and the seniors opposing them. One gentleman threatened his nephew to discard him from his house, if he attended their meetings—but finding this ineffectual, he shook him by the throat, and not until he besought him with great condescension, could he prevail upon him to attend on the sixth Sabbath only—which he ever after continued.

Measures were now adopted to induce them to relax their strictness and godly deportment, which were the greatest possible libel upon the majority of the residents in the university. It was reported that the censors of the college were about to blow up the Godly Club:—this circumstance actuated Mr. Wesley, as the opposition to their measures assumed a serious aspect—to consult his father and some other gentlemen of piety and learning, upon the propriety of their conduct—and what ought to be their future steps? The answers which they received were of the most flattering kind—they were exhorted to be stedfast in their mode of life, and to continue in the performance of their useful duties.

The first letter from his father is dated September 21, 1730.

" As to your own designs and employments, what can I say less of them than *valde probo;* and that I have the highest reason to bless God, that he has given me two sons together at Oxford, to whom he has given grace and courage to turn the war against the world and the Devil, which is the best way to conquer them. Go on then in God's name in the path to which your Saviour has directed you. Walk as prudently as you can, though not fearfully, and my heart and prayers are with you."

The second letter was written on December 1st.

" This day I received both yours, and this evening, in the course of our reading, I thought I found an answer that would be more proper than any I myself could dictate; " Great is my glorying of you. I am filled with comfort." On the present view of your actions and designs, my daily prayers are that God would keep you humble: and then I am sure that if you continue to suffer for righteousness sake, though it be but in a lower degree, the Spirit of God and of glory shall in some good measure rest upon you. And you cannot but feel such a satisfaction in your own minds as you would not part with for all the world.—Be never weary of well-doing : never look back, for you know the prize and the crown are before you : be not high-minded, but fear. Preserve an equal temper of mind under whatever treatment you meet with, from not a very just or good-natured world. Bear no more sail than necessary, but steer steady. The less you value yourselves for these unfashionable duties, the more all good and wise men will value you ; or, which is infinitely more, he by whom actions and intentions are weighed, will both accept, esteem, and reward you.

" I hear my son John has the honour of being styled the Father of the Holy Club : if it be so, I am sure I must be the Grand-father of it; and I need not say, that I had rather any of my sons should be so dignified and distinguished, than to have the title of *His Holiness*."

The bishop of Oxford and the officiating minister at the Castle Mr. Gerald, sanctioned their proceedings.— A clergyman of great wisdom and piety was appealed to, and his answer was such as to confirm them in the path in which they had begun to walk.—Mr. Wesley senior when an under graduate at Oxford, had frequently visited the prisoners at the Castle with the same benevolent intentions. Samuel Wesley the brother, in his reply to the application made to him, says, " I think you are now in that state, wherein he who is not for you is against you. I do not know how often you meet together, yet I would rather straiten than slacken the string now, if it might be done without breaking. I cannot say, I thought you always, in every thing right; but I must now say that rather than you and Charles should give over your whole course, especially what relates to the prisoners in the Castle, I would chuse to follow either of you, nay both of you to your graves.

" I cannot advise you better than in the words which I proposed as a motto to a pamphlet. " Stand thou stedfast, as a beaten anvil to the stroke, for it is the part of a good champion to be flayed alive, and to conquer."

Is it not an extraordinary fact, that in a public institution devoted to the instruction of youth, for the important station of pastors of Christ's Church—holiness of life, a scrupulous attention to the injunctions of the New Testament—and a charity, which induced its possessors to submit to great personal deprivations, should be scoffed at with all the malevolence of the impious, ridiculed with all the buffoonery of the deist, and gravely opposed by those identical men who enjoyed honour, wealth, and ease, that they might have additional opportunities to enforce upon those committed to their charge an attention to their incumbent duties?

Had the university in general, followed their example, instead of persecuting them—they would not so long have been the disgrace of Christianity, and the seat of vice.—To silence the general clamour against their conduct, they proposed the following questions to their friends and to their opponents :—

" 1. Whether it does not concern all men of all conditions, to imitate him as much as they can, *who went about doing good?*

Whether all Christians are not concerned in that command, " *While we have time, let us do good to all men.*"

Whether we shall not be more happy hereafter, the more good we do now?

2. Whether we may not try to do good to our acquaintance among the young gentlemen in the university? Particularly, whether we may not endeavour to convince them of the necessity of being Christians, and of being scholars?

Whether we may not try to convince them of the necessity of method and industry, in order to either learning or virtue?

Whether we may not try to persuade them to confirm and increase their industry, by communicating as often as they can?

Whether we may not mention to them the authors whom we conceive to have written best on those subjects?

Whether we may not assist them as we are able, from time to time, to form resolutions upon what they read in those authors, and to execute them with steadiness and perseverance?

3. May we not try to do good to those who are hungry, naked or sick? If we know any necessitous family, may we not give them a little food, clothes or physic, as they want?

If they can read, may we not give them a Bible, a Common-Prayer Book, or a Whole Duty of Man?

May we not inquire, now and then, how they have used them; explain what they do not understand, and enforce what they do?

May we not enforce upon them the necessity of private prayer, and of frequenting the Church and Sacrament?

May we not contribute what we are able, towards having their children clothed and taught to read?

4. May we not try to do good to those who are in prison? May we not release such well-disposed persons as remain in prison for small debts?

May we not lend small sums to those who are of any trade, that they may procure themselves tools and materials to work with?

May we not give to them who appear to want it most, a little money, or clothes, or physic?"

Mr. Samuel Wesley, in a second letter to his brother, adverted to his conduct, and intimated that he was rather too precise ; that he might excite prejudices ; and that a little relaxation from his strictness might be favourable to his object. This produced a reply, dated November 17, 1731. "Considering the other changes that I remember in myself, I shall not at all wonder if the time comes, when we differ as little in our conclusions as we do now in our premises. In most we seem to agree already; especially as to rising, not keeping much company, and sitting by a fire, which I always do, if any one in the room does, whether at home or abroad. But these are the very things about which others will never agree with me. Had I given up these, or but one of them, rising early, which implies going to bed early, though I never am sleepy now, and keeping so little company, not one man in ten of those who are offended at me, as it is, would ever open their mouth against any of the other particulars. For the sake of these, those are mentioned ; the root of the matter lies here—would I but employ a third of my money, and about half my time as other folks do, smaller matters would be easily overlooked. But I think, ' *Nil tanti est*.'

" I have often thought of a saying of Dr. Hayward's, when he examined me for priest's orders ; ' Do you know what you are about ? You are bidding defiance to all mankind. He that would live a Christian priest, ought to know, whether his hand be against every man or no, he must expect every man's hand should be against him.' It is not strange that every man's hand, who is not a Christian, should be against him that endeavors to be so. But is it not hard that even those who are with us should be against us ; that a man's enemies, in some degree, should be those of the same household of faith ? Yet so it is. From the time that a man sets himself to this business, very many even of those who travel the same road, many of those who are before as well as behind him, will lay stumbling blocks in his way. One blames him for not going fast enough, another for having made no greater progress; another for going too far, which perhaps, strange as it is, is the more common charge of the two. For this comes from people of all sorts; not only infidels, not only half Christians, but some of the best of men are very apt to make this reflection, ' he lays unnecessary burdens upon himself; he is too precise; he does what God has no where required to be done.' True, he has not required it of those who are perfect; and even as to those who are not, all men are not required to use all means; but every man is required to use those which he finds most useful to himself. And who can tell better than himself, whether he finds them so or no? Who knoweth the things of a man better than the spirit of a man that is in him?

"This being a point of no common concern, I desire to explain myself upon it once for all, and to tell you freely and clearly, those general positions on which I ground all those practices, for which, as you would have seen had you read that paper through, I am generally accused of singularity. 1st. As to the end of my being; I lay it down for a rule, that I cannot be too happy and therefore too holy; and thence I infer that the more steadily I keep my eye upon the prize of our high calling, and the more of my thoughts and words and actions are directly pointed at the attainment of it, the better. 2. As to the instituted means of attaining it, I likewise lay it down for a rule, that I am to use them every time I may. 3. As to prudential means, I believe this rule holds of things indifferent in themselves; whatever I know to do me hurt, that to me is not indifferent, but resolutely to be abstained from: whatever I know to do me good, that to me is not indifferent, but resolutely to be embraced.

"But it will be said, I am whimsical. True, and what then? If by *whimsical* be meant simply *singular*, I own it; if singular without any reason, I deny it with both my hands, and am ready to give a reason to any one that asks me, of every custom wherein I differ from the world. I grant in many single actions I differ unreasonably from others, but not wilfully; no, I shall extremely thank any one who will teach me how to help it.

"As to my being *formal;* if by that be meant that I am not easy and unaffected enough in my carriage, it is very true; but how shall I help it?—If by formal be meant that I am serious, this too is very true; but why should I help it? Mirth I grant is very fit for you; but does it follow that it is fit for me? Are the same tempers, any more than the same words and actions fit for all circumstances? If you are to *rejoice evermore*, because you have put your enemies to flight, am I to do the same while they continually assault me? You are very glad because you are *passed from death to life;* well but let him be afraid who knows not whether he is to live or die. Whether this be my condition or no, who can tell better than myself? Him who can, whoever he be, I allow to be a proper judge, whether I do well to be generally as serious as I can."

In April, 1732, the little society was increased by the junction of Messrs. Clayton, Ingham, Broughton, Hervey, and one or two of Mr. C. Wesley's, and his own pupils. During the latter part of Mr. Wesley's residence at Oxford, both he and his brother Charles maintained a close intimacy with Mr. Law. Twice or thrice in the year, they travelled about sixty miles on foot, that they might save the more money for the poor, in order to visit him. Mr. Law once observed to Mr. John Wesley, "You would have a philosophical religion, but there can be no such thing. Religion is the most plain, simple thing in the world. It is only, *we love him, because he first loved us.*" Another time Mr. Law perceiving Mr. Wesley much dejected, inquired the reason. " Because," said he, " I see so little fruit of all my labours." My dear friend," replied Mr. Law, " you reverse matters from their proper order. You are to follow the divine light, wherever it leads you, in all your conduct. It is God alone that gives the blessing. I pray you, always mind your own work, and go on with cheerfulness : and God, you may depend upon it, will take care of his. Besides, sir, I perceive you would fain convert the world. But you must wait God's own time. Nay, if after all he is pleased to use you only as *a hewer of wood or drawer of water*, you should submit, yea, you should be thankful to him that he has honoured you so far."

During this summer, Mr. Wesley twice visited Epworth; and in the first journey narrowly escaped death by the falling of a garden wall upon which he was standing. The object of his second attendance there, was to be present with all the family previous to his father's death and his brother's removal to Tiverton. Mr. Wesley returned to Oxford on the 23d of September ; where he received a letter from Mr. Morgan's father, who informed him of the departure of his son. He left the college on the 25th of June, and died in Dublin on the 26th of August, after a decline of more than twelve months, which the university-railers attributed to his fasting in conformity to Mr. Wesley's advice. To obviate the evils which such a report might produce, should it have reached Mr. Morgan senior, Mr. Wesley wrote to him, dated October 18th. " The occasion," says he, " of giving you this trouble, is of a very extraordinary nature. On Sunday last I was informed, as no doubt you will be ere long, that my brother and I had killed your son ; that the rigorous fasting which he had imposed upon himself by our advice, had increased his illness and hastened his death. Now, though considering in itself, *it is a very small thing with me to be judged of man's judgment;* yet as the being thought guilty of so mischievous an imprudence, might make me less able to do the work I came into the world for, I am obliged to clear myself of it, by observing to you, as I have done to others, that your son left off fasting about a year and a half since, and that it is not yet half a year since I began to practise it.

" I must not let this opportunity slip of doing my part towards giving you a juster notion of some other particulars, relating both to him and myself, which have been industriously misrepresented to you.

" In March last he received a letter from you, which not being able to read, he desired me to read to him; several of the expressions I perfectly remember, and shall do, till I too am called hence.—In one practice for which you blamed your son, I am concerned as a friend, not as a partner. Your own account of it was in effect this : ' He frequently went into poor people's houses about Holt, called their children together and instructed them in their duty to God, their neighbour, and themselves. He likewise explained to them the necessity of private as well as public prayer, and provided them with such forms as were best suited to their several capacities'; and being well apprized how the success of his endeavours depended on their good will towards him, he sometimes distributed among them a little of that money which he had saved from gaming and other fashionable expences of the place.' This is the first charge against him, and I will refer it to your own judgment, whether it be fitter to have a place in the catalogue of his faults or of those virtues for which he is *now numbered among the sons of God.*

" If all the persons concerned in that ridiculous society, whose follies you have so often heard repeated, could but give such a proof of their deserving the glorious title which was once bestowed upon them, they would be contented that their *lives too should be counted madness, and their end thought to be without honour.* But the truth is, their title to holiness stands upon much less stable foundations; as you will easily perceive when you know the ground of this wonderful outcry, which it seems England itself is not wide enough to contain.

"As for the names of Methodists, Supererogation-men, and so on, with which some of our neighbours are pleased to compliment us, we do not conceive ourselves to be under any obligation to regard them, much less to take them for arguments. To the law and to the testimony we appeal, whereby we ought to be judged. If by these it can be proved we are in error, we will immediately and gladly retract it: if not, *we have not so learned Christ*, as to renounce any part of his service, though men should say all manner of evil against us, with more judgment, and as little truth as hitherto. We do indeed use all the lawful means which we know, to prevent the good which is in us from being evil spoken of; but if the neglect of known duties, be the condition of securing our reputation, why fare it well. We know whom we have believed, and what we thus lay out, he will pay us again. Your son already stands before the judgment seat of him who judges righteous judgment, at the brightness of whose presence the clouds remove; his eyes are open, and he sees clearly whether it was, ' Blind zeal and a thorough mistake of true religion that hurried him on in the error of his way,' or whether he acted like a faithful and wise servant, who from a just sense that his time was short, made haste to finish his work before his Lord's coming, that when *laid in the balance*, he might not *be found wanting.*"

This letter fully satisfied Mr. Morgan, and gave him a better opinion of the society with which his son had been connected. His answer is dated November 25:—

" Your favour of the 20th past was delayed in its passage, I believe by contrary winds, or it had not been so long unanswered. I give entire credit to every thing and every fact you relate. It was ill-judged of my poor son to take to fasting with regard to his health, which I knew nothing of, or I should have advised him against it. He was inclined to piety and virtue from his infancy. I must own I was much concerned at the strange accounts which were spread here, of some extraordinary practices of a religious society which he had engaged in at Oxford, which you may be sure lost nothing in the carriage, lest through his youth and immaturity of judgment, he might be hurried into zeal and enthusiastic notions that would prove pernicious. But now indeed, that piety and holiness of life which he practised, affords me some comfort in the midst of my affliction for the loss of him; having full assurance of his being for ever happy.

" The good account you are pleased to give of your own and your friends' conduct in point of duty and religious offices, and the zealous approbation of them by the good old gentleman your father, signified in a manner and style becoming the best of men, reconciles and recommends that method of life to me, and makes me almost wish that I were one amongst you. I am very much obliged to you, for the great pains you have been at in transcribing so long and so particular an account for my perusal, and shall be always ready to vindicate you from any calumny or aspersion that I shall hear cast upon you. I am much obliged for your and your brother's great civilities and assistances to my dearest son: and I thank the author of those lines you sent me, for regard he has shewn to his memory. If ever I can be the serviceable to any of you in this kingdom, I beg you will let me know."

A correspondence took place between Mr. Wesley and Mr. Morgan, and the year following Mr. Morgan sent his only son to Oxford, and placed him under Mr. Wesley's care; the strongest proof which he could possibly give, that he approved of his conduct.

January 1st 1733, Mr. Wesley preached before the university at St. Mary's, his sermon *on the circumcision of the heart:* he soon after visited Epworth: in his journey his horse fell from the bridge into a stream of water near Daintry, but Providence preserved his life.

On the 21st of September 1733, Mr. Wesley began the practice of reading as he travelled on horseback, which he continued nearly forty years, until his infirmities obliged him to travel in a carriage. His frequent journies, often on foot as well as on horseback, and the great and constant labour of preaching, reading, visiting, &c. wherever he was, with close study and a very abstemious diet, had now very much affected his health. His strength was greatly reduced, and he had frequent returns of spitting of blood. In the night of the 16th of July, he had a return of it, and the sudden, unexpected manner of its attack, with the solemnity of the night season, made eternity seem near. He cried to God; " O! prepare me for thy coming, and come when thou wilt." His friends began to be alarmed for his safety, and his mother wrote two or three letters blaming him for the general neglect of his health. He now took the advice of a physician or two, and by proper care and prudent management of his daily exercise, he gradually lost his complaints, and recovered his strength.

Mr. Wesley's father had been declining some years, and as the close of life appeared to be approaching, he expressed much anxiety that the living of Epworth should remain in the family. When the subject was first mentioned to Mr. Wesley in the beginning of the year 1734, he was undecided respecting his coalescing.

with his father's wish. The latter wrote to him in the fall of the year, requesting him to apply for the next presentation—but he had then altogether determined not to accept the living even if he could obtain it. To the wishes of a parent, were superadded the desires of the people—the interest and the welfare of his family:—but these arguments were urged in vain—he had conceived so inspuerable an attachment to Oxford and anticipated so much benefit from his friends and advantages in the colleges, that he resolved not to accede to his request.

This denial was succeeded by a correspondence between his father, his brother, and himself—in which the two former laboured to persuade him, of the futility of his objections—and of the numerous claims which this situation had upon him.

Although no person can doubt that he was not induced to this refusal by any sordid motives, yet it is questionable how far he was right in the opinions which he adopted.—Of the worldly interest in either case, probably there was little difference:—and the extra labour it is nedless to mention—as in whatever situation Providence might have permitted him to have moved, he would have been, as he was for sixty years, industry and diligence embodied.

In the view of a serious mind however, it must be allowed, that the opinion and desire of a venerable father, the comfort of a dependent and numerous family—and the unanimous request of a whole parish, are considerations of great moment—and although he was himself convinced, and Providence admitted it for the most wise designs—yet it cannot be disputed—that in Providential difficulties, where the impressions of the party in doubt are opposed by the most sensible men, the best judges, and other friends allied by the strongest ties, and endeared by natural affection; when to this is joined the voice of a congregation, it behoves a man to pause, and if he do not resign his judgment, to suspend his decision. Nevertheless a perusal of that correspondence, will demonstrate to every person that he acted with the utmost integrity, and that with a good conscience he could not have swerved from his determination.

The living of Epworth was disposed of in May 1735 immediately after the decease of Mr. Wesley's father, who had desired him to present his commentary on Job to the Queen. Whilst in London on this occasion—the Trustees of Georgia strongly solicited him and his brother to sail thither as missionaries, and introduced him to Mr. Oglethorpe the Governor. He gave them no positive answer, but wished to know the opinion of his friends. The chief of his objections respected his mother. " I am," says he, " the staff of her age, her chief support and comfort." It was asked in reply, " Will you go, if your mother's consent can be obtained?" This he thought impossible: however, he permitted the trial, settling it in his heart that if she was willing, he would receive it as the call of God. Her answer was worthy of her: " Had I," said she, " twenty sons, I should rejoice that they were all so employed, though I should never see them more."

His mother, sister, brother, and other friends consenting to his acceptance of the proposal, he determined upon the mission; which occasioned the following letters from Dr. Burton, who had been chiefly instrumental in engaging him to resign his pupils, and to leave his friends and country. " It was with no small pleasure, that I heard your resolution on the point under consideration. I am persuaded, that an opportunity is offered of doing much good in an affair, for the conducting of which we can find but few proper instruments. Your undertaking it adds greater credit to our proceedings; and the propagation of religion will be the distinguishing honour of our colony. This has ever, in like cases, been the *desideratum* : a defect seemingly lamented, but scarcely ever remedied. With greater satisfaction therefore, we enjoy your readiness to undertake the work. When it is known, that good men are thus employed, the pious and charitable will be the more encouraged to promote the work. You have too much steadiness of mind, to be disturbed by the light scoffs of the idle and profane. Let me put a matter to be considered by your brother Charles. Would it not be more adviseable that he were in Orders?"

On the 28th of the same month, a few days before Mr. Oglethorpe intended to sail, Dr. Burton wrote again to Mr. Wesley, giving him advice respecting his future situation. " Under the influence of Mr. Oglethorpe, giving weight to your endeavours, much may be effected under the present circumstances. The apostolical manner of preaching, from house to house, will, through God's grace, be effectual to turn many to righteousness. The people are babes in the progress of their Christian life, and must be fed with milk instead of strong meat ; and the wise householder will bring out of his stores, food proportioned to the necessities of his family. The circumstances of your present Christian pilgrimage will furnish the most affecting subjects of discourse ; and what arises *pro re nata*, will have greater influence than a laboured discourse on a subject, in which men think themselves not so immediately concerned. With regard to your behaviour and manner of address, that must be determined according to the different circumstances of persons, &c. But you will always, in the use of means, consider the great end, and therefore your applications will of course vary. You will keep in view the pattern of that gospel preacher St. Paul, who became all things to all men, that he might gain some. Here is a nice trial of Christian prudence :

accordingly, in every case you will distinguish between what is essential, and what is merely circumstantial to Christianity; between what is indispensable, and what is variable; between what is of divine, and what is of human authority. I mention this, because men are apt to deceive themselves in such cases, and we see the traditions and ordinances of men frequently insisted on, with more rigour than the commandments of God, to which they are subordinate. Singularities of less importance, are often espoused with more zeal, than the weighty matters of God's law. As in all points we love ourselves, so especially in our hypotheses.

Where a man has, as it were, a property in a notion, he is most industrious to improve it, and that in proportion to the labour of thought he has bestowed upon it; and as its value rises in imagination, we are in proportion more unwilling to give it up, and dwell upon it more pertinaciously, than upon considerations of general necessity and use. This is a flattering mistake, against which we should guard ourselves. I hope to see you at Gravesend if possible. I write in haste what occurs to my thoughts—*disce docendus adhuc, quæ censet amiculus.* May God prosper your endeavours for the propagation of his gospel!"

The following narrative by Mr. Gambold, an intimate acquaintance of the two brothers, was composed during their absence in Georgia :—" About the middle of March 1730, I became acquainted with Mr. Charles Wesley, of Christ-Church. I had been for two years before in deep melancholy; so it pleased God to disappoint and break a proud spirit, and to embitter the world to me as I was inclining to relish its vanities. During this time, I had no friend to whom I could open my mind; no man did care for my soul, or none at least understood her paths. The learned endeavoured to give me right notions, and the friendly to divert me.

One day an old acquaintance entertained me with some reflections on the whimsical Mr. Charles Wesley; his preciseness, and pious extravagancies. Upon hearing this, I suspected he might be a good Christian. I therefore went to his room, and without ceremony desired the benefit of his conversation. I had so large a share of it afterwards, that hardly a day passed while I was at College, but we were together once, if not oftener.

" After some time, he introduced me to his brother John, of Lincoln-College : ' For he is somewhat older,' said he, ' than I am, and can resolve your doubts better.' I never observed any person have a more real deference for another than he had for his brother; which is the more remarkable, because such near relations, being equals by birth, and conscious to each other of all the little familiar passages of their lives, commonly stand too close, to see the ground there may be for such submission. Indeed he followed his brother entirely; could I describe one of them I should describe both. I shall therefore say no more of Charles, but that he was a man formed for friendship; who by his cheerfulness and vivacity would refresh his friend's heart: with attentive consideration would enter into, and settle all his concerns as far as he was able: he would do any thing for him, great or small, and by a habit of mutual openness and freedom, would leave no room for misunderstanding.

" The Wesleys were already talked of for some religious practices, which were first occasioned by Mr. Morgan, of Christ-Church. He was a young man of an excellent disposition. He took all opportunities to make his companions in love with a good life; to create in them a reverence for the public worship: to tell them of their faults with a sweetness and simplicity that disarmed the worst tempers. He delighted much in works of charity; he kept several children at school; and, when he found beggars in the street, would bring them into his chambers, and talk to them. From these combined friends began a little society. Mr. John Wesley was the chief manager, for which he was very fit: for he had not only more learning and experience than the rest, but he was blest with such activity as to be always gaining ground, and such steadiness that he lost none. What proposals he made to any, were sure to alarm them; because he was so much in earnest; nor could they afterwards slight them, because they saw him always the same. What supported this uniform vigour, was the care he took to consider well every affair before he engaged in it; making all his decisions in the fear of God, without passion, humour, or self-confidence. For though he had naturally a very clear apprehension, yet his exact prudence depended more on his humility and singleness of heart. He had, I think, something of authority in his countenance, yet he never assumed any thing to himself above his companions; any of them might speak their mind, and their words were as strictly regarded by him as his words were by them.

" Their undertaking included these several particulars: to converse with young students; to visit the prisons; to instruct some poor families; to take care of a school and a parish workhouse. They took great pains with the younger members of the University, to rescue them from bad company, and to encourage them in a sober studious life. They would get them to breakfast, and over a dish of tea endeavour to fasten some good hint upon them. They would bring them acquainted with other well-disposed young men, give them assistance in the difficult parts of their learning, and watch over them with the greatest tenderness.

Some or other of them went to the Castle every day, and another most commonly to Bocardo. Whoever went to the Castle was to read in the Chapel to as many prisoners as would attend, and to talk apart to the man or men whom he had taken particularly in charge. When a new prisoner came, their conversation with him for four or five times was close and searching.—If any one was under sentence of death, or appeared to have some intentions of a new life, they came every day to his assistance, and partook in the conflict and suspense of those who should now be found able, or not able to lay hold on salvation. In order to release those who were confined for small debts, and to purchase books and other necessaries, they raised a little fund, to which many of their acquaintance contributed quarterly. They had prayers at the Castle most Wednesdays and Fridays, a sermon on Sunday, and the sacrament once a month.

" When they undertook any poor family, they saw them at least once a week ; sometimes gave them money, admonished them of their vices, read to them, and examined their children. The school was, I think, of Mr. Wesley's own setting up ; however he paid the mistress, and clothed some, if not all the children. When they went thither, they inquired how each child behaved, saw their work, heard them read and say their prayers, or catechism, and explain part of it. In the same manner they taught the children in the workhouse, and read to the old people as they did to the prisoners.

" They seldom took any notice of the accusations brought against them for their charitable employments; but if they did make any reply, it was commonly such a plain and simple one, as if there was nothing more in the case, but that they had just heard such doctrines of their Saviour, and had believed and done accordingly. Sometimes they would ask such questions as the following: " Shall we be more happy in another life, the more virtuous we are in this? Are we the more virtuous the more intensely we love God and man? Is love, of all habits, the more intense, the more we exercise it? Is either helping or trying to help man for God's sake, an exercise of love to God or man? particularly, is feeding the hungry, clothing the naked, visiting the sick, or prisoners, an exercise of love to God or man? Is endeavouring to teach the ignorant, to admonish sinners, to encourage the good, to comfort the afflicted, and reconcile enemies, an exercise of love to God or man? Shall we be more happy in another life, if we do the former of these things, and try to do the latter; or if we do not the one, nor try to do the other?"

" I could say a great deal of his private piety; how it was nourished by a continual recourse to God; and preserved by a strict watchfulness in beating down pride, and reducing the craftiness and impetuosity of nature, to child-like simplicity; and in a good degree crowned with divine love, and victory over the whole set of earthly passions. He thought prayer to be more his business than any thing else; and I have seen him come out of his closet with a serenity of countenance that was next to shining; it discovered what he had been doing, and gave me double hope of receiving wise directions, in the matter about which I came to consult him. In all his motions he attended to the will of God. He had neither the presumption, nor the leisure to anticipate things whose season was not now; and would shew some uneasiness whenever any of us, by impertinent speculations, were shifting off the appointed improvement of the present minute. By being always cheerful, but never triumphing, he so husbanded the secret consolations which God gave him, that they seldom left him, and never but in a state of strong and long-suffering faith. Thus the repose and satisfaction of the mind being otherwise secured, there were in him no idle cravings, no chagrin or fickleness of spirit, nothing but the genuine wants of the body to be relieved by outward accommodations and refreshments. When he was just come home from a long journey, and had been in different companies, he resumed his usual employments, as if he had never left them; no dissipation of thought appeared, no alteration of taste: much less was he discomposed by any slanders or affronts; he was only afraid lest he should grow proud of his conformity to his Master. In short, he used many endeavours to be religious, but none to seem so; with a zeal always upon the stretch and a most transparent sincerity, he addicted himself to every good word and work.

"Because he required such a regulation of our studies, as might devote them all to God, he has been accused as one that discouraged learning. Far from that, for the first thing he struck at in young men, was that indolence which will not submit to close thinking. He earnestly recommended to them, a method and order in all their actions. The morning hour of devotion was from five to six, and the same in the evening. On the point of early rising, he told them, the well spending of the day would depend. For some years past he and his friends have read the New Testament together in the evenings; and after every portion of it, having heard the conjectures the rest had to offer, he made his own observations on the phrase, design, and difficult places; and one or two wrote these down from his mouth.

"If any one could have provoked him, I should; for I was very slow in coming into his measures, and very remiss in doing my part. I frequently contradicted his assertions; or, which is much the same, distinguished upon them. I hardly ever submitted to his advice at the time he gave it, though I relented afterwards. One time he was in fear I had taken up notions that were not safe, and pursued my spiritual improvement in an erroneous, because inactive way; so he came over and staid with me near a week. He condoled with me the incumbrances of my constitution, heard all I had to say, and endeavoured to pick out my meaning, and yielded to me as far as he could. I never saw more humility in him than at this time.

"Mr. Wesley had not only friends at Oxford to assist but a great many correspondents. He set apart one day at least in the week, to write letters, and he was no slow composer; in which, without levity or affectation, but with plainness and fervour, he gave his advice in particular cases, and vindicated the strict original sense of the gospel precepts.

"He is now gone to Georgia as a Missionary, where there is ignorance that aspires after divine wisdom, but no false learning that is got above it. He is I confess, still living; and I know that an advantageous character is more decently bestowed on the deceased. But, besides that his condition is very like that of the dead, being unconcerned in all we say, I am not making any attempt on the opinion of the public, but only studying a private edification. A family picture of him, his relations may be allowed to keep by them. And this is the idea of Mr. Wesley, which I cherish for the service of my own soul, and which I take the liberty likewise to deposit with you."

Mr. *Wesley's Mission to Georgia.*

ON Tuesday, the 14th of October 1735, Mr. Wesley embarked for Georgia, on board the Simmonds at Gravesend. His companions were Mr. Ingham of Queen's College, Mr. Delamotte, and Mr. Charles Wesley: General Oglethorpe was a passenger in the same vessel. He wrote to his brother Samuel on the following day, informing him that he had presented his father's commentary on Job to the Queen. In this letter he declares his sentiments concerning the use of the heathen poets in large schools. "The uncertainty of having another opportunity to tell you my thoughts in this life, obliges me to tell you what I have often thought of, and that in as few and plain words as I can. Elegance of style is not to be weighed against purity of heart; purity both from the lusts of the flesh, the lusts of the eye, and the pride of life. Therefore, whatever has a tendency to impair that purity, is not to be tolerated, much less recommended for the sake of that elegance. But of this sort are most of the classics usually read in great schools: I beseech you therefore, by the mercies of God, who would have us holy as he is holy, that you banish all such poison from your school, that you introduce in their place such Christian authors as will work together with you in building up your flock in the knowledge and love of God.

"So many souls are committed to your charge by God, to be prepared for a happy eternity. You are to instruct them, not only in the beggarly elements of Greek and Latin, but much more in the gospel. You are to labour with all your might to convince them that Christianity is not a negation, or an external thing, but a new heart, a mind conformed to that of Christ; faith, working by love."

Every judicious Christian will here join with Mr. Wesley; and it must be regretted, that in most of our academies those authors which are introduced as the means of instruction in the language, tend only to vitiate the mind, and usurp the place of those works, which if studied, would contribute to the highest moral improvement. Ovid, Horace, some parts of Virgil, Terence, and others of the poets, are very improper school books; and yet they are generally preferred to the historians and the moralists.

The vessel remaining in the river, he preached without notes, and administered the Lord's Supper upon deck, on Friday the 17th. He had once before departed from the usual practice: this happened when he upon some occasion attended at Allhallows' to hear Dr. Heylin: the Doctor not coming, Mr. Wesley was requested to supply for him—and being unprovided with a sermon, delivered his address extempore.

Having sailed from Gravesend they reached the Downs on the 21st. " Now," says Mr. Wesley, " We began to be a little regular. Our common way of living was this: from four in the morning until five, each of us used private prayer. From five until seven we read the bible together, carefully comparing it with the writings of the earliest ages. At seven we breakfasted—at eight were the public prayers—from nine to twelve I usually learned German, and Mr. Delamotte, Greek. My brother wrote sermons, and Mr. Ingham instructed the children. At twelve we met to give an account to one another of what we had done since our last meeting, and of what we designed to do before our next. About one we dined. The time from dinner to four, we spent in reading to those of whom each of us had taken charge, or in speaking to them severally, as need required. At four were the evening prayers: when either the second lesson was explained, or the children catechised and instructed before the congregation. From five to six we again used private prayer. From six to seven I read in our cabin to two or three of the passengers, and each of my brethren to a few more in theirs. At seven I joined with the Germans in their public service; while Mr. Ingham was reading between the decks, to as many as desired to hear. At eight we met again, to exhort and instruct one another. Between nine and ten we went to bed, where neither the roaring of the sea nor the motion of the ship could take away the refreshing sleep which God gave us." The heavy gales and contrary winds usual at that season of the year retarded them until the 10th of December, on which day they departed from Cowes.

On Thurday, the 15th of January 1736, complaint being made to Mr. Oglethorpe of the unequal distribution of water to the passengers, new officers were appointed, and the old ones were highly exasperated against Mr. Wesley, who as they supposed, had made the complaint.—From the 17th to the 25th, they had violent storms, the sea going frequently over the ship, and breaking the cabin windows. On these occasions he found the fear of death brought him into some degree of bondage: at the same time he could not but observe the lively victorious faith which appeared in the Germans, and which kept their minds in a state of tranquility and ease, to which he and the English on board were strangers: " I had long before observed the great seriousness of their behaviour. Of their humility they had given a continual proof, by performing those servile offices for the other passengers which none of the English would undertake; for which they desired, and would receive no pay; saying, "It was good for their proud hearts, and their loving Saviour had done more for them." And every day had given them occasion of shewing a meekness, which no injury could move. If they were pushed, struck, or thrown down, they rose again and went away; but no complaint was found in their mouth. There was now an opportunity of trying whether they were delivered from the spirit of fear, as well as from that of pride, anger, and revenge. In the midst of the psalm wherewith their service began, the sea broke over, split the main-sail in pieces, covered the ship, and poured in between the decks, as if the great deep had already swallowed us up. A terrible screaming began among the English. The Germans calmly sung on. I asked one of them afterwards, "Was you not afraid?" He answered, "I thank God, no." I asked, "But were not your women and children afraid? He replied mildly, "No, our women and children are not afraid to die."

The following anecdote is preserved as an excellent trait in the character of Mr. Wesley. He hearing an unusual noise in the cabin of general Oglethorpe, stepped in to inquire the cause of it: on which the general immediately addressed him, " Mr. Wesley you must excuse me, I have met with a provocation too great for man to bear. You know, the only wine I drink is Cyprus wine, as it agrees with me the best of any. I therefore provided myself with several dozens of it, and this villain Grimaldi," his foreign servant, who was present, and almost dead with fear, " has drank up the whole of it. But I will be revenged of him. I have ordered him to be tied hand and foot, and to be carried to the man of war which sails with us. The rascal should have taken care how he used me so, for *I never forgive.*" " Then, I hope sir," said Mr. Wesley, looking calmly at him, " *You never sin.*" The general was quite confounded at the reproof; and putting his hand into his pocket, took out a bunch of keys which he threw at Grimaldi, saying, " There villain, take my keys, and behave better for the future."

They saw the land on the 4th of February 1736, and on the morning of the 6th, landed on a small island in Savannah River; immediately after their landing they all prostrated themselves and returned thanks to God for his goodness manifested to them during a perilous passage. Whilst at sea Mr. Wesley discontinued the use of flesh and wine, confining himself to vegetables, rice and biscuit, he also desisted from eating suppers, and slept upon the floor of the cabin, his bed having been wetted, without inconvenience. February 7, Mr. Oglethorpe retunrned from Savannah, with Mr. Spangenberg, one of the German Pastors. " I soon found," says Mr. Wesley, " what spirit he was of; and asked his advice with regard to my own conduct. He said, " My brother, I must first ask you one or two questions. Have you the witness within yourself? Does the spirit of God bear witness with your spirit, that you are the child of God?" I was surprised and knew not what to answer. He observed it, and asked, " Do you know Jesus Christ?" I paused and said, I know he is the Saviour of the world. " True; replied he; but do you know he has saved you?" I answered, I hope he has died to save me. He only added, " Do you know yourself?" I said, I do. But I fear they were vain words."—On the 14th, some Indians came to them, and shook them by the hand, one of them saying, " I am glad you are come. When I was in England, I desired that some would speak the great word to me, and my nation then desired to hear it; but now we are all in confusion. Yet I am glad you are come. I will go up and speak to the wise men of our nation; and I hope they will hear. But we would not be made Christians, as the Spaniards make Christians: we would be taught, before we are baptized." Mr. Wesley answered, " There is but one, he that sitteth in " heaven, who is able to teach man wisdom. Though " we are come so far, we know not whether he will " please to teach you by us or not. If he teach you, " you will learn wisdom; but we can do nothing."

The house at Savannah in which they were to reside not being ready, Mr. Wesley with Mr. Delamotte, took up their lodging with the Germans. Here they had an opportunity of being better acquainted with them, and of closely observing the whole of their behaviour, from morning till night. Mr. Wesley gives them an excellent character. " They were always employed, always cheerful themselves, and in good humour with one another. They had put away all anger, and strife, and wrath, and bitterness, and clamour, and evil-speaking. They walked worthy of the vocation wherewith they were called, and adorned the Gospel of our Lord in all things." " Feb. 28. They met to consult concerning the affairs of their church. After several hours spent in conference and prayer, they proceeded to the election and ordination of a bishop. The great simplicity, as well as solemnity of the whole, almost made me forget the seventeen hundred years between, and imagine myself in one of those assemblies where form and state were not; but Paul the tent-maker, or Peter the fisherman presided; yet with the demonstration of the spirit and of power."

Sunday, March 7, He entered on his ministry at Savannah, by preaching on the epistle for the day, being the 13th of the first of Corinthians. In the second lesson, Luke xviii. was our Lord's prediction of the treatment which he himself, and consequently his followers, should meet with from the world.—He adds, " Yet notwithstanding these plain declarations of our Lord; notwithstanding my own repeated experience; notwithstanding the experience of all the sincere followers of Christ, whom I have ever talked with, read, or heard of: nay and the reason of the thing, evincing to a demonstration, that all who love not the light must hate him who is continually labouring to pour it in upon them: I do here bear witness against myself, that when I saw the number of people crowding into the church, the deep attention with which they received the word, and the seriousness that afterwards sat on all their faces; I could scarce refrain from giving the lie to experience and reason and scripture all together. I could hardly believe that the greater, the far greater part of this attentive serious people, would hereafter trample under foot that word, and say all manner of evil falsely of him that spake it."

April 4th, Mr. Wesley left Savannah to visit his brother Charles at Frederica—the pettiawga came to an anchor on the passage—wrapping himself up in his cloak, he slept on the deck, and in the course of the night, rolling out of his cloak, fell into the sea, so fast asleep, that until his mouth was filled with water, he did not perceive his situation—He then swam to the boat and gained the vessel.

Not finding as yet any open door for pursuing his design of preaching to the Indians, he consulted with his companions, in what manner they might be most useful to the little flock at Savannah. It was agreed, 1. To advise the more serious among them, to form themselves into a little society, and to meet once or twice a week, to reprove, instruct, and exhort one another. 2. To select out of these a smaller number for a more intimate union with each other; which might be forwarded partly by their conversing singly with each, and inviting them altogether to Mr. Wesley's house: and this accordingly they determined to do every Sunday in the afternoon.

The mode of instructing the children is detailed by him in a letter to some gentlemen who had presented the colony with a library: " Our gener l method of catechising, is this; a young gentleman who came with me teaches between thirty and forty children to read, write, and cast accounts. Before school in the morning, and after school in the afternoon, he catechises the lowest class, and endeavours to fix something of what was said in their understanding, as well as in their memories. In the evening he instructs the larger children. On Sunday in the afternoon I catechise them all. The same I do on Sunday before the evening-service: and in the church immediately after the second lesson, a select number of them having repeated the catechism, and been examined in some part of it, I endeavour to explain at large, and enforce that part, both on them and the congregation.

" Some time after the evening-service, as many of my parishioners as desire it, meet at my house and spend about an hour in prayer, singing, and mutual exhortation. A smaller number, mostly those who design to communicate the next day, meet here on Saturday evenings: and a few of these come to me on the other evenings, and pass half an hour in the same employment."

Mr. Wesley's labours on the Lord's day, are thus related by himself, " The English service lasted from five till half an hour past six. The Italian began at nine. The second service for the English, including the sermon and the holy communion, continued from half an hour past ten, till about half an hour past twelve. The French service began at one. At two I catechised the children. About three began the English service. After this was ended, I joined with as many as my large room would hold, in reading, prayer and singing. And about six the service of the Germans began; at which I was glad to be present, not as a teacher, but as a learner."

His health was astonishingly preserved during his visit to Georgia; and the hardships which he suffered improved his constitution. He continued his custom of eating little, of sleeping less, and of leaving not a moment of his time unemployed. He exposed himself with the utmost indifference to every change of season, and to all kinds of weather. Snow and hail, storm and tempest, had no effect on his body. He frequently slept on the ground in the summer, under the heavy dews of the night; and in the winter with his hair and clothes frozen to the earth in the morning. He would wade through swamps, and swim over rivers in his clothes, and then travel on till they were dry, without any apparent injury to his health.

His stay at Savannah was embittered, and his usefulness altogether hindered by a dispute which was excited by some persons who disliked his strict deportment, and by the dissolution of his connection with Mr. Causton's family. Those circumstances hastened his departure from Georgia. Numberlesss improprieties were laid to his charge, and he was persecuted by Mr. Causton the chief magistrate of Savannah with every degree of intemperate virulence. The narratives of his biographers differ very materially on the subject of his acquaintance with Mrs. Williamson; but it seems certain, that two females of whom she previous to her marriage was one, were appointed to allure him from the path of strict propriety—that he felt some attachment to Miss Causton—and that from her disappointment proceeded much of the bitter usage which he afterwards experienced. They asserted that he embezzled the publick money; he therefore wrote to the Georgia Trustees from whom he received this reply:

Dear Sir,

"I communicated your letter to the Board this morning. We are surprised at your apprehensions of being charged with the imputation of having embezzled any publick or private monies. I cannot learn any ground for even suspicion of any thing of this kind. We beg you not to give weight to reports or private insinuations. The Trustees have a high esteem of your good services, and on all occasions will give further encouragement: and would not have the express mention of the fifty pounds, in lieu of the same sum formerly advanced by the Society for propagation, so understood, as not to admit of enlargement upon proper occasions. I am ordered by all the members present to acquaint you of this, and to give you assurance of their approbation 'of your conduct, and readiness to assist you. The V. Prov. of Eton has given you ten pounds, for your private use and doing works of charity. Mr. Whitefield, will shortly, and by the next convenient opportunity go over to Georgia. There are three hundred acres granted to the church in Frederica. Be not discouraged by hasty insinuations; but hope the best. In good time matters will bear a better face. God strengthen your hands, and give efficacy to your honest endeavours. I am, yonr affectionate friend,

" J. BURTON."

Having in conformity with the Rubrick refused to administer the Lord's supper to Mrs. Williamson because she would not comply with the regulations of the church; he was apprehended by a warrant—and at the succeeding session after much artifice on Mr. Causton's part was presented to the court by the Grand Jury upon charges not within their jurisdiction—having in vain endeavoured to procure a trial at six successive courts, he determined to leave Savannah, and to return home. In September, he was encouraged to persist by a clergyman of Charleston, and about the same time he received a consolatory letter from Doctor Cutler of Boston, " I am sorry, Sir," says he, " for the clouds hanging over your mind, respecting your undertaking and situation : but I hope God will give an happy increase to that good seed you have planted and watered, according to his will. The best of men in all ages, have failed in the success of their labour; and there will ever be found too many enemies to the cross of Christ : for earth will not be heaven. This reminds us of that happy place, where we shall not see and be grieved for transgressors ; and where, for our wellmeant labours, our judgment is with the Lord, and our reward with our God. And you well know, Sir, that under the saddest appearances, we may have some share in the consolations which God gave Elijah ; and may trust in him, that there is some wickedness we repress or prevent; some goodness by our means, weak and unworthy as we are, beginning and increasing in the hearts of men, at present ; perhaps like a grain of mustard-seed, that in God's time may bud forth, and spread, and flourish : and that, if the world seems not the better for us, it might be worse without us. Our low opinion of ourselves is a preparative to these successes ; and so the modest and great Apostle found it.

" No doubt, Sir, you have temptations where you are, nor is there any retreat from them ; they hint to us the care we must take, and the promises we must apply to : and blessed is the man that endureth temptation.

" I rejoice in the good character you give, which I believe you well bestow, of Mr. Whitefield, who is coming to you—but I question not, but his labours will be better joined with, than supersede yours : and even his, and all our sufficiency and efficiency is of God.

" It is the least we can do to pray for one another ; and if God will hear me, a great sinner, it will strengthen your interest in him. I recommend myself to a share in your prayers, for his pardon, acceptance, and assistance; and beg that my family—may not be forgotten by you."

After a pretended opposition made to his departure by the magistrates, he left Savannah for Charleston, on the 2nd of December, 1737. His relation of the journey is very interesting : " Saturday, December 3. We came to Purrysburg early in the morning, and endeavoured to procure a guide for Port-Royal. But none being to be had, we set out without one, an hour before sun-rise. After walking two or three hours, we met with an old man, who led us into a small path, near which was a line of blazed trees, i. e. marked by cutting off part of the bark, by following which, he said we might easily come to Port-Royal in five or six hours.

" We were four in all ; one of whom intended to go for England with me ; the other two to settle in Carolina. About eleven we came into a large swamp, where we wandered about till near two. We then found another blaze, and pursued it, till it divided into two ; one of these we followed through an almost impassable thicket, a mile beyond which it ended. We made through the thicket again, and traced the other blaze, till that ended too. It now grew toward sunset, so we sat down, faint and weary, having had no food all day, except a ginger-bread cake, which I had taken in my pocket. A third of this we had divided among us at noon ; another third we took now ; the rest we reserved for the morning ; but we had met with no water all the day. Thrusting a stick into the ground, and finding the end of it moist, two of our company fell a digging with their hands, and at about three feet depth found water. We thanked God, drank, and were refreshed. The night was sharp ; however, there was no complaining among us ; but after having commended ourselves to God, we lay down close together, and I at least slept till near six in the morning.

"Sunday, December 4. God renewing our strength, we arose neither faint nor weary, and resolved to make one trial more, to find a path to Port-Royal. We steered due East; but finding neither path nor blaze, and the woods growing thicker and thicker, we judged it would be our best course to return, if we could, by the way we came. The day before, in the thickest part of the woods, I had broke many young trees, I knew not why, as we walked along; these we found a great help in several places, where no path was to be seen; and between one and two God brought us safe to Benjamin Arien's House, the old man we left the day before.

"In the evening I read French prayers to a numerous family, a mile from Arien's; one of whom undertook to guide us to Port-Royal. In the morning we set out. About sun-set, we asked our guide if he knew where he was? Who frankly answered, No. However, we pushed on, till about seven we came to a plantation, and the next evening, after many difficulties and delays we landed on Port-Royal Island.

"Wednesday 7. We walked to Beaufort; where Mr. Jones, the minister of Beaufort, with whom I lodged during my short stay here, gave me a lively idea of the old English hospitality. On Thursday, Mr. Delamotte came; with whom, on Friday 9th, I took a boat for Charleston. After a slow passage by reason of contrary wind, and some conflict, our provisions falling short, with hunger as well as cold, we came thither early in the morning, on Tuesday the 13th."

He here separated from his friend, Mr. Delamotte, from whom he had been but a few days absent since their departure from England.

On the 22nd he bade farewell to America, after having preached the gospel in Savannah during one year and nine months.

To the testimonies already adduced in favour of Mr. Wesley's conduct in Georgia, the following extract from Mr. Whitefield, who visited Savannah in May, 1738, is added: " Many praying people were in the congregation, which, with the consideration that so many charitable people in England had been stirred up to contribute to Georgia, and such faithful labourers as Messrs. Wesleys and Ingham had been sent, gave me great hopes, that, unpromising as the aspect at present might be, the colony might emerge in time out of its infant state. Some small advances Mr. Ingham had made towards converting the Indians, who were at a small settlement about four miles from Savannah. He went and lived among them for a few months, and began to compose an Indian Grammar; but he was soon called away to England; and the Indians who were only some run-away Creeks were, in a few years, scattered or dead. Mr. Charles Wesley, had chiefly acted as Secretary to General Oglethorpe, but he soon also went to England to engage more labourers; and, not long after, his brother, Mr. John Wesley, having met with unworthy treatment, both at Frederica and Savannah, soon followed. All this I was apprized of, but think it most prudent not to repeat grievances. Mr. Garden thanked me most cordially and apprised me of the ill treatment Mr. Wesley had met with in Georgia, and assured me, that, were the same arbitrary proceedings to commence against me, he would defend me with his life and fortune."

During his voyage to England, Mr. Wesley entered into a close and severe examination of himself. " By the most infallible of proofs, inward feeling, I am convinced, 1. Of unbelief; having no such faith in Christ, as will prevent my heart from being troubled.—2. Of pride, throughout my life past; inasmuch as I thought I had, what I find I have not. 3. Of gross irrecollection; inasmuch as, in a storm I cry to God every moment; in a calm, not. 4. Of levity and luxuriancy of spirit—appearing by my speaking words not tending to edify; but most, by my manner of speaking of my enemies——Lord save, or I perish! Save me, 1. By such a faith as implies peace in life and death. 2. By such humility, as may fill my heart from this hour for ever, with a piercing uninterrupted sense, *Nihil est quod hactenus feci,* that, *hitherto I have done nothing.* 3. By such a recollection as may enable me to cry to thee every moment. 4. By steadiness, seriousness, sobriety of spirit, avoiding as fire, every word that tendeth not to edifying, and never speaking of any who oppose me, or sin against God, without all my own sins set in array before my face."

January 29. They once more saw English land, and Feb. 1, Mr. Wesley landed at Deal; where he was informed that Mr. Whitefield had sailed the day before for Georgia. He read prayers, and explained a portion of Scripture to a large company at the Inn, and on the third arrived in London.

CHAPTER III.

Mr. Wesley's labours until the first Methodist Conference in 1744.

AFTER his return from Georgia, Mr. Wesley was detained several weeks in London, by the trustees, and here he detailed the reasons which induced him so hastily to re-visit England.—The relation which he gave to the trustees, was so different from the flattering accounts of others, that they were highly displeased with him.

About this time he received a letter from a friend in Lincolnshire, intreating him to serve the church of a Mr. Hume, sometime before deceased, during its vacancy. The occasion of this letter, with all the circumstances connected with it, is very extraordinary.

When Mr. Samuel Wesley's Parsonage-house was burnt at Epworth, as formerly related, many of the neighbouring gentry, who held Mr. Wesley in very high esteem, opened their houses to him and his family. One gentleman received Mr. and Mrs. Wesley, another one of the children: and thus the whole family was accommodated. Mr. John Wesley, who was then six years old only, was received into the house of Mr. Hume, a neighbouring Clergyman. There he continued for a year, till his father's house was rebuilt: and confessed that he loved that family, while he resided among them, as much as he ever loved his own. Mr. Hume had four sons and one daughter. Three of the sons were educated at Oxford, and entered into holy orders: the other went into the Guinea-trade, and settled on the Coast of Africa.

Mr. Wesley having read the letter above-mentioned, inquired of one of his Lincolnshire friends, whether Mr. Hume was dead. " Have you not been informed of the calamities of that family," replied his friend ? " I have not," said Mr. Wesley. " I will then," said he, " relate them to you."

" About nine months ago Mr. Hume was riding out : and watering his horse at a large pond, the unruly beast plunged out of his depth ; by which Mr. Hume was so wetted, that he caught a violent cold, which was followed by a fever that caused his death. Lord ——, the patron of Mr. Hume's living, was determined that it should remain in the family as long as possible ; and therefore gave the eldest son a presentation of it. Mr. Hume, the father, had just rebuilt the parsonage-house before he died : the son took possession before it was dry, and the dampness of it occasioned his speedy death. The second son was then presented to the living ; and he died also a few weeks after his induction. The third son, his brother dying suddenly, immediately left Oxford to receive the presentation. In his way he slept at the house of an old acquaintance of his father. The gentleman of the house had a beautiful daughter, to whom young Mr. Hume immediately became attached : he therefore, before he departed, begged permission to return, and make proposals ; to which the father consented. Mr. Hume, after his induction to his living, returned according to his engagement, and in a few days the marriage was completed. But in six weeks after the nuptials the lady was brought to bed ; and Mr. Hume soon after died with grief.

" Now, Sir," said the Lincolnshire gentleman, " You may have a living and a wife : for Lord ——, has declared that if Miss Hume is married to a clergyman within six months from the death of her brother, the living shall be part of her fortune ; and Miss Hume has consented with much apparent satisfaction, that you should be invited to supply the church." But Mr. Wesley was too much impressed with the thoughts of eternity, to pay any attention to this proposal.

The conclusion must not be omitted. Mrs. Hume, soon after the death of her third son, received a letter from the only remaining one, informing her he was just about to sail from Africa to England with a fortune sufficient to make the whole family comfortable: and in a few days after, she received a letter from the captain of a swift-sailing vessel, who had been hailed by the ship in which her son sailed; by whom she was informed that her son had died on his passage of a disorder which then raged in the ship. Mrs. Hume, sinking under the weight of such a complication of misfortunes, soon died of a broken heart. Miss Hume, about a month after the death of her mother, was in company with a physician, who looking stedfastly at her observed, " Madam, you take opium: I know it by your eyes; and I am afraid you have put it out of my power to recover you." She confessed that the misfortunes of the family had so entirely deprived her of rest, that she had taken laudanum, to obtain a little repose. The physician prescribed. In a fortnight she recovered her appetite, her colour, and in a good measure her health. The physician then advised her to take a table-spoonful of a julap he had ordered for her, whenever she found herself inclined to be sick. A few days after this she desired the servant to bring her a spoonful of the julap. The servant mistaking the bottle of laudanum for the julap, brought her a spoonful of the laudanum, which she drank; and immediately fell asleep to awake no more.

When Mr. Wesley received information of the death of the last of the family, he recollected a remarkable observation made to him by his mother many years previous. He had been commending to her in very strong terms Mr. Hume and his amiable family. "John," replied Mrs. Wesley. "depend upon it, that family will come to an untimely end." Mrs. Wesley was a woman so far from being given to censure, that Mr. Wesley asked with some surprise, "Madam, why do you speak so severely of so lovely a family?" "John," said she, "I will tell you why. I have observed in various instances in the course of my life, that where persons have grossly violated the fifth commandment, and afterwards have been brought to the fear of God, the Lord has reversed the promise, and punished them for their transgression with temporal death. Mr. Hume and his family lie under this censure. I remember the time when his mother lived under his roof. He used her cruelly. He grudged every bit of meat she put into her mouth, and the whole family partook of his spirit. And, depend upon it, God will remember them for this."

Mr. Wesley now indulged himself in a social intercourse with his friends and relations, and became acquainted with Peter Bohler, Schulius Richter, and other Moravians who had lately arrived from Germany, and with whom he was much gratified. He then visited his brother at Oxford, reported to be in his last moments, but he found him recovered. Here he again met Bohler, and by him, he was convinced of the want of that faith, by which alone we are saved—and in conformity with his advice, he now began to preach, "salvation by faith alone." Bohler's words to him were very curious; "preach faith till you have it; and then because you have it, you will preach faith." The first address in which he inculcated the necessity of that faith which the Gospel describes, was to a prisoner under the sentence of death.

He spent much of this spring in travelling with Mr. Kinchin, of Corpus Christi college—They visited Manchester, Holms Chapel, Newcastle, and many other towns, frequently preaching and exhorting " *in season and out of season*"—in public and in private, in inns and in stables, and with different success—The novelty of their conduct produced a diversity of effects; some were astonished at the boldness of their reproofs and the energy of their exhortations, whilst others were grateful and desirous to be farther instructed.

In the beginning of April, he dismissed in part his use of the form of prayer. Mr. Kinchin and himself were visiting a prisoner in the Castle at Oxford, when this change commenced—having used the form, they prayed with him extempore—And on April 1st he resolved to use a form or not as might appear to him most suitable.

From this period he studied the scriptures, with much constancy and earnestness that he might ascertain what foundation there was in the scripture for the doctrine upon which Bohler had so much insisted—and on the 22d of April he says, that he was convinced of the truth of instantaneous conversion, by the testimony of many living witnesses. May 1. They began to form themselves into a religious society, which met in Fetter-Lane. This has been called the first methodist society in London. Mr. Wesley distinguishes the origin of Methodism, into three distinct periods. " The first rise of Methodism, was in November 1729, when four of us met together at Oxford: the second was at Savannah, in April 1736, when twenty or thirty persons met at my house: the last was at London, on this day, when forty or fifty of us agreed to meet together every Wednesday evening, for free conversation, begun and ended with singing and prayer." Their rules were printed under the title of *Orders* of a *Religious Society*, meeting in Fetter-Lane; in obedience to the command of God by St. James, and by the advice of Peter Bohler.

Wherever Mr. Wesley was now invited to preach in the churches, he boldly offered to all, a free salvation through faith in the blood of Christ. At most of those, he was soon told, " Sir, you must preach here no more."

How absurd and preposterous does this appear! An orator who is desirous to awaken in his auditors a proper sense of the importance of the Christian religion, to be dismissed from those temples which were professedly raised as houses of devotional exercises, and worship to its founder.

The peculiar point which seems to have produced this dislike was the doctrine of " *saving faith,*" of which truth he was first convinced on Monday, March the 6th 1738, he began to preach it immediately. He says," that greater effects were produced by this doctrine than by any other part of his ministerial work"—How much need was there of such preachers, when that truth which is one of the peculiar characteristics of the Redeemer's gospel, and the very life of religion in the soul, was so unknown as to be despised, and so disliked as to be discarded by those who were solemnly sworn to enforce it.

" So true," says he, " did I find the words of Mr. Gambold in a letter to my Brother at this time : " I have seen upon this occasion, more than ever I could have imagined, how intolerable the doctrine of faith is to the mind of man ; how peculiarly intolerable to the most religious men. One may say the most unchristian things, even down to deism ; the most enthusiastic things, so they proceed but upon mental raptures, lights and unions ; the most severe things, even the whole rigour of ascetic mortification ; and all this will be forgiven. But if you speak of faith, in such a manner as makes Christ a Saviour to the utmost, a most universal help and refuge ; in such a manner as takes away glorying, but adds happiness to wretched man; as discovers a greater pollution in the best of us, than we could before acknowledge, but brings a greater deliverance from it, than we could before expect: if any one offers to talk at this rate he is heard with the same abhorence as if he were going to rob mankind of their salvation, their mediator, or their highest happiness. I am persuaded, that a Montanist, or a Novation, who from the height of his purity should look with contempt upon poor sinners, and exclude them from all mercy, would not be thought such an overthrower of the gospel, as he who learns from the author of it to be a friend to publicans and sinners, and to sit down upon the level with them as soon as they begin to repent. But this is not to be wondered at. For all religious people have a quantity of righteousness, acquired by much painful exercise, and formed at last into current habits, which is their wealth both for this world and the next. Now all other schemes of religion are either so complaisant as to tell them they are very rich, and have enough to triumph in; or else only a little rough, but friendly in the main, by telling them their riches are not sufficient, but by such arts of self-denial and mental refinement, they may enlarge the stock. But the doctrine of faith is a downright robber; it takes away all this wealth, and tells us, it is deposited for us with somebody else, upon whose bounty we must live like mere beggars. Indeed they who are truly beggars, vile and filthy sinners till very lately, may stoop to live in this dependent condition; it suits them well enough: but they who have long distinguished themselves from the heard of vicious wretches, or have even gone beyond moral men; for them to be told that they are either not so well; or but the same needy, impotent, insignificant vessels of mercy with others, this is more shocking to reason than transubstantiation. For reason had rather resign its pretensions to judge what is bread or flesh, than have this honour wrested from it, to be the architect of virtue and righteousness.—But where am I running ? My design was only to give you warning, that wherever you go, this foolishness of preaching will alienate hearts from you, and open mouths agrinst you. What are you then to do, my dear friend ? I will not exhort you to courage ; we need not talk of that, for nothing that is approaching is evil. I will only mention the prejudice we shall be under, if we seem in the least to lay aside universal charity, and modesty of expression. Though we love some persons more than we did, let us love none less : and the rather because we cannot say any one is bad, or destitute of divine grace, for not thinking as we do. Indignation at mankind, is a temper unsuitable to this cause. If we are at peace with God in Christ, let it soften our demeanour still more, even towards gainsayers—What has been most offensive hitherto, is what perhaps may best be spared ; as some people's confident and hasty triumphs in the grace of God ; not by way of humble thankfulness to him for looking upon them, or acknowledgment of some peace and strength unknown before, which they hope will be increased to them ; but insisting on the completeness of their deliverance already from all sin, and taking to them every apostolical boast in the strongest terms.—Let us speak of every thing in such manner as may convey glory to Christ, without letting it glance on ourselves by the way. Let us profess, when we can with truth, how really the christian salvation is fulfilled in us, rather than how sublimely."

Mr. Wesley now hungered and thirsted more and more after the righteousness which is of God by faith. He saw the promise of justification and life was the free gift of God through Jesus Christ. The nearer he approached to the enjoyment of it, the more distinctly he perceived, and the more strongly felt, his own sinfulness, guilt, and helplessness.

Mr. Wesley continued in this state, till Wednesday, May 24. " I think," says he, " it was about five this morning, that I opened my Testament on those words, *There are given unto us, exceeding great and precious promises, that by these ye might be partakers of the divine nature.*

" In the evening I went very unwillingly to a society in Aldersgate-Street, where one was reading Luther's preface to the Epistle to the Romans. About a quarter before nine, while he was describing the change which God works in the heart through faith in Christ, I felt my heart strangely warmed. I felt I did trust in Christ, Christ alone for salvation : and an assurance was given me, that he had taken away my sins, even mine, and saved me from the law of sin and death.

" I began to pray with all my might, for those who had in a more especial manner despitefully used me, and persecuted me. I then testified openly to all there, what I now first felt in my heart. But it was not long before the enemy suggested, ' This cannot be faith, for where is thy joy.' Then was I taught, that peace and victory over sin, are essential to faith in the Captain of our Salvation : but, that as to the transports of joy, that usually attend the beginning of it, especially in those who have mourned deeply, God sometimes giveth, sometimes with-holdeth them, according to the councils of his own will."

About this time Bohler departed for America—and Mr. John Wesley being anxious concerning the state of his soul before God, determined upon an excursion into Germany, that he might by intercourse with the Moravian brethren, have his doubts removed and be establish-in the faith. Mr. Wesley took leave of his mother, and embarked on Thursday the 13th of June 1738, accompanied by Mr. Ingham ; on Thursday they landed at Rotterdam—and on the 4th of July, arrived at Marienbeen, where they were introduced to Count Zinzendorf. He then visited Hernhuth; and by attending the meetings of the brethren, attained that knowledge of which he wished to be informed.

September 16. He arrived again in London, having no intention but to preach the gospel in the churches; and accordingly wherever he was invited, he boldly declared, *by grace ye are saved through faith*. This doctrine was opposed by most of the clergy; and the genteel part of the congregation was offended at the crowds that followed him.

He exhorted and preached three or four times daily in Newgate, and in different parts of the city, and made several excursions into the country.

The reproaches of one party, and the opposition of others stimulated his courage, and inflamed his zeal. With all the spirit and labour of Luther, and with apostolic gravity and energy he persisted in his career, inattentive to contempt or applause, and alike careless both of popularity and persecution.

Whilst the worldlings reputed his undertaking to be the offspring of folly, he called it " the work of God," and defined it to be " the conversion of sinners from sin unto holiness."

December 11. Hearing Mr. Whitefield was returned from Georgia, he met him in London. January 1, 1739. He was present at a love-feast in Fetter-lane, together with Messrs. Hall, Kinchin, Ingham, Whitefield, Hutchins, and his brother Charles; and nearly sixty of the brethren. " About three in the morning," says he, " as we were continuing instant in prayer, the power of God came mightily upon us insomuch that many cried out for exceeding joy, and many fell to the ground. As soon as we were recovered a little from that awe and amazement at the presence of his Majesty, we broke out with one voice, *We praise Thee, O God, we acknowledge Thee to be the Lord.*"

In the spring, Mr. Whitefield went down to Bristol, and there first began to preach in the open air, to incredible numbers of people. Mr. Wesley continued his labours in London and Oxford alternately, and occasionally in the neighbouring places. In the latter end of March, he received a letter from Mr. Whitefield, who intreated him in the most pressing manner to visit Bristol. At first he was not willing to comply with the request; and his brother Charles, and some others, warmly opposed his journey from an unaccountable apprehension that it would prove fatal to him. At length Mr. Wesley freely gave himself up, to whatever the Lord should appoint. It was a rule of the society, " That any person who desired, or designed to take a journey, should first, if it were possible, have the approbation of the Bands." Accordingly on the 28th, the matter was laid before them, and after some debate they determined that he should comply with Mr. Whitefield's request. He left London the next day, and on the 31st arrived in Bristol.

April 1. Mr. Whitefield having left Bristol, Mr. Wesley began to expound to a little society in Nicholas-Street, our Lord's sermon on the mount ; " One pretty remarkable precedent, of field-preaching, though I suppose there were churches at that time also. Monday the second, I submitted to be more vile, and proclaimed in highways the glad-tidings of salvation, speaking from a little eminence in a ground adjoining to the city, to about three thousand people."—His preaching was attended with surprising success, so that in a very short time, a few, and afterwards a greater number agreed to meet together, to edify and strengthen one another, as the people already did in London.

Mr. Wesley continued in Bristol and the neighbouring places till June. He thus describes his public labours through the week. " My ordinary employment in public, was as follows: every morning I read prayers and preached at Newgate. Every evening I expounded a portion of scripture, at one or more of the societies. On Monday in the afternoon I preached abroad near Bristol : on Tuesday at Bath and Two Mile-Hill, alternately. On Wednesday at Baptist-Mills. Every Thursday, near Pensford. Every other Friday, in another part of Kingswood On Saturday in the afternoon, and Sunday morning, in the Bowling-Green. On Sunday at eleven, near Hannam-Mount ; at two at Clifton ; at five, at Rose-Green. And hitherto, as my day is, so is my strength."—He could scarcely reconcile himself at first to this preaching in the fields, of which Mr. Whitefield had set him the example ; " Having been till very lately, so tenacious of every point relating to decency and order, that I should have thought the saving of souls almost a sin, if it had not been done in a church."

During this summer, his preaching at Bristol was attended with some extraordinary circumstances, which gave great offence. Under the sermon, some persons trembled from head to foot : others fell down and cried out with a loud and bitter cry : whilst others became speechless, and seemed convulsed as if in the agonies of death. After prayer for them, many rose up rejoicing in God, and testifying that they had redemption through the blood of Christ, even the forgiveness of sins, according to the riches of his grace.

His brother Samuel having written to him on this head, his answer was as follows :

" The question between us turns chiefly, if not wholly, on matter of fact. You deny, that God does now work these effects: at least, that he works them in this manner. I affirm both; because I have heard these things with my own ears, and seen them with my eyes. I have seen, as far as a thing of this kind can be seen, very many persons changed in a moment, from the spirit of fear, horror, and despair, to the spirit of love, joy and peace; and from sinful desire, till then reigning over them, to a pure desire of doing the will of God. These are matters of fact, whereof I have been, and almost daily am, an eye or ear-witness. What I have to say, touching visions or dreams, is this: I know several persons, in whom this great change was wrought in a dream, or during a strong representation to the eye of their mind, of Christ either on the cross or in glory. This is the fact; let any judge of it as they please. And that such a change was then wrought, appears not from their shedding tears only, or falling into fits, or crying out: these are not the fruits, as you seem to suppose, whereby I judge, but from the whole tenor of their life, till then many ways wicked, from that time, holy; just and good.

"I will shew you him that was a lion till then, and is now a lamb; him that was a drunkard, and is now exemplarily sober: the whoremonger that was, who now abhors the very garment spotted by the flesh. These are my living arguments for what I assert, viz. *That God does now, as aforetime, give remission of sins, and the gift of the Holy Ghost, even to us and to our children:* if it be not so, I am found a false witness before God. For these things I do, and by his grace, will testify."

After eight or nine days absence, in which he visited London, Mr. Wesley returned to Bristol, and continued his labours with increasing success. October 15. Upon a pressing invitation he visited Wales. The churches were here shut against him, as in England, and he preached in private houses, or in the open air to a willing people.—" I have seen," says he, " no part of England so pleasant for sixty or seventy miles together, as those parts of Wales I have been in : and most of the inhabitants are indeed ripe for the gospel. I mean, they are earnestly desirous of being instructed, and as utterly ignorant of it as any Creek or Cherokee Indians. I do not mean, that they are ignorant of the name of Christ · many of them can say both the Lord's prayer, and the belief; some, all the catechism : but take them out of the road of what they have learned by rote, and they know no more either of gospel salvation, or of that faith whereby alone we can be saved, than *Chicali*, or *Tomo Chachi*. Now what spirit is he of, who had rather these poor creatures should perish for lack of knowledge, than that they should be saved, even by the exhortations of Howell Harris, or an itinerant preacher. The word did not fall to the ground. Many repented and believed the gospel ; and joined together, to strengthen each others hands in God, and to provoke one another to love and to good works."

November 3. Mr. Wesley came to London, where the society was greatly divided, by means of some new notions which the Moravian preachers had introduced among them, concerning degrees of faith, and the use of the ordinances, as means of grace. On the 9th, he tells us, " All this week I endeavoured by private conversation, to comfort the feeble-minded, and to bring back the lame who had been turned out of the way, that at length they might be healed.—Sunday, November 11. I preached at eight, to five or six thousand, on the spirit of bondage, and the spirit of adoption : and at five in the evening to seven or eight thousand, in the place which had been the King's Foundery for cannon.

The Society which had been formed soon after his return from Georgia had increased in numbers, and consisted of many pious characters; but doctrinal disputes interrupted that harmony which ought to have subsisted amongst them. Mr. Wesley had been in London several times without being able to put an end to them: and a great majority of the society were more and more estranged from him. He returned to London in June, and laboured with them till the 20th of July; when, finding it was to no purpose, he read a paper, of which this was the substance:

"About nine months ago, certain of you began to speak contrary to the doctrine we had till then received. The sum of what you asserted is this: 1. That there is no such thing as weak faith; that there is no justifying faith, where there is ever any doubt or fear; or where there is not, in the full sense, a new, a clean heart. 2. That a man ought not to use those ordinances of God, which our church terms means of grace, before he has such a faith as excludes all doubt and fear, and implies a new, a clean heart. 3. You have often affirmed, that to search the scriptures, to pray, or to communicate, before we have this faith, is to seek salvation by works: and till these works are laid aside, no man can receive faith.

"I believe these assertions to be flatly contrary to the word of God. I have warned you hereof again and again, and besought you to turn back to the law and to the testimony. I have born with you long, hoping you would turn. But as I find you more and more confirmed in the error of your ways, nothing now remains, but that I should give you up to God. You that are of the same judgment follow me.—I then, without saying any thing more withdrew, as did eighteen or nineteen of the society."

July 23. "Our little company met at the Foundery, instead of Fetter-Lane. About twenty-five of our brethren God hath given us already, all of whom think and speak the same thing; seven or eight and forty likewise, of the fifty women that were in band, desired to cast in their lot with us."

Until the year 1740, Mr. Wesley and Mr. Whitefield had been perfectly united in their Evangelical work. They preached in the same pulpits, and had one common design only, to promote christian knowledge, and a holy conversation among the people, without entering into the discussion of particular opinions. But about this time Mr. Wesley printed a sermon against the Calvinistic notion of predestination, and sent a copy to Commissary Garden at Charlestown, where Mr. Whitefield met with it. He had already embraced that opinion; and though the subject was treated in that sermon, in a general way, without naming, or pointing at any individual, yet he found himself hurt, that Mr. Wesley should bring forward the controversy, and publicly oppose an opinion which he believed to be agreeable to the word of God. On his passage to England, he wrote to Mr. Charles Wesley, expostulating with him and his brother on the subject. " My dear, dear brethren, why did you throw out the bone of contention? Why did you print that sermon against predestination? Why did you in particular, my dear brother Charles, affix your hymn, and join in putting out your late hymn-book? How can you say, you will not dispute with me about election, and yet print such hymns, and your brother sent his sermon over against election, to Mr. Garden, and others in America?—Do not you think, my dear brethren, I must be as much concerned for truth, or what think truth, as you? God is my judge, I always was, and hope I always shall be desirous that you may be preferred before me. But I must preach the gospel of Christ, and that I cannot now do, without speaking of election."—He then tells Mr. Charles, that in Christmas week he had written an answer to his brother's sermon, " Which is now printing at Charlestown; another copy I have sent to Boston, and another I now bring with me to print in London. If it occasion a strangeness between us, it shall not be my fault. There is nothing in my answer exciting to it, that I know of. O my dear brethren, my heart almost bleeds within me! Methinks I could be willing to tarry here on the waters for ever, rather than come to England to oppose you."

On this occasion, a separation took place between Mr. Wesley and Mr. Whitefield, so far as to have different places of worship: but their good opinion of each other's integrity and usefulness, founded on long and intimate acquaintance, could not be injured by such a difference of sentiment; and their mutual affection was obscured only by a cloud, for a season.

In the latter end of the following year, Mr. Whitefield wrote to him as follows: " I long to hear from you and write this hoping to have an answer. I rejoice to hear the Lord blesses your labours. May you be blessed in bringing souls to Christ, more and more! I believe we shall go on best when we only preach the simple gospel, and do not interfere with each other's plan. Our Lord exceedingly blesses us at the Tabernacle. I doubt not but he deals in the same bountiful manner with you. I was at your letter-day on Monday. Brother Charles has been pleased to come and see me twice. Behold what a happy thing it is for brethren to dwell together in unity! That the whole christian world may all become of one heart and one mind: and that *We* in particular, though differing in judgment, may be examples of mutual, fervent, undissembled affection, is the hearty prayer of your most affectionate, though most unworthy younger brother in the kingdom and patience of Jesus."

From this time their mutual regard and friendly intercourse suffered no interruption till Mr. Whitefield's death; who says in his will, which was written with his own hand about six months before he died, " I leave a mourning-ring to my honoured and dear friends, and disinterested fellow-labourers, the Rev. Messrs. John and Charles Wesley, in token of my indissoluble union with them in heart and christian affection, notwithstanding our difference in judgment about some particular points of doctrine." When the news of Mr. Whitefield's death reached London, Mr. Keen, one of his executors, recollected that he had often said to him, " If you should die abroad whom shall we get to preach your funeral sermon ? Must it be your old friend, the Rev. Mr. John Wesley ?" And having constantly received for answer, " He is the man ;" waited on Mr. Wesley, and engaged him to preach it; in which he bore ample testimony to the undissembled piety, the ardent zeal, and the extensive usefulness of his much loved and honoured friend.

After Mr. Wesley had separated from the Moravians, Mr. Gambold and some others left him, and even his brother Charles was at this period wavering. On this occasion Mr. Wesley sent him the following letter. " I am settling the regular method of visiting the sick here: eight or ten have offered themselves for the work ; who are likely to have full employment ; for more and more are taken every day. Our Lord will thoroughly purge his floor.

" I rejoice in your speaking your mind freely. O let our love be without dissimulation. I am not clear, that brother Maxfield should not expound at Greyhound-Lane ; nor can I as yet do without him."

From this time, the number of laymen employed gradually increased in proportion to the growth of the so-

R

cieties and the want of preachers; the clergy generally standing at a distance from a plan of so much irregularity, and labour.

In June, Mr. Wesley took a journey as far as Nottingham, where he preached in the market-place to an immense multitude of people.

Some however, were offended at these proceedings. A complaint was made in form to Mr. Wesley, and he hastened to London to silence the Laymen. His mother then lived in his house, adjoining to the Foundery. When he arrived, she perceived that his countenance was expressive of dissatisfaction, and inquired the cause. " Thomas Maxfield," said he abruptly, " has turned preacher, I find." She looked attentively at him, and replied, " John, you know what my sentiments have been. You cannot suspect me of favouring readily any thing of this kind. But take care what you do with respect to that young man, for he is as surely called of God to preach, as you are. Examine what have been the fruits of his preaching: and hear him also yourself." He did so. His prejudice bowed before the force of truth : and he could only say, " *It is the Lord : let him do what seemeth him good.*"

July 15, Mr. Wesley reached Bristol, " For, a spirit of enthusiasm was breaking in upon many, who charged their own imaginations on the will of God, and that, not written, but impressed on their hearts. If these impressions be received as the rule of action, instead of the written word, I know nothing so wicked or absurd, but we may fall into, and that without remedy."

The public attention was soon drawn to the leader of the party: thus many weak-headed people wished to persuade the government, that he was an agent for the Pretender; a Frenchman, and a Jesuit; and his disciples Papists and seditious: in a short time they declared that he had been fined for selling gin contrary to the statute; and lastly they upbraided him as an idiot, a driveller, and an illiterate enthusiast.

His opponents in general, derived little credit from the manner in which they attacked him: their heads and their hearts in this controversy appear very contemptible. They strived to inflame the resentment of the populace against him, by slander and defamation. The magistrates joined the throng, and manifested dispositions which would have done honour to the Roman Inquisitors. They refused to take informations, to grant warrants, and thus encouraged the brutality of the ignorant, irreligious and riotous multitude: in addition to this, these distributers of justice, sworn to see the laws executed, not only refused to protect them from assault, and to punish the "sons of Belial," but actually professed their delight and gratification with the enormities of the mob, and with all their illegal deeds.

The labourers as yet being few, Mr. Wesley staid but a short time in one place, being continually travelling between London, Bristol, and Wales; the last of which he visited twice in the autumn. In London, they had been long disturbed in their places of worship by a riotous mob; but on the last day of this year, Sir John Ganson called upon him, and said, "Sir, you have no need to suffer these riotous mobs to molest you; I, and all the other Middlesex magistrates have orders from above, to do you justice whenever you apply to us." Two or three weeks after they did apply. Justice was done, though not with rigour: and from that time the Methodists had peace in London.

April 9. They had the first watch-night in London. "We commonly choose, for this solemn service, the Friday night nearest the full moon, either before or after, that those of the congregation who live at a distance among the Colliers at Kingswood, he long had a desire to visit those about Newcastle, and now accomplished his wish. He was not known to any person in Newcastle; and therefore he and John Taylor, who travelled with him, put up at an inn. On walking through the town, after taking some refreshment he observes, " I was surprised: so much drunkenness, cursing, and swearing, even from the mouths of little children, do I never remember to have seen and heard before in so short a time."

Sunday, May 30. At seven in the morning, he walked down to Sandgate, the poorest and most contemptible part of the town, and standing at the end of the street with John Taylor, began to sing the hundredth psalm. " Three or four people came out to see what was the matter, who soon increased to four or five hundred. I suppose there might be twelve or fifteen hundred before I had done preaching: to whom I applied those solemn words, *He was wounded for our transgressions, he was bruised for our iniquities; the chastisement of our peace was upon him, and by his stripes we are healed.*

" Observing the people when I had done, to stand gaping and staring upon me with the most profound astonishment, I told them, if you desire to know who I am, my name is John Wesley. At five in the evening, with God's help, I design to preach here again.—At five, the hill on which I designed to preach, was covered from the top to the bottom. I never saw so large a number of people together, either in Moorfields, or at Kennington-Common. I knew it was not possible for the one half to hear, although my voice was then strong and clear; and I stood so as to have them all in view, as they were ranged on the side of the hill. The word of God which I set before them was, *I will heal their backsliding, I will love them freely.* After preaching, the poor people were ready to tread me under foot, out of pure love and kindness. I was some time before I could possibly get out of the press. I then went back another way than I came. But several were got to our inn before me; by whom I was vehemently importuned to stay with them, at least a few days: or however one day more. But I could not consent; having given my word to be at Birstal, with God's leave, on Tuesday night."

Monday 31. Mr. Wesley left Newcastle, and preached at various places as he returned through Yorkshire. June 5. He rode to Epworth. "It being many years since I had been in Epworth before, I went to an inn, in the middle of the town, not knowing whether there were any left in it now, who would not be ashamed of my acquaintance. But an old servant of my father, with two or three poor women, presently found me out. I asked her, do you know any in Epworth who are in earnest to be saved? She answered, "I am by the grace of God; and I know I am saved through faith." I asked, have you then peace with God? Do you know that he has forgiven your sins? She replied, "I thank God, I know it well, and many here can say the same thing."

Sunday 6. A little before the service began, he offered his assistance to Mr. Romley the curate, but it was not accepted. In the afternoon, the church was exceedingly full, a report being spread, that Mr. Wesley was to officiate. After sermon, John Taylor stood in the church-yard, and gave notice, as the people came out, that Mr. Wesley, not being permitted to address them in the church, designed to preach there at six o'clock. "Accordingly at six, I came, and found such a congregation as, I believe, Epworth never saw before. I stood near the east end of the church, upon my father's tombstone, and cried, *The kingdom of Heaven is not meat and drink; but righteousness, and peace, and joy in the Holy Ghost.*"

"On the 9th I rode over to a neighbouring town, to wait upon a justice of the peace, a man of candor and understanding; before whom, I was informed, their angry neighbours had carried a whole waggon-load of these new *heretics*. But when he asked, ' what have they done?' there was a deep silence; for that was a point their conductors had forgotten. At length one said, ' why they pretend to be better than other people: and besides they pray from morning to night.' Mr. S. asked, ' But have they done nothing besides?' Yes, Sir, said an old man: An't please your worship, they have *converted* my wife. Till she went among them, she had such a tongue! and now she is as quiet as a lamb.' "Carry them back, carry them back," replied the justice, "and let them convert all the scolds in the town."

"Friday 11. I preached again at Epworth on Ezekiel's vision of the resurrection of the dry bones. And great indeed was the shaking among them: lamentation and great mourning were heard; God bowing the hearts, so that on every side, as with one accord, they lifted up their voices and wept aloud.

"Saturday 12. I preached on the righteousness of the law and the righteousness of faith. While I was speaking several dropped down as dead: and among the rest, such a cry was heard of sinners groaning for the righteousness of faith, as almost drowned my voice. But many of these soon lifted up their heads with joy, and broke out into thanksgiving; being assured, that they now had the desire of their souls, the forgiveness of their sins.

"I observed a gentleman there, who was remarkable for not pretending to be of any religion at all. I was informed he had not been at public worship of any kind for upwards of thirty years. Seeing him stand as motionless as a statue; I asked him abruptly, '· Sir, are you a sinner?" He replied with a deep and broken voice, " Sinner enough," and continued staring upwards, untill his wife and a servant or two, who were all in tears, put him into a chaise and carried him home.

" Sunday 13. At six I preached for the last time in Epworth church-yard, to a vast multitude gathered together from all parts, on the beginning of our Lord's sermon on the mount. I continued among them for near three hours : and yet we scarce knew how to part. O let none think his labour of love is lost, because the fruit does not immediately appear. Near forty years did my father labour here. But he saw little fruit of all his labour. I took some pains among this people too : and my strength also seemed spent in vain. But now the fruit appeared. There were scarce any in the town, on whom either my father or I had taken any pains formerly, but the seed sown so long since, now sprung up, bringing forth repentance and remission of sins."

From Epworth Mr. Wesley proceeded to Sheffield, and preaching constantly on the way, arrived at Bristol on the 28th of June : after a visit to Wales, he laboured chiefly in London, Bristol and their viciuities, until November, on the 13th of which month he was at Newcastle, where his brother had been engaged several weeks with great success, and had formed a society.

At Newcastle, in 1743, he was employed in erecting the Orphan house, a heavy pile appropriated to publick worship. The expences of building this, like all the other houses of worship, were defrayed by contribution—and whilst it was raising he was often moneyless ; but it was his office to provide for all demands. " In me *domus inclinata recumbit ;*" and he observes, " that if it had not been for the report of his great riches, although unfounded, his work must have been stopped."

S

"How unsearchable art thou, O God; and thy ways past finding out!"

It gave him much trouble to procure ground for the building, and when this had been purchased, it was with some difficulty that he attained possession. The following letter written to the owner on that occasion, is worthy of preservation here, both as it is strongly characteristick of the writer, and a remarkable specimen of the laconick.

Sir,

I am surprized. You give it under your hand, that you will put me into possession of a piece of ground, specified in an article between us, in fifteen days time. Three months are passed, and that article is not fulfilled. And now you say, you cannot conceive what I mean by troubling you. I mean to have that article fulfilled. I think my meaning is very plain.

I am, Sir,
Your servant,
JOHN WESLEY.

January 1, 1743. He reached Epworth; and the next day being Sunday, he preached at five in the morning; and again at eight, from his father's tomb-stone. "Many," says he, "from the neighbouring towns, asked, if it would not be well, as it was Sacrament-Sunday, for them to receive it? I told them, by all means; but it would be more respectful first to ask Mr. Romley, the curate's leave. One did so, in the name of the rest. To whom he said, pray tell Mr. Wesley, I shall not give *him* the sacrament; for he is *not fit*." This Mr. Romley owed his all in this world, to the tender love which Mr. Wesley's father had shewn to his father, as well as personally to *himself*.

January 8. He went to Wednesbury in Staffordshire which his brother had already visited. At seven in the evening he preached in the town-hall. It was crowded with deeply attentive hearers. Mr. Egginton, the minister, seemed friendly disposed; and the prospect of doing much good, was fair and promising.—Hence Mr. Wesley went to Bristol and thence to London. February 19th, he reached Newcastle: and here, and in the neighbouring towns and villages he spent nearly six weeks, in preaching and exhorting, in praying and conversing with the people, and in regulating the societies. A great number of these societies were already formed exactly on the same principles in various parts of the kingdom, though at a considerable distance from each other. But hitherto no general rules had been made to govern the whole. The two brothers, therefore, framed a set of rules which should be observed by the members of all their societies, and tend to unite them all into one body; so that a member at Newcastle, knew the rules of the society in London, as well as at the place where he resided. They were printed under the title of, " *The Nature, Design, and General Rules, of the United Societies, in London, Bristol, Newcastle upon Tyne,* &c."

On his return from Newcastle, Mr. Wesley again visited Wednesbury, where he found the society already increased to several hundreds. But a cloud was gathering over them which threatened a dreadful storm. Mr. W———s, had so exasperated Mr. Egginton the minister, that his former love was turned into hatred. But he had not yet had time to excite the rage and madness which afterwards appeared.—On the Sunday following the scene began to open. " I think," says Mr. Wesley, " I never heard so wicked a sermon, and delivered with such bitterness of voice and manner, as that which Mr. Egginton preached in the afternoon. I knew what effect this must have in a little time, and therefore judged it expedient to prepare the poor people for what was to follow, that when it came, they might not be offended.

Accordingly, I strongly enforced those words of our Lord, *If any man come after me, and hate not his father and mother—yea, and his own life, he cannot be my disciple. And whosoever doth not bear his cross and come after me, cannot be my disciple.*"

Having visited Bristol and Wales, he returned to London. After having inspected the classes, and set in order such things as required his care and attention, he proceeded for the North, taking the societies in Staffordshire, and various other places in his way to Newcastle, and again reached London in the latter end of July.

Mr. Wesley now visited Cornwall, where his brother and two of the preachers had already laboured with great success: but he made no considerable stop, till he came to St. Ives. Some time before, captain Turner of Bristol had put in here, and was agreeably surprised to find a little society formed, who constantly met together. They were greatly refreshed and strengthened by him, and this was the occasion of introducing the Methodists to this place. Mr. Wesley spake severally with those of the society, about a hundred and twenty; near a hundred of whom had found peace with God. He spent three weeks in preaching here, and in Zennor, Morva, St. Just, Sennan, St. Mary's, Gwenap, and on several of the Downs throughout the west of Cornwall.

October 3, he returned to Bristol, and now received full information of the riots at Wednesbury. Mr. Egginton, assisted by two neighbouring justices, Mr. Lane of Bentley-Hall, and Mr. Persehouse of Walsal, having stirred up the basest of the people, such outrages followed as were a scandal to the Christian name. Riotous mobs were summoned together by the sound of the horn; men, women, and children were abused in the most shocking manner, being beaten, stoned, and covered with mud; some, even pregnant women, were treated most brutally. In the mean time their houses were broken open by any that pleased, and their goods spoiled or carried away, the owners standing by, but not daring to oppose, as it would have been at the peril of their lives. Mr. Wesley thought it was his duty to visit this harassed people in their distress, and on the 20th, having preached at Birmingham, he rode to Wednesbury, and addressed them at noon in a ground near the middle of the town, on *Jesus Christ, the same yesterday, to day, and for ever.*— " No creature offered to molest us, either going or coming: the *Lord fought for us*, and we *held our peace*."

" I was writing at Francis Ward's in the afternoon, when the cry arose, that the mob had beset the house. We prayed that God would disperse them: and so it was; one went this way, another that, so that in half an hour not a man was left. I told our brethren now is the time to go: but they pressed me exceedingly to stay. So that I might not offend them, I sat down, though I foresaw what would follow. Before five the mob surrounded the house again, and in greater numbers than ever. The cry of one and all was, ' Bring out the minister, we will have the minister.' I desired one to take the captain by the hand and bring him into the house. After a few sentences interchanged between us, the lion was become a lamb. I desired him to go, and bring one or two of the most angry of his companions. He brought in two, who were ready to swallow the ground with rage: but in two minutes they were as calm as he. I then bade them make way, that I might go out among the people. As soon as I was in the midst of them, I called for a chair, and asked, " What do any of you want with me?" Some said, we want you to go with us to the justice. I replied, that I will with all my heart. I then spoke a few words, which God applied; so that they cried out with might and main,

"'The gentleman is an honest gentleman, and we will spill our blood in his defence. I asked shall we go to the justice to night, or in the morning? Most of them cried, ' To night, to night:' on which I went before, and two or three hundred followed, the rest returning whence they came.

" The night came on before we had walked a mile, together with heavy rain. However, on we went to Bentley-Hall, two miles from Wednesbury. One or two ran before, to tell Mr. Lane, that they had brought Mr. Wesley before his worship.' Mr. Lane replied, ' What have I to do with Mr. Wesley: Go and carry him back again.' By this time the main body came up, and began knocking at the door. A servant told them, Mr. Lane was in bed. His son followed, and asked, what was the matter? One replied, " Why, an't please you, they sing psalms all day; nay, and make folks rise at five in the morning. And what would your worship advise us to do?" To go home, said Mr. Lane, and be quiet.

" Here they were at a full stop, till one advised to go to Justice Persehouse at Walsal. All agreed to this: so we hastened on, and about seven came to his house. But Mr. Persehouse likewise sent word, that he was in bed. Now they were at a stand again: but at last they all thought it the wisest course to make the best of their way home. About fifty of them undertook to convoy me. But we had not got a hundred yards, when the mob of Walsal came pouring in like a flood, and bore down all before them. The Darlston mob made what defence they could; but they were weary, as well as out-numbered: so that, in a short time, many being knocked down, the rest went away, and left me in their hands.

" To attempt speaking was vain; for the noise on every side was like the roaring of the sea. So they dragged me along till we came to the town : where seeing the door of a large house open, I attempted to go in ; but a man catching me by the hair, pulled me back into the middle of the mob. They made no more stop till they had carried me through the main street, from one end of the town to the other. I continued speaking all the time to those within hearing, feeling no pain or weariness. At the west end of the town, seeing a door half open, I made towards it, and would have gone in. But a gentleman in the shop would not suffer me, saying, they would pull the house to the ground. However, I stood at the door and asked, are you willing to hear me speak ? Many cried out, 'No, no ! knock his brains out : down with him : kill him at once.' Others said, ' Nay ; but we will hear him speak first.' I began asking, what evil have I done ? Which of you all have I wronged in word or deed ? and continued speaking for above a quarter of an hour, till my voice suddenly failed. Then the floods began to lift up their voice again ; many crying out, ' Bring him away, bring him away.'

" In the mean time my strength and my voice returned, and I broke out aloud into prayer. And now the man who had just before headed the mob, turned and said, ' Sir, I will spend my life for you. Follow me, and not one soul here shall touch a hair of your head.' Two or three of his fellows confirmed his words, and got close to me immediately. At the same time the gentleman in the shop cried out, ' For shame, for shame, let him go.' An honest butcher, who was a little further off, said it was a shame they should do thus: and pulled back four or five, one after another, who were running on the most fiercely. The people then, as if it had been by common consent, fell back to the right and left : while those three or four men took me between them, and carried me through them all. But on the bridge the mob rallied again ; we therefore went on one side, over the mill-dam, and thence through the meadows: till a little before ten, God brought me safe to Wednesbury : having lost only one flap of my waistcoat, and a little skin from one of my hands.

" When I came back to Francis Ward's, I found many of our brethren waiting upon God. Many also whom I had never seen before, came to rejoice with us. And the next morning as I rode through the town, in my way to Nottingham, every one I met expressed such a cordial affection, that I could scarcely believe what I saw and heard.

" In April, 1744," says Mr. Wesley, " I took a second journey into Cornwall, and went through many towns which I had not seen before. Since my former visit, there had been hot persecution both of the preachers and the people. The preaching-house at St. Ives, was pulled to the ground : one of the preachers pressed and sent for a soldier, as were several of the people ; over and above being stoned, covered with dirt, and the like, which was the treatment many of them experienced from day to day.

" I rode to Falmouth. About three in the afternoon I went to see a gentlewoman who had been indisposed. Almost as soon as I sat down, the house was beset on all sides by an innumerable multitude of people. A louder or more confused noise could hardly be at the taking of a city by storm. At first Mrs. B. and her daughter endeavoured to quiet them. But it was labour lost. They might as well have attempted to still the raging of the sea, and were therefore soon glad to shift for themselves. The rabble roared with all their throats, " bring out the *Conorum !* Where is the *Conorum ?*" an' unmeaning word which the Cornish rabble then used instead of *Methodist*. No answer being given, they quickly forced open the outer door, and filled the passage. Only a wainscot-partition was between us, which was not likely to stand long. I immediately took down a large looking-glass which hung against it, supposing the whole side would fall in at once. They began their work with abundance of bitter imprecations. A poor girl who was left in the house, was utterly astonished, and cried out, " O Sir, what must we do?" I said, " We must pray." Indeed at that time, to all appearance, our lives were not worth an hour's purchase. She asked, " But, Sir, is it not better for you to hide yourself? To get into the closet?" I answered, " No. It is best for me to stand just where I am." Among those without, were the crews of some privateers, which were lately come into the harbour. Some of these, being angry at the slowness of the rest, thrust them away, and coming up altogether, set their shoulders to the inner door, and cried out, " Avast, lads, avast!" Away went all the hinges at once, and the door fell back into the room. I stepped forward into the midst of them and said, " Here I am. Which of you has any thing to say to me? To which of you have I done any wrong? To you? Or you? Or you?" I continued speaking, till I came into the middle of the street, and then raising my voice, said, " Neighbours, countrymen! Do you desire to hear me speak?" They cried vehemently, ", Yes, yes. He shall speak. He shall. Nobody shall hinder him." But having nothing to stand on, and no advantage of ground, I could be heard by few only. However I spoke without intermission; and as far as the sound reached, the people were still: till one or two of their captains turned about and swore, " Not a man shall touch him."— Mr. Thomas, a clergyman, then came up, and asked, " Are you not ashamed to use a stranger thus?" He was soon seconded by two or three gentlemen of the town, and one of the Aldermen; with whom I walked down the town, speaking all the time, till I came to Mrs.

Maddern's house. The gentlemen proposed sending for my horse to the door, and desired me to step in and rest the mean time. But on second thoughts, they judged it not advisable to let me go out among the people again. So they chose to send my horse before me to Penryn, and to send me thither by water; the sea running close by the backdoor of the house in which we were.

" I never saw before, no, not at Walsal itself, the hand of God so plainly shewn as here. There I had many companions, who were willing to die with me: here not a friend, but one simple girl; who likewise was hurried away from me in an instant, as soon as ever she came out of Mrs. B's house. There I received some blows, lost part of my clothes, and was covered with dirt. Here, although the hands of perhaps some hundreds of people were lifted up to strike or throw, they were one and all stopped in the midway, so that not a man touched me with one of his fingers. Neither was any thing thrown from first to last: so that I had not even a speck of dirt on my clothes. Who can deny, that God heareth the prayer? or that he hath all power in heaven and earth?"

The preachers in the different parts of the kingdom were permitted to drink of the same cup, yea, in many instances suffered greater persecution than Mr. Wesley himself. Stones, dirt and rotten eggs were the common weapons of the mob. In some instances, as in that of Mr. Thomas Mitchell, they were thrown into ponds of water, and held down till they were nearly drowned. Applications were made for redress to the neighbouring magistrates, but generally in vain. They then, under the patronage of Mr. Wesley, had recourse to the Court of King's Bench, and in every instance found the most ample justice. The judges of that court acted on all occasions with the greatest uprightness and impartiality: the consequence of which was, that peace was nearly restored.

About the time of these persecutions, John Nelson of Birstal in Yorkshire, and Thomas Beard an honest industrious man, were pressed and sent off, as soldiers, for no other crime either committed or pretended, than that of calling sinners to repentance. John Nelson was after much ill usage released by an order from the secretary at war, and preached the Gospel many years. But Thomas Beard sunk under his oppressions. He was then lodged in the hospital at Newcastle, where he praised God continually. His fever increasing, he was bled. His arm festered, mortified, and was cut off: two or three days after which, God signed his discharge, and called him to his eternal home.

"All this year the alarms were uninterrupted, from the French on the one hand, and the rebels on the other: and a general panick ran through the nation, from the east to the west, from the north to the south. I judged it the more needful to visit as many places as possible, and avail myself of the precious opportunity. My brother and our preachers were of the same mind: they spoke and spared not. They rushed through every open door, " And cried, Sinners behold the Lamb !" And their work did not fall to the ground: they saw abundant fruit of their labour. I went through many parts of Wales: through most of the midland counties: and then through Lincolnshire and Yorkshire, to Newcastle-upon-Tyne. And multitudes who were utterly careless before, did now *prepare to meet* their God."

" The persecution of St. Ives, was owing in great measure to the indefatigable labours of Mr. Hoblin, and Mr. Simmons: gentlemen worthy to be had in everlasting remembrance, for their unwearied endeavours to destroy heresy."

The riots in Staffordshire still continued in the beginning of this year. The mob of Walsal, Darlston and Wednesbury, hired for the purpose by their betters, broke open their poor neighbours' houses at their pleasure, by day and by night, extorting money from the few that had it; taking away or destroying their victuals and goods; beating and wounding their bodies; abusing their women, and openly declaring that they would destroy every Methodist in the country.

From Cornwall, Mr. Wesley passed over into Wales; on his return he made a short stay at Bristol, and then visited most of the societies in his way to Newcastle. June 20, he arrived in London, where he met his brother, two or three other clergymen, and a few of the preachers, whom he had appointed to come from various parts, to confer with them on the affairs of the societies. He observes, " Monday, June 25, and the five following days we spent in conference with our preachers, seriously considering, by what means we might the most effectually save our own souls and them that hear us. And the result of our consultations we set down, to be the RULE *of our future practice*."—This was the first Methodist-Conference.

From the year 1744, *until the establishment of the Conference, in* 1784.

THE plan on which Mr. Wesley had hitherto governed the societies and the preachers, was imperfect. When the preachers at first went out to exhort and speak, it was by Mr. Wesley's permission and authority; some from one part of the kingdom and some from another: and though strangers, yet on his credit and sanction alone, they were received and provided for as friends, by the societies wherever they came. But having little or no communication or intercourse with each other, nor any subordination among themselves, they were under a continual necessity of recurring to Mr. Wesley, how and where each one was to labour. By calling them together to a conference, he brought them into a closer union with each other, and made them sensible of the utility of acting in concert and harmony under his direction and appointment. He soon found it necessary, however, to bring their itinerancy under certain regulations, and to reduce it to some fixed order; both to prevent confusion, and for his own ease. He therefore took fifteen or twenty societies, more or less, which lay round some principal society in that part, and which were so situated, that the greatest distance from one to the other was not much more than twenty miles, and united them into what was called a circuit. At the yearly conference, he appointed two, three, or four preachers to one of these circuits, according to its extent, which at first was often very considerable, sometimes taking in a part of three or four counties. Here, and here only, they were to labour for one year, that is, until the next conference. One of the preachers on every circuit, was called the Assistant, for the reason before mentioned. He took charge of all the societies with him. Having received a list of the societies forming his circuit, he took his own station in it, gave to the other preachers a plan of it, and pointed out the day when each should be at the place fixed for him, to begin a progressive motion round it, in such order as the plan directed. They then followed through all the societies belonging to the circuit at stated distances of time: all being governed by the same rule, and undergoing the same labour.

On Friday, August 24, 1744, Mr. Wesley preached for the last time at Oxford before the University. He had addressed them twice before, since the time he began to declare the truth in the fields and highways. Those sermons are printed in the first volume of his Works, and are well worthy of a serious perusal. "I am now," says he, " clear of the blood of those men. I have fully delivered my own soul. And I am well pleased that it should be the very day, on which, in the last century, near two thousand burning and shining lights were put out at one stroke. Yet what a wide difference is there between their case and mine! They were turned out of house and home, and all that they had: whereas I am only hindered from preaching, without any other loss: and that in a kind of honourable manner: it being determined, that when my next turn to preach came, they would pay another person to preach for me. And so they did twice or thrice: even to the time that I resigned my fellowship."

During this summer the preachers and people in Cornwall, bore hard service; the war against the Methodists being carried on more vigorously than that against the Spaniards. In September, Mr. Wesley received the following letter from Mr. Henry Millard, one of the preachers in Cornwall, giving some account of their difficulties. " The word of God, has free course here: it runs and is glorified. But the Devil rages horribly. Even at St. Ives, we cannot shut the door of John Nance's house to meet the society, but the mob immediately threaten to break it open. And in other places it is worse. I was going to Crowan on Tuesday, and within a quarter of a mile of the place where I was to preach, when some met me, and begged me not to go up: saying, ' If you do, there will surely be murder; if there is not already: for many were knocked down, before we came away.' By their advice I turned back to the house where I had left my horse. We had been there but a short time, when many people came in very bloody. But the main cry of the mob was, " Where is the preacher ?" whom they sought for in every part of the house ; swearing bitterly, ' If we can but knock him on the head, we shall be satisfied.'

" Not finding me, they said, ' However we shall catch him on Sunday at Cambourn.' But it was Mr. Westall's turn to be there. While he was preaching at Mr. Harris's, a tall man came in, and pulled him down. Mr. Harris demanded his warrant; but he swore, ' Warrant or no warrant, he shall go with me.' So he carried him out to the mob, who took him away to the church-town. They kept him there till the Tuesday morning, when the Rev. Dr. Borlase wrote his mittimus, by virtue of which he was to be committed to the house of correction at Bodmin, as a 'vagrant. So they took him as far as Cambourn that night, and the next day to Bodmin."

The justices who met at the next quarter-sessions in Bodmin, knowing a little more of the laws of God and man, or at least shewing more regard for them, than Dr. Borlase, declared Mr. Westall's commitment to be contrary to all law, and immediately set him at liberty.

1745. March 11, Mr. Wesley observes, "many persons still representing the Methodists as enemies to the clergy, I wrote to a friend the real state of the case, in as plain a manner as I could.

"1. About seven years since, we began preaching inward, present salvation, as attainable by faith alone. 2. For preaching this doctrine we were forbidden to preach in most of the churches. 3. We then preached in private houses, and when the houses could not contain the people, in the open air. 4. For this many of the clergy preached or printed against us, as both heretics and schismatics. 5. Persons who were convinced of sin, begged us to advise them more particularly, how to flee from the wrath to come? We desired them, being many, to come at one time, and we would endeavour it. 6. For this we were represented both from the pulpit and press, as introducing Popery, and raising sedition. Yea all manner of evil was said both of us, and of those who used to assemble with us. 7. Finding that some of these did walk disorderly, we desired them not to come to us any more. 8. And some of the others we desired to overlook the rest, that we might know whether they walked worthy of the gospel. 9. Several of the clergy now stirred up the people, to treat us as outlaws or mad dogs. 10. The people did so, both in Staffordshire, Cornwall, and many other places. 11. And they do so still wherever they are not restrained by fear of the magistrates.

"Now what can we do, or what can you or your brethren do, towards healing this breach? Desire of us any thing which we can do with a safe conscience, and we will do it immediately. Will you meet us here? Will you do what we desire of you, so far as you can with a safe conscience.

"Do you desire us, 1. To preach another, or to desist from preaching this doctrine? We cannot do this with a safe conscience.

"Do you desire us, 2. To desist from preaching in private houses, or in the open air? As things are now circumstanced, this would be the same as desiring us not to preach at all.

"Do you desire us, 3. Not to advise those who meet together for that purpose? To dissolve our societies? We cannot do this with a safe conscience; for we apprehend many souls would be lost thereby.

"Do you desire us, 4. To advise them one by one? This is impossible because of their number.

"Do you desire us, 5. To suffer those who walk disorderly, still to mix with the rest? Neither can we do this with a safe conscience: for evil communications corrupt good manners.

"Do you desire us, 6. To discharge those leaders as we term them, who overlook the rest? This is, in effect, to suffer the disorderly walkers still to remain with the rest.

"Do you desire us, lastly, to behave with tenderness, both to the characters and persons of our brethren the clergy? By the grace of God, we can and will do this: as indeed we have done to this day.

"If you ask, what we desire of you to do? We answer, 1. We do not desire any of you, to let us preach in your church, either if you believe us to preach false doctrine, or if you have the least scruple. But we desire any who believes us to preach true doctrine, and has no scruple in the matter, not to be either publickly or privately discouraged from inviting us to preach in his church.

U

2. "We do not desire, that any who thinks it his duty to preach or print against us, should refrain therefrom. But we desire, that none will do this, till he has calmly considered both sides of the question; and that he would not condemn us unheard, but first read what we say in our own defence.

3. "We do not desire any favour, if either Popery, sedition, or immorality be proved against us. But we desire you would not credit without proof, any of those senseless tales that pass current with the vulgar: that if you do not credit them yourselves, you will not relate them to others: yea, that you will discountenance those who still retail them abroad.

4. "We do not desire any preferment, favour, or recommendation, from those that are in power, either in church or state. But we desire, 1. That if any thing material be laid to our charge, we may be permitted to answer for ourselves. 2. That you would hinder your dependents from stirring up the rabble against us, who are certainly not the proper judges in these matters: and, 3. That you would effectually suppress and discountenance all riots and popular insurrections, which evidently strike at the foundation of all government, whether of church or state.

"Now these things you certainly can do, and that with a safe conscience. Therefore till these things be done, the continuance of the breach, if there be any, is chargeable on you, and on you only."

On August 1, and the following days, Mr. Wesley held the second Conference, with as many of the preachers as could conveniently be present. They reviewed their doctrines, and added such rules of discipline as the increase of the work required, or prudence suggested.

In October he was at Newcastle-upon-Tyne, where the English army lay, to oppose the progress of the rebels. Observing with great concern, the drunkenness and profane swearing which prevailed among the soldiers, he wrote the following letter to Alderman Ridley.

" Sir,

" The fear of God, the love of my country, and the regard I have for his Majesty, constrain me to write a few plain words to one, who is no stranger to these principles of action.

" My soul has been pained day by day, even in walking the streets of Newcastle, at the senseless, shameless wickedness, and the ignorant profaneness of the poor men to whom our lives are intrusted. The continual cursing and swearing, the wanton blasphemy of the soldiers in general, must needs be a torture to the sober ear, whether of a Christian or an honest infidel. Can any that either fear God or love their neighbour, bear this without concern? Especially if they consider the interest of our country, as well as of these unhappy men themselves? For can it be expected, that God should be on their side who are daily affronting him to his face? And if God be not on their side, how little will either their number, or courage, or strength avail.

" Is there no man that careth for these souls? Doubtless there are some who ought so to do. But many of these, if I am rightly informed, receive large pay, and do just nothing.

" I would to God it were in my power, in any degree, to supply their lack of service. I am ready to do what in me lies, to call those poor sinners to repentance, once or twice each day, while I remain in these parts, at any hour at any place. And I desire no pay at all for doing this: unless what my Lord shall give me at his appearing.

" If it were objected, that I should only fill their heads with peculiar whims and notions? That might easily be known. Only let the officers hear with their own ears: and they may judge, whether I do not preach the plain principles of manly, rational religion.

"Having myself no knowledge of the General, I took the liberty to make this offer to you. I have no interest herein: but I should rejoice to serve, as I am able, my king and country. If it be judged that this will be of no real service, let the proposal die and be forgotten. But I beg you, Sir, to believe, that I have the same glorious cause, for which you have shewn so becoming a zeal, earnestly at heart: and that therefore I am, with warm respect,

"Sir,

"Your most obedient servant.

This letter was written on the 26th, and on the 31st, Mr. Wesley preached on Newcastle Town-Moor, at a small distance from the English camp. November 1, he addressed them again on a little eminence before the camp, and continued this practice occasionally until the 30th, on which day his congregation was larger than any before; "Were it only for the sake of this hour, I should not have thought," says he, "much of staying at Newcastle longer than I intended. Between one and two in the afternoon, I went to the camp once more. Abundance of people now flocked together, horse and foot, rich and poor, to whom I declared, *There is no difference; for all have sinned and come short of the glory of God.* I observed many Germans standing disconsolate in the skirts of the congregation. To these I was constrained, though I had discontinued it so long, to speak a few words in their own language. Immediately they gathered up close together, and drank in every word." Of the colliers in the neighbourhood of Newcastle he remarks, "Our Lord gives us the poor, wherever we go: they are our perquisite, such a loving dirty company you never saw with your eyes; but by and by they shall be as white as snow."

" All this year the work of God gradually increased in the Southern counties, as well as in the North of England. Many were awakened in a very remarkable manner: many were converted to God. Many were enabled to testify, that *the blood of Jesus cleanseth from all sin.* Mean time we were in most places tolerably quiet, as to popular tumults."

Mr. Wesley, continued his labours with the same zeal and diligence, through the most distant parts of the kingdom during the year 1746. Methodism spread rapidly on every side: the societies flourished, and the people increased in number, and in the knowledge and love of the truth. At this period the lay-preachers had not been blessed with opportunities of improving their minds by an early education, or by much reading. In general their knowledge extended not beyond the first principles of religion, and the practical consequences deducible from them. *Repentance towards God, faith towards our Lord Jesus Christ;* and the fruits which follow. *Righteousness, and peace, and joy in the Holy Ghost,* were the subjects of their daily discourses, in which there was little variety. But such was the low state of religious knowledge among the people, that they were not prepared for any thing higher. It was absolutely requisite to make them well acquainted with first principles, and to give these principles a practical influence on the heart and life. Hence the limited knowledge of the preachers so far from being an inconvenience, was an unspeakable advantage; as it necessarily confined them to the fundamental points of experimental and practical religion. To enforce the necessity of repentance, and of salvation by grace alone through a Redeemer, the preacher would often draw a picture of human nature in such strong and natural colours, that every one who heard him saw his own likeness in it, and was ready to say, he hath shewn me all that was in my heart. The people found themselves under every discourse, emerging from the thickest darkness into a region of light. Mr. Wesley foresaw, that as knowledge increased among the people, it ought to augment in a greater proportion among the preachers. He therefore began to think of forming a collection of books in the English language, treating of the various branches of practical divinity. He was conscious, that the plan of his own education, and the prejudices which he had early imbibed against the non-conformists of the last century, had excluded him from many writings, which might be very useful on this occasion. This induced him to request Dr. Doddridge to give him a list of such books as he might think proper for the improvement of young preachers. March 15, the Doctor wrote to him, apologising for the delay in complying with the request. "I am quite grieved and ashamed, that any hurry, publick or private, should have prevented my answering your very obliging letter from Newcastle; especially as it has a face of disrespect, where I am sure I ought to express the very reverse, if I would do justice either to you, or to my own heart. But you have been used to forgive greater injuries.

" I have been reading the fourth edition of your Further Appeals : concerning which, I shall only say, that I have written upon the title page, " How forcible are RIGHT WORDS." I am daily hurried by my printer, to finish the third volume of my Family Expositor : and I have unwillingly, a secular affair on my hands, in consequence of a guardianship, which calls me away from my usual business for some days next week : on which account I must beg your patience for a little while longer, as to the list of books you desire me to send you. But if God permit, you shall be sure to have it in a few weeks.

"I lately published a thansgiving sermon, for the retreat of the rebels, which if you think it worth calling for, at Mr. Waugh's, at the Turk's Head in Gracechurch Street, I shall desire you to accept. I was willing to greet the first openings of mercy; and so much the rather, as I think with Lord Somerville, who first made the reflection in one of his letters; that, had the blow at Falkirk been pursued, our whole army had been destroyed.—The wisest and best of men, I know, agree to fear: oh! that they could also agree in their efforts to save! I trust I can call God to record on my soul, that to bring sinners to believe in Christ, and universally to obey him from a principle of grateful love, is the reigning desire of my heart, and has been the main business of my life. But alas, that it is so unsuccessful a labour! Yet God knows, that could I have fore-seen only the tenth part of that little success I seem to have had, I would have preferred the ministry, with ten times the labours and sorrows I have gone through in it, to any other employment or situation in life. I shall never forget Colonel Gardner's words, speaking of a much despised and persecuted, but very useful Minister, 'I had rather be that man, than Emperor of the world!'

"But I must conclude. May God, even your own God, continue to increase all his blessings on your head, heart, and labours; and may he sometimes lead you to remember in your prayers,

"Reverend and dear Sir,

"Your affectionate Brother and Servant,

"P. DODDRIDGE.

P. S. "I presume the list you desire is chiefly Theological. Perhaps my desire of making it too particular, has hindered me from setting about it, till I had a leisure time, which I have not yet found. But under the impression which your book made upon me, I could not delay writing one post longer. Let me know in one word, how you do, what your success is, and what your apprehensions are. I fear we must have some hot flame to melt us."

This letter was written in the time of the rebellion, when the English nation was in the greatest consternation. June 18, Dr. Doddridge sent the list of books, which Mr. Wesley had requested, and the next day wrote to him as follows : " I send this by way of Postscript, to thank you for the entertaining account you gave me of that very extraordinary turn which our affairs took in the battle of Falkirk.—I perceive our rebel enemies were as confident of victory as possible, just before the action at Culloden, which proved so fatal to them. A friend of mine thence, brings word that just as the armies joined, an officer was sent back to make proclamation at the Market-Cross at Inverness, that every householder should bake a bushel of bread, that it might be ready to refresh the prince's victorious army on its return ; which was required on pain of military execution. The consequence of this was, that our army found much better provision for their refreshment after the fatigue of that glorious day, than they could otherwise have done. I have also reason to believe, that a day or two before this action, Lord Kilmarnock having quartered himself and some of his chief officers at a minister's house of the Scotch established church in those parts, obliged the master of the house and his eldest son, to wait upon them at table, and in a profane manner undertook to say grace himself; which was, ' May God d—n and confound all Presbyterian parsons, their wives and children, and families, henceforth and for evermore. Amen.'—It is not to be wondered, that such a deliverance after such circumstances as these, should make a strong impression on the mind of ministers and people in general, which I am assured it does. I heartily pray God that the impression may be lasting and that it may produce that reformation which is so much needed among them as well as amongst us.

"I shall not be at all surprised, if the next winter should open upon us a much more afflictive scene than the last, if we will not be reformed by such judgments and deliverances as these. Yet I think with you, dear Sir, that God will not make a full end of us. I look upon every sinner converted from the error of his ways, by the power of God working in his gospel, as a token for good, that we shall not be utterly forsaken.

"I am, dear Sir,
"Most faithfully and affectionately yours,
"P. DODDRIDGE."

Mr. Wesley continued his frequent visits to the most distant parts of the kingdom. No season of the year, no change of weather, could either prevent or retard his journies. He generally preached two or three times each day, and regulated the societies wherever he came. His whole heart was in the work, and his fixed resolution surmounted every difficulty. In February 1747, being in Yorkshire, he met with a clergyman, who told him, "some of the ministers had frequently preached in his parish; and his judgment was, 1. That their preaching had done some good, but more harm. Because, 2. Those who had attended it, had only turned from one wickedness to another: they had only exchanged sabbath-breaking, swearing or drunkenness, for slandering, backbiting, and evil speaking: and 3. Those who did not attend it, were provoked hereby to return evil for evil. So that the former were, in effect, no better, the latter worse than before."

"The same objection, in substance," says Mr. Wesley, "has been made in most other parts of England. It therefore deserves a serious answer, which will equally hold in all places. It is allowed, 1. That our preaching has done some good; common swearers, sabbath-breakers, drunkards, thieves, fornicators, having been reclaimed from those outward sins. But it is affirmed, 2. That it has done more harm; the persons so reclaimed, only changing one wickedness for another: and their neighbours being so provoked thereby, as to become worse than they were before.

"Those who have left their outward sins, you affirm, have only changed drunkenness or sabbath-breaking, for backbiting or evil-speaking. I answer, if you affirm this of them all, it is notoriously false: many we can name, who left cursing, swearing, backbiting, drunkenness, and evil-speaking altogether, and who are to this day, just as fearful of slandering, as they are of cursing and swearing. And if some are not yet enough aware of this snare of the Devil, we may hope they will be ere long. Meantime bless God for what he has done, and pray that he would deliver them from this death also.

"You affirm further, 'That their neighbours are provoked hereby, to return evil for evil; and so while the former are no better, the latter are worse than they were before.'

"I answer, 1. 'These are worse than they were before.' But why? Because they do fresh despite to the spirit of grace: because they despise that long-suffering love of God which would lead them, as it does their neighbours, to repentance. And in laying the blame of this on those who will no longer run with them to the same excess of riot, they only fulfil the scriptures, and fill up the measure of their own iniquity.

"I answer, 2. There is still no proportion at all between the good on the one hand, and the harm on the other: for they who reject the goodness of God, were servants of the Devil before; and they are but servants of the Devil still. But they who accept it, are brought from the power of Satan, to serve the living and true God."

In April, Mr. Wesley, on his return from the North, spent an hour with the same clergyman, pressed him to make good his assertion, that the preaching of the Methodists had done more harm than good. This he did not choose to pursue; but enlarged on the harm it might occasion in succeeding generations. Wesley adds, " I cannot see the force of this argument. I dare not neglect the doing certain present good, for fear of some probable ill consequences, in the succeeding century."

" February 10, 1747. My brother returned from the North, and I prepared to supply his place there.

" I was wondering at the mildness of the weather, such as seldom attends me in my journeys. But my wonder now ceased: the wind turned full North, and blew so exceeding hard and keen, that when we came to Hatfield, neither my companions nor I had much use of our hands or feet. After resting an hour, we bore up again through the wind and snow, which drove full in our faces. But this was only a squall. In Baldock-field the storm began in earnest. The large hail drove so vehemently in our faces, that we could not see, nor hardly breathe. However before two o'clock we reached Baldock, where one met and conducted us safe to Potten. About six I preached to a serious congregation.

" On the 17th, we set out as soon as it was well light. But it was really hard work to get forward. For the ice would not well bear or break. And the untracked snow covering all the road, we had much ado to keep our horses on their feet. Mean time the wind rose higher and higher, till it was ready to overturn both man and beast. However after a short bait at Bugden, we pushed on, and met in the middle of an open field with so v[?] a storm of rain and hail, as we had not had befo[re] It drove through our coats, great and small, [?] and every thing, and froze as it fell, even upon o[ur] eye-brows: so that we had scarce either strength [or] motion left, when we came into the Inn at Stilton.

"[We n]ow gave up our hopes of reaching Grantham, the s[now] falling faster and faster. However we took the a[dva]ntage of a fair blast, and made the best of our way [to] Stamford-Heath. But here a new difficulty aros[e] from the snow lying in large drifts. Sometimes hor[se] and men were well nigh swallowed up. Yet in les[s t]han an hour we were brought safe to Stamford. B[ein]g willing to get as far as we could, we made but a sh[or]t stop here; and about sun-set came, cold and weary, yet well, to a little town called Brig-casterton.

"On the 18th, our servant came up and said, "Sir, there is no travelling to-day. Such a quantity of snow has fallen in the night, that the roads are quite filled up." I told him, "At least we can walk twenty miles a day, with our horses in our hands." So in the name of God we set out. The North East wind was piercing as a sword, and had driven the snow into such uneven heaps, that the main road was not passable. However we kept on, a foot or on horseback, till we came to the White Lion at Grantham. Some from Grimsby had appointed to meet us here. But not hearing any thing of them, for they were at another house by mistake, after an hour's rest we set out straight for Epworth.

" On the 19th, the frost was not so sharp: so that we had little difficulty till we came to Haxey-Car. But here the ice which covered the dikes and great part of the common, would not bear, nor readily break. Nor did we know, there being no track of man or beast, what parts of the dike were fordable. However we committed ourselves to God, and went on. We hit all our fords exactly, and without any fall or considerable hinderance came to Epworth in two hours, full as well as when we left London.

In the spring and summer of this year, Mr. Wesley and the Preachers were invited into many parts of Yorkshire, Lancashire, Derbyshire, and Cheshire, where they had not before travelled. Mr. John Bennet was a most indefatigable and successful labourer for several years, in these parts of the country; a man of sound judgment, and of considerable abilities. From a letter which he wrote to Mr. Wesley, we may form some notion of the labours of the Preachers. " Many doors are opened for preaching in these parts, but cannot be supplied for want of Preachers. I think some one should be sent to assist me, otherwise we shall lose ground.—My circuit is one hundred and fifty miles in two weeks; during which time I preach publickly thirty-four times, besides meeting the societies, visiting the sick and transacting the temporal business. The above is too much for me, considering my weak constitution."

This was great labour; but Mr. Wesley, and his brother Mr. Charles Wesley, laboured still more.— They preached as often, did all the other business, and frequently travelled nearly treble the distance in the same space of time. Hitherto they had been enabled to labour, and form societies with the assistance of the other Preachers, in most parts of England, though frequently at the peril of their lives: but now their mission was stretched a little farther. One of the Lay-Ministers had gone to Dublin, and after preaching there for some time, had formed a society. He wrote an account of his success to Mr. Wesley, who determined to visit Ireland immediately. Accordingly, August 4, he departed from Bristol, and passing through Wales, arrived in Dublin on Sunday the 9th, about ten o'clock in the forenoon. Mr. Wesley observes: "Soon after we landed, hearing the bells ringing for church, I went thither directly.—About three I wrote a line to the curate of St. Mary's, who sent me word he should be glad of my assistance. So I preached there, another gentleman reading prayers, to as gay and senseless a congregation as ever I saw. After sermon Mr. R. thanked me very affectionately, and desired I would favour him with my company in the morning. Monday 10, Between eight and nine I went to Mr. R. the curate of St. Mary's: he professed abundance of good-will, commended my sermon in strong terms, and begged he might see me again the next morning. But at the same time he expressed the most rooted prejudice against Lay-Preachers, or preaching out of a church; and said, the archbishop of Dublin was resolved to suffer no such irregularities in his diocese."

The next day Mr. Wesley waited upon the archbishop at New-Bridge, and conversed with him two or three hours; in which time he answered many of his objections.

The house wherein they worshipped at this time, was originally designed for a Lutheran church, and contained about four hundred people: but abundantly more might stand in the yard. Mr. Wesley preached morning and evening to many more than the house could contain; and had more and more reason to hope, that they would not all be unfruitful hearers. Monday the 17th, he began to examine the society, which contained about two hundred and fourscore members, many of whom had found peace with God. "The people in general," says Mr. Wesley, "are of a more teachable spirit than in most parts of England: but on that very account, they must be watched over with the more care, being equally susceptible of good and ill impressions."

Mr. Wesley proceeds. "Sunday the 23d, I began in the evening before the usual time; yet were a multitude of people got together, in the house, yard, and street: abundantly more than my voice could reach. I cried aloud to as many as could hear, *All things are ready; come ye to the marriage.* Having delivered my message, about eleven I took ship for England, leaving J. Trembath, then a burning and a shining light, a workman that needed not to be ashamed, to water the seed which had been sown. Wednesday 26, about two in the afternoon we landed at Holyhead. Saturday 29, I preached at Garth, in Brecknockshire, in the evening, where I met my brother, in his way to Ireland".—The remaining part of this year, Mr. Wesley spent in Bristol, London, Salisbury, and the neighbouring places.

In 1747, Mr. Wesley experienced God's providential care in the following perilous accident. "I took horse," says he, "in Bristol for Wick, where I had appointed to preach at three in the afternoon. I was riding by the wall through St. Nicholas' gate my horse having been brought to the house where I dined just as a cart turned short from St. Nicholas street, and came swiftly down the hill. There was just room to pass between the wheel of it and the wall; but that space was taken up by the carman. I called to him to go back, or I must ride over him. But the man, as if deaf, walked straight forward. This obliged me to hold back my horse. In the mean time the shaft of the cart came full against his shoulder, with such a shock as beat him to the ground. He shot me forward over his head, as an arrow out of a bow, where I lay with my arms and legs, I knew not how, stretched out in a line, close to the wall. The wheel ran by, near my side, but only dirtied my clothes, I found no flutter of spirit, but the same composure as if I had been sitting in my study. When the cart was gone, I rose. Abundance of people gathered round, till a gentleman desired me to step into his shop. After cleaning myself a little, I took horse again, and was at Wick by the time appointed. I returned to Bristol, where the report of my being killed had spread far and wide, time enough to praise God in the great congregation, and to preach on, *Thou, Lord, shalt save both man and beast.*"

"February 12, 1748. After preaching at Oakhill, a village in Somersetshire, I rode on to Shepton-Mallet, but found the people all under a strange consternation. A mob, they said, was hired, and made sufficiently drunk to do all manner of mischief. I began preaching between four or five; and none hindered or interrupted at all. We had a blessed opportunity, and the hearts of many were exceedingly comforted. I wondered what was become of the mob. But we were quickly informed, they mistook the place, imagining that I should alight, as I used to do, at William Stone's house, and summoned by drum all their forces together to meet me at my coming. But Mr. Swindells, one of the preachers, innocently carrying me to the other end of the town, they did not find their mistake till I had done preaching.

"However they attended us from the preaching-house to William Stone's, throwing dirt, stones and clods in abundance; but they could not hurt us, only Mr. Swindells had a little dirt on his coat, and I a few specks on my hat.

"After we had gone into the house, they began throwing large stones, in order to break the door. But perceiving this would require some time, they dropped that design for the present. They then broke all the tiles on the Pent-house over the door, and poured in a shower of stones at the windows. One of their captains, in his great zeal, had followed us into the house, and was now shut in with us. He did not like this, and would fain have gone out; but it was not possible. So he kept as close to me as he could, thinking himself safest when he was near me. But staying a little behind, when I went up two pair of stairs, and stood close on one side, where we were a little sheltered, a large stone struck him on the forehead, and the blood spouted out like a stream. He cried out, " O Sir, are we to die to-night? What must I do? What must I do?" I said, " Pray to God. He is able to deliver you from all danger." He took my advice and began praying, I believe, as he had scarcely ever done before.

" Mr. Swindells and I then went to prayer: after which I told him, " We must not stay here. We must go down immediately." He said, " Sir we cannot stir, you see how the stones fly about." I walked straight through the room, and down the stairs; and not a stone came in, till we were at the bottom. The mob had just broken open the door, when we came into the lower room; and while they burst in at one door, we walked out at the other. Nor did one man take any notice of us, though we were within five yards of each other.

" They filled the house at once, and proposed setting it on fire. But one of them remembering that his own house was next, persuaded them not to do it. Hearing some person cry out, " They are gone over the grounds," I thought the hint was good. So we went over the grounds to the far end of the town, where a friend waited, and undertook to guide us to Oakhill.

"I was riding on in Shepton-Lane, it being now quite dark, when he cried out, " Come down: come down from the bank." I did as I was desired; but the bank being high, and the side almost perpendicular, I came down all at once, my horse and I tumbling one over another. But we both rose unhurt. In less than an hour we came to Oakhill, and the next morning to Bristol."

February 15, he left Bristol, and proceeded through Wales on his way to Ireland. On the 24th, he reached Holyhead, where he was detained about twelve days. He did not remain idle; but preached every day in the neighbourhood.

March 8, about one o'clock in the morning, they sailed, and reached Dublin in the evening, where Mr. Wesley found his brother. On the 16th, he inquired into the state of the society. "Most pompous accounts," says Mr. Wesley, "had been sent me from time to time, of the great numbers that were added to it; so that I confidently expected to find therein, six or seven hundred members. And how is the real fact? I left three hundred and ninety four members; and I doubt if there are now, three hundred and ninety six!"

On the 30th, he left Dublin, and rode to Philip's-Town. The street was soon filled with those who flocked from every side. And even at five in the morning, he had a large congregation. After worship he spoke severally to those of the society; of whom forty were troopers. At noon he addressed a larger congregation than that in Dublin.

The following days he preached at Tullamore, Tyrrell's-Pass, Claro, Temple-Maqueteer, Moat; and on April 2d, came to Athlone.

"May 3, I rode to Birr, twenty miles from Athlone; and the key of the Sessions-house not being to be found, declared *The grace of our Lord Jesus Christ*, in the street, to a dull, rude, senseless multitude. Many laughed the greater part of the time. Some went away just in the middle of a sentence. And yet when one cried out, a Carmelite Friar, Clerk to the Priest, "You lie:" the zealous Protestants cried out, "Knock him down." And it was no sooner said than done. I saw some bustle, but knew not what was the matter, till the whole was over."

On the 10th, he left Athlone, when he drew near to the turnpike, about a mile from the city, a multitude waited for him at the top of the hill. They fell back on each side, to make him way, and then joined, and inclosed him. After singing two or three verses, he advanced and on a sudden he was surprised by such a cry of men, women and children, as he had never heard before. "Yet a little while," said he, "and we shall meet to part no more; and sorrow and sighing shall flee away for ever."

On his return he spent some time in Dublin, previous to his departure for England. On one of these days, while he was preaching on the green near the barrack, a man cried out, " Aye, he is a Jesuit: that's plain." To which a popish priest, who happened to be near, replied, " No, he is not: I would to God he were!"

On the 24th of June, Mr. Wesley opened the Kingswood School with a sermon from the wise man's admonition, " Train up a child in the way that he should go, and when he is old, he will not depart from it": at the conclusion, the Lord's supper was celebrated by a very large congregation.

This institution, is supported by an annual collection through all the societies; the preacher's sons forming three fourths of the pupils, who are boarded, clothed, and instructed.

In July, Mr. Wesley was at Newcastle-upon-Tyne; and thence travelled to Berwick upon Tweed. Here he preached three or four times, in a large green space, near the governor's house. A little society had been formed in this town some time before, which was now considerably increased: and several members of it, walked worthy of the vocation wherewith they were called. On the 23d, he returned to Newcastle.

During the summer, there was a large increase of the work of God, in Northumberland, Durham, Yorkshire, and in the most savage parts of Lancashire.

"On August 26th," says Mr. Wesley, "while I was speaking to some quiet people at Roughley, near Coln, in Lancashire, a drunken rabble came, the captain of whom said he was a deputy constable, and I must go with him. I had scarce gone ten yards, when one of his company struck me in the face with all his might. Another threw his stick at my head: all the rest were like as many ramping and roaring lions. They brought me, with Mr. Grimshaw, the minister of Haworth; Mr. Colbeck of Kighley, and Mr. Mackford of Newcastle, who never recovered the abuse he then received, into a public-house at Barrowford, a neighbouring village, where all their forces were gathered together.

"Soon after Mr. Hargrave, the high constable, came, and required me to promise I would come to Roughley no more. This I flatly refused. But upon saying, I will not preach here now, he undertook to quiet the mob. While he and I walked out at one door, Mr. Grimshaw, and Mr. Colbeck, went out at the other. The mob immediately closed them in, tossed them to and fro with the greatest violence, threw Mr. Grimshaw down, and loaded them both with dirt and mire of every kind. The other quiet harmless people, who followed me at a distance, they treated full as ill. They poured upon them showers of dirt and stones, without any regard to age or sex. Some of them they trampled in the mire, and dragged by the hair of the head. Many they beat with their clubs without mercy. One they forced to leap from a rock, ten or twelve feet high, into the river. And when he crept out, wet and bruised, were hardly persuaded, not to throw him in again.

Such was the recompense we frequently received from our countrymen, for our labour of love."

The year 1749 is distinguished by no important occurrence in Mr. Wesley's life. His labours were as usual incessant, his journies regular, and his exertions in the cause of his master unwearied.

In the beginning of the year 1750, having been informed of the violence of the mobs at Cork, against both the preachers and people, and being in nothing terrified by the adversaries, he determined to visit the scene of riot. Accordingly, on April 7th, he landed in Dublin. Here he received a full account of the shocking outrages which had been committed at Cork, for several months together; and which the *good* magistrates had encouraged rather than opposed. At the Lent assizes, several depositions were laid before the grand jury, against the rioters: yet they did not find any of those bills! But they presented a poor baker, who when the mob were discharging a shower of stones upon him, fired a pistol without ball over their heads, which put them into such bodily fear, that they all ran away, without looking behind them.

Having rested ten or twelve days in Dublin, Mr. Wesley began his journey through the country societies towards Cork, where he arrived on May the 19th. The next day, understanding that the house was small, he went about eight o'clock, to Hammond's-Marsh; here he preached, to a large and deeply attentive congregation. In the afternoon, two of the ministers went to the mayor, and asked, if it would be disagreeable to him, that Mr. Wesley should preach on the Marsh? He answered, "Sir, I will have no more mobs and riots." One of them replied, Sir, Mr. Wesley has made none. He then spake plainly, "Sir, I will have no more preaching. And if Mr. Wesley attempts it, I am prepared for him." "I would not therefore, attempt to preach on the Marsh, but began in our own house about five. The good mayor, mean time, was walking on the Change, and giving orders to his serjeants and the town drummers, who immediately came down to the house, with an innumerable mob attending him. They continued drumming, and I continued preaching, till I had finished my discourse. When I came out, the mob presently inclosed me. Observing one of the serjeants standing by me, I desired him to keep the king's peace. But he replied, ' Sir, I have no orders to do that.' As soon as I came into the open street, the rabble threw whatever came to hand. But all went by me, or over my head; nor do I remember that any thing touched me. I walked straight through the midst of the rabble, looking every man before me in the face; and they opened to the right and left, till I came near Dant's Bridge. A large party had taken possession of this: but when I came up, they likewise shrunk back, and I walked through them to Mr. Jenkins's house. But a stout Papist-woman stood just within the door, and would not let me come in, till one of the mob, aiming I suppose at me, knocked her down flat. I then went in, and God restrained the wild beasts, so that no one attempted to follow me.

"But many of the congregation were more roughly handled; particularly Mr. Jones, who was covered with mud, and escaped with his life almost by a miracle. Finding the mob were not inclined to disperse, I sent to alderman Pembrook, who immediately desired alderman Wenthrop, his nephew, to go down to Mr. Jenkins's: with whom I walked up the street, none giving an unkind or disrespectful word.

"All the following week it was at the peril of his life, if any Methodist stirred out of doors. And the case was much the same, during the whole mayoralty of

Mr. Crone. But the succeeding mayor, declared in good earnest, ' There shall be no more mobs or riots in Cork.' And he did totally suppress them. So that from that time forward, even the Methodists enjoyed the same liberty with the rest of his Majesty's subjects.

" In the mean time the work of God went on with little opposition, both in other parts of the county of Cork, at Waterford, and Limerick; as well as in Mountmelick, Athlone, Longford, and most parts of the province of Leinster. On my return from Cork, I had an opportunity of visiting all these. And I had the satisfaction of observing, how greatly God had blessed my fellow-labourers, and how many sinners were saved from the error of their ways.

" All this time God gave us great peace at Bandon, notwithstanding the unwearied labours, both public and private of Dr. B. to stir up the people. But Saturday 26, many were under great apprehensions of what was to be done in the evening. I began preaching in the main street at the usual hour, but to more than twice the usual congregation. After I had spoken about a quarter of an hour, a clergyman, who had planted himself near me, with a very large stick in his hand, according to agreement opened the scene. Indeed his friends assured me, ' he was in drink, or he would not have done it.' But before he had uttered many words, two or three resolute women, by main strength pulled him into an house, and after expostulating a little, sent him away through the garden.—The next champion that appeared, was a young gentleman of the town.— But his triumph too was short: for some of the people quickly bore him away, though with much gentleness and civility. The third came on with far greater fury: but he was encountered by a butcher of the town, not one of the Methodists, who used him as he would an ox, bestowing one or two heavy blows on his head, This cooled his courage, especially as none took his part. So I quietly finished my discourse."

Mr. Wesley continued his labours in Ireland, till July 22, when he sailed for Bristol. He staid there a few days only, and then visited the societies through the West of England, as far as Cornwall.

Previous to this period, Mr. Wesley had formed a resolution to marry. But Mr. Charles Wesley, found means to prevent the marriage, for reasons which appeared to him of sufficient importance to authorize him to interfere. Mr. John Wesley, however, thought otherwise, and this was the first breach of that union and harmony which had now subsisted between the two brothers, without interruption, during twenty years. Notwithstanding this disappointment, Mr. Wesley having fixed his choice of a partner, proposed the matter to Mr. Perronet. February 2, 1775, he received Mr. Perronet's answer, in favour of the marriage. Immediately after, he married Mrs. Vizelle, a widow, lady of independent fortune. But before the wedding, he settled her fortune upon herself, refusing to have the command of one shilling of her property. Mr. Wesley's constant habit of travelling through Great Britain and Ireland, the number of persons who visited him, and his extensive correspondence with the members of the society, were circumstances unfavourable to that social intercourse, mutual openness and confidence, which form the basis of happiness in the married state. These circumstances, indeed, would not have been very important, had he espoused a woman who could have entered into his views, and accommodated herself to his situation: but had he searched the whole kingdom, he could not have found a woman more unsuitable in these respects, than the lady whom he married.

She first left him, in 1771: and they finally separated at four years after that occurrence. When she was told that she had left his house, determined never to return, he said, " non eam reliqui ; non dimisi ; non revocabo." She died in October 1781, and bequeathed her fortune to Mr. Vizelle—To Mr. Wesley she gave a ring.

On March 27, Mr. Wesley commenced his Northern journey. He travelled through the societies as far as Whitehaven, and on April 20, arrived at Newcastle. On the 24th, he proceeded to pay his first visit to Scotland. He was invited thither by colonel Galatin, who was then quartered at Musselborough. Mr. Wesley having mentioned this to Mr. Whitefield, he replied, " You have no business there : for your principles are so well known, that if you spoke like an angel, none would hear you. And if they did, you would have nothing to do but to dispute with one and another from morning to night." He answered, " If God sends me, people will hear. And I will give them no provocation to dispute : for I will studiously avoid controverted points, and keep to the fundamental truths of christianity. And if any still begin to dispute, they may : but I will not dispute with them."

" I had no intention," says he, " to preach in Scotland ; not imagining that there were any that desired I should. But I was mistaken. Curiosity, if nothing else, brought abundance of people together in the afternoon. And whereas in the kirk, Mrs. Galatin informed me, there used to be laughing and talking, and all the marks of the grossest inattention ; it was far otherwise here. They remained as statues from the beginning of the sermon to the end. I preached again at six in the evening, on, *Seek ye the Lord while he may be found.* I used great plainness of speech towards high and low : and they all received it in love : so that the prejudice which had been several years planting, was torn up by the roots in one hour. After preaching, one of the bailiffs of the town, with one of the elders of the kirk, came to me, and begged I would stay with them a while; nay, if it were but two or three days, and they would fit up a larger place than the school, and prepare seats for the congregation. Had not my time been fixed, I should gladly have complied. All that I could now do, was to give them a promise, that Mr. Hopper should come back the next week and spend a few days with them. And it was not without a fair prospect. The congregations were very numerous: many were cut to the heart; and several joined together in a little society."

That activity, diligence, and success which had marked Mr. Wesley's labours and travels during several years, were evinced throughout the whole of the year 1752, in various districts both in England and Ireland.

In April, 1753, he again visited Scotland by the invitation of Dr. Gillies of Glasgow, in whose kirk he preached to very large and attentive congregations: "Who would have believed," says he, "five and twenty years ago, either that the minister would have desired, or that I should have consented to preach in a Scotch kirk!" In July, Mr. Wesley crossed over to the Isle of Wight. From Cowes, he went to Newport.— He here found a little society in tolerable order: several of whom had found peace with God, and walked in the light of his countenance. At half an hour after six he addressed in the market-place a numerous congregation: the children made much noise; and many grown persons were talking aloud during the time of worship. "There was a large congregation again at five in the morning: and every person therein, seemed to know that this was the word whereby God would judge him in the last day. In the evening the congregation was more numerous, and far more serious than the night before; only one drunken man made a little disturbance, but the mayor ordered him to be taken away."

October 19, Mr. Wesley returned to London, and the next day found himself unwell. In a short time his complaint appeared to be an ague. Before he was perfectly recovered, he was threatened with a rapid consumption. In consequence of Dr. Fothergill's advice, he retired to Lewisham : and wishing " to prevent vile panegyrick" in case of death, he wrote as follows :

" Here lieth
The body of *John Wesley*,
A brand plucked out of the burning :
Who died of a consumption in the fifty-first year of
his age.
Not leaving after his debts are paid, ten pounds behind
him :
Praying,
God be merciful to me an unprofitable servant !"

He ordered that this, if any inscription, should be placed on his tomb-stone.

While Mr. Wesley was confined, he received the following letter from Mr. Whitefield.

" *Rev. and very dear Sir*,

" If seeing you so weak when leaving London distressed me, the news and prospect of your approaching dissolution hath quite weighed me down. I pity myself and the church, but not you : a radient throne awaits you, and ere long you will enter into your Master's joy : yonder he stands with a massy crown, ready to put it on your head amidst an admiring throng of saints and angels. But I, poor I, that have been waiting for my dissolution these nineteen years, must be left behind to grovel here below ! Well ! this is my comfort : it cannot be long ere the chariots will be sent even for worthless me. If prayers can detain them, even you, rev. and very dear sir, shall not leave us yet: but if the decree has gone forth, that you must now fall asleep in Jesus, may he kiss your soul away, and give you to die in the embraces of triumphant love! If in the land of the living, I hope to pay my last respects to you next week. If not, rev. and dear sir, farewell. Ego sequar, etsi non passibus æquis. My heart is too big, tears trickle down too fast, and you are I fear too weak for me to enlarge. Underneath you may there be Christ's everlasting arms. I commend you to his never-failing mercy, and am,

Rev. and very dear sir,
Your most affectionate, sympathizing,
And afflicted younger brother,
In the Gospel of our common Lord,
G. WHITEFIELD."

On May 6, 1755, the conference began at Leeds. "The point," says Mr. Wesley, "on which we desired all the preachers to speak their minds at large, was, whether we ought to separate from the church? Whatever was advanced on one side or the other, was seriously and calmly considered: and on the third day we were all fully agreed, that, whether it was lawful or not, it was by no means expedient."

"August 6, I mentioned to our congregation in London, a means of increasing serious religion, which had been frequently practised by our forefathers, the joining in a covenant to serve God with all our heart and with all our soul. I explained this for several mornings following; and on Friday many of us kept a fast unto the Lord, beseeching him to give us wisdom and strength, that we might *promise unto the Lord our God and keep it.* On Monday at six in the evening we met for that purpose, at the French church in Spitalfields. After I had recited the tenour of the covenant proposed, in the words of that blessed man, Richard Allyen, all the people stood up, in token of assent, to the number of about eighteen hundred. Such a night I scarcely ever knew before. Surely the fruit of it shall remain for ever."—The covenant has been renewed once every year, since that period.

January 1756. The general expectation of publick calamities in the ensuing year, spread a general seriousness over the British nation. " We endeavoured," says Mr. Wesley, " in every part of the kingdom, to avail ourselves of the apprehensions which we frequently found it was impossible to remove, in order to make them conducive to a nobler end, to that *fear of the Lord which is the beginning of wisdom.*—February 6, " The fastday was a glorious day, every church in the city was more than full: and a solemn seriousness sat on every face. Surely God heareth prayer: and there will yet be a lengthening of our tranquillity."

In the latter end of March, he visited Ireland again, and after inspecting the societies in Leinster and Munster, went with Mr. Walsh into the provinces of Ulster and Connaught.

August 25, Mr. Wesley returned to Bristol, where he found about fifty preachers, who had collected to hold a conference.

Mr. Wesley's journeys and labours of love, in preaching the gospel of peace through all parts of the three kingdoms, were continued with the same unremitting diligence; while the duties of his situation in some other respects, increased every year upon him. New societies were frequently formed in various places; which naturally called for an increase of ministers. These, however, were more easily procured, than a stranger would imagine; for the class and band meetings were a fruitful nursery, where the most zealous and pious young men soon grew up to the requisite standard, to be transplanted into a higher situation, among the local or itinerant preachers.

In the spring and summer of the year 1760, Mr. Wesley was in Ireland. He remained in Dublin about twenty days, and travelled through the greater part of that kingdom.

In 1761, Mr. Wesley visited several parts of Scotland, as far as Aberdeen; where he was favourably received and treated with much respect by the principal and other eminent persons of the university. He preached first in the college-close, and then in the hall, which was crowded even at five in the morning! In every place some desired to unite with him, to meet together weekly, and to *provoke each other to love and to good works.*

"May 4. About noon, I took a walk to King's college. Going up to see the hall, we found a large company of ladies with several gentlemen. They looked, and spoke to one another, after which one of the gentlemen took courage, and came to me. He said, "We came last night to the college-close, but could not hear, and should be extremely obliged, if you would give us a short discourse here." I knew not what God might have to do, and so began without delay, on *God was in Christ reconciling the world unto himself.* I believe, the word was not lost. It fell as dew on the tender grass."

In the beginning of July, he reached York on his return, and was desired to call on a poor prisoner in the castle. "I had formerly," says Mr. Wesley, "occasion to take notice of an hideous monster, called a chancery-bill; I now saw the fellow to it, called a declaration. The plain fact was this. Some time since, a man who lived near Yarm, assisted others in running some brandy. His share was worth nearly four pounds. After he had wholly left off that work, and was following his own business, that of a weaver, he was arrested, and sent to York gaol. And not long after came down a declaration, " That Jac. Wh— had landed a vessel laden with brandy and geneva, at the port of London, and sold them there, whereby he was indebted to his majesty five hundred and seventy-seven pounds, and upwards. And to tell this worthy story, the lawyer takes up thirteen or fourteen sheets of treble stampt paper.

" O England ! Will this reproach never be rolled away from thee ? Is there any thing like this to be found, either among Turks, or Heathens ? In the name of justice, mercy, and common sense, I ask, 1. Why do men lie, for lying sake ? Is it only to keep their hands in ? What need else of saying it was the port of London ? when every one knew the brandy was landed above three hundred miles thence. What a monstrous contempt of truth does this shew, or rather hatred to it ? 2. Where is the justice of swelling four pounds, into five hundred and seventy-seven ? 3. Where is the common sense, of taking up fourteeen sheets to tell a story, that may be told in ten lines ? 4. Where is the mercy, of thus grinding the face of the poor beggared prisoner. Would not this be execrable villainy, if the paper and writing together were only six-pence a sheet, when they have stript him already of his little all, and not left him fourteen groats in the world ?"

It is certain that nothing can be said in defence of some of our law proceedings. They are often absurd, highly oppressive to the subject, and disgraceful to a civilized nation. In criminal cases, how often does the indictment magnify and exaggerate both the crime and every circumstance connected with it, beyond all the bounds of truth and probability ? Hence it becomes extremely difficult for jurymen to discharge their duty with a good conscience; and we seldom see punishments duly proportioned to the crimes committed. What shall we say in other cases, where the tautology and circumlocution peculiar to the language of our law, the delay of judgment in the courts, and the tergiversation permitted through the whole proceedings, render it almost impossible for an honest man in middling life to obtain his right against a villain, without the utmost danger of being ruined? A man who robs on the highway is hanged; but a villain who robs by means of the chicanery, delay and expence of the law, escapes with impunity, and is applauded.

During the two following years, there was much noise throughout the societies concerning perfection: but more especially in London, where two or three persons who stood at the head of those professing to have attained that state, fell into some extravagant notions and forms of expression. One of the persons was George Bell, who was supported, by Mr. Maxfield; and they soon raised a party.

Mr. Wesley did not, at first, oppose these extravagances with sufficient firmness; by which the persons who favoured them daily increased in number. At length, however, he found it absolutely necessary to give it an effectual check: but now it was too late to be done, without the risk of a separation in the society. This, being the least of the two evils, accordingly took place: Mr. Maxfield withdrew from his connection with Mr. Wesley, with nearly two hundred of the people.

At this time the societies were so multiplied, and so widely spread, that they formed twenty-five extensive circuits in England, eight in Ireland, four in Scotland, and two in Wales; on which about ninety preachers were daily employed.

Mr. Wesley continued his travels and labours, with his usual diligence and punctuality through all the societies in Great-Britain, Ireland, and Wales; and his health and strength were wonderfully preserved. In October 1765, he observes, " I breakfasted with Mr.

Whitefield, who seemed to be an old man, being fairly worn out in his Master's service, though he has hardly seen fifty years. And yet it pleases God, that I, who am now in my sixty-third year, find no disorder, no weakness, no decay, no difference from what I was at five and twenty: only that I have fewer teeth, and more grey hairs!"—Soon after he adds, " Mr. Whitefield called upon me. He breathes nothing but peace and love. Bigotry cannot stand before him, but hides its head wherever he comes."

Mr. Wesley received sixty pounds per annum from the society in London, which is the salary that every clergyman receives who officiates among them. But individuals in various places frequently gave him money; legacies were sometimes left him, and the produce of his books in the latter part of life, was considerable. It is well known however, that he hoarded nothing at the end of the year. He even contracted his expences as much as possible, and gave the surplus to the poor, and to those who might, through misfortunes, be in want. His charitable disposition may appear from the following little circumstance, which strongly evinces the tender feelings of his mind, under a consciousness that he had not given in proportion to the person's want. In November 1766, a foreigner in distress called upon him, and presented a Latin letter, begging some relief. Shortly after, Mr. Wesley, reflecting on the case, wrote on the back of the letter, " I let him go with five shillings: I fear he is starving. Alas!"

In 1770, the society had increased in Great-Britain and Ireland to forty-nine circuits, one hundred and twenty-two itinerant, and two hundred local ministers.

Some of the preachers being now in America, and several societies having been formed, they earnestly requested Mr. Wesley, once more to cross the Atlantic. In the beginning of this year, he wrote to Mr. Whitefield on that subject: "Mr. Keen informed me some time since, of your safe arrival in Carolina; of which indeed I could not doubt for a moment, notwithstanding the idle report of your being cast away, which was so current in London. I trust our Lord has more work for you to do in Europe, as well as in America. And who knows, but before your return to England, I may pay another visit to the new world? I have been strongly solicited by several of our friends in New-York and Philadelphia. They urge many reasons; some of which seem to be of considerable weight. And my age is no objection at all: for, I bless God, my health is not barely good, but abundantly better, in several respects, than when I was five and twenty. But there are so many reasons on the other side, that as yet, I can determine nothing; so I must wait till I have further light. Here I am; let the Lord do with me as seemeth to him good. For the present, I must beg of you to supply my lack of service: by encouraging the preachers as you judge best, who are as yet comparatively young and inexperienced: by giving them such advices as you think proper: and above all, by exhorting them, not only to love one another, but if it be possible, as much as lieth in them, to live peaceably with all men."—Hence it is evident that he had a strong inclination once more to visit America. Being one day asked in company, if he did intend to go to America? He answered, "If I go to America, I must do a thing which I hate as bad as I hate the Devil." What is that, Sir, said one present? "I must keep a secret."

Mr. Wesley, and those associated with him, were called Arminians, because they maintained that Jesus Christ died for the salvation of all men: Mr. Whitefield, and those in connexion with him, were denominated Calvinists, because they maintained that Christ died for a determinate number only, who must finally be saved. Hence the propositions at the conclusion of the minutes kindled what before was jealousy and suspicion only, into a flame of contention and strife. The Calvinists were alarmed, and Mr. Shirley wrote a circular letter to all the serious clergy throughout the land. In June 1771, Mr. Fletcher sent a copy of this letter to Mr. Wesley. On Tuesday, August 6, the conference began at Bristol; on Thursday, Mr. Shirley and his friends were admitted: and although the parties had manifested much violence in their writings, yet the interview with the conference during two hours, was conducted with great temper and moderation, but without effect. The dispute was continued some time, but committed almost wholly to Mr. Fletcher; who managed it with astonishing temper and success. He was devout and pious, to a degree seldom equalled since the days of the Apostles: and displayed great knowledge of his subject. His letters were published under the title of " Checks to Antinomianism:" they exhibit a beautiful model for controversy on religious topics, and will ever bear ample testimony to the goodness of Mr. Fletcher's head and heart.

In January 1773, Mr. Wesley offered the joint authority in the direction of the society to Mr. Fletcher, but he determined not to assume so responsible a station.

In 1775, Mr. Wesley visited Ireland, and in June, on his return from Londonderry, was attacked by a more severe illness than he had ever experienced.—— " Tuesday 13, I was not very well in the morning, but supposed it would soon go off. In the afternoon, the weather being extremely hot, I lay down on the grass in Mr. Lark's orchard at Cockhill. This I had been accustomed to do for forty years, and never remember to have been hurt by it. Only I never before lay on my face, in which posture I fell asleep. I waked a little, and but a little out of order, and preached with ease to a multitude of people. Afterwards I was a good deal worse: however, the next day I went on a few miles to the Grange. The table was placed there in such a manner, that all the time I was preaching, a strong and sharp wind blew on the left side of my head. And it was not without a good deal of difficulty that I made an end of my sermon. I now found a deep obstruction in my breast: my pulse was exceedingly weak and low. I shivered with cold, though the air was sultry hot, only now and then burning for a few minutes. I went early to bed, drank a draught of treacle and water, and applied treacle to the soles of my feet. I lay till seven on Thursday the 15th, and felt considerably better. But I found nearly the same obstruction in my breast: I had a low, weak pulse: I burned and shivered by turn, and if I ventured to cough it jarred my head exceedingly. In going on to Derry Anvil, I wondered what was the matter, that I could not attend to what I was reading; no, not for three minutes together, but my thoughts were perpetually shifting. Yet all the time I was preaching in the evening, though I stood in the open air, with the wind whistling round my head, my mind was as composed as ever. Friday 16, in going to Lurgan, I wondered again that I could not fix my attention to what I read: yet while I was preaching in the evening on the parade, I found my mind perfectly composed; although it rained a great part of the time, which did not well agree with my head. Saturday 17, I was persuaded to send for Dr. Laws, a sensible and skilful physician. He told me, 'I was in a high fever, and advised me to lie by.' I told him, that could not be done; as I had appointed to preach in several places, and must preach as long as I could speak. He then prescribed a cooling draught, with a grain or two of camphor, as my nerves were universally agitated. This I took with me to Tangragee: but when I came there, I was not able to preach: my understanding being quite confused, and my strength gone. Yet I breathed freely, and had not the least thirst, nor any pain from head to foot.

"I was now at a full stand; whether to aim at Lisburn, or to push forward for Dublin? But my friends doubting whether I could bear so long a journey, I went to Derry-Aghy, a gentleman's seat on the side of a hill, three miles beyond Lisburn. Here nature sunk, and I took my bed: but I could no more turn myself therein, than a new-born child. My memory failed as well as my strength, and well nigh my understanding. Only those words ran in my mind, when I saw Miss Gayer on one side of the bed, looking at her mother on the other,

'She sat, like patience on a monument
'Smiling at grief.'

"I can give no account of what followed for two or three days, being more dead than alive. Only I remember it was difficult for me to speak, my throat being exceedingly dry. But Joseph Bradford tells me, I said on Wednesday, 'It will be determined before this time to-morrow—That my tongue was much swoln, and as black as a coal; that I was convulsed all over, and for some time my heart did not beat perceptibly, neither was any pulse discernible.'

"In the night of Thursday the 22d, Joseph Bradford came to me with a cup, and said, 'Sir, you must take this.' I thought I will, if I can, to please him; for it will do me neither harm nor good. Immediately it made me vomit; my heart began to beat, and my pulse to play again. And from that hour, the extremity of the symptoms abated. The next day I sat up several hours, and walked four or five minutes across the room. On Saturday I sat up all day, and walked across the room many times, without any weariness. "On Sunday I came down stairs, and sat several hours in the parlour. On Monday I walked before the house: on Tuesday I took an airing in the chaise: and on Wednesday, trusting in God, to the astonishment of my friends, I set out for Dublin."

In 1776 an order was made by the House of Lords, "That the Commissioners of His Majesty's Excise do write circular letters to all such persons whom they have reason to suspect to have plate, as also, to those who have not paid regularly the duty on the same," &c. In consequence of this order, the Accomptant-General for Household Plate, sent Mr. Wesley, a copy of the order, with a letter, desiring an immediate reply.

Mr. Wesley answered:

"Sir,

I have two Silver tea-spoons in London, and two in Bristol. This is all the Plate which I have at present: and I shall not buy any more, while so many round me want bread.

I am, Sir,
Your most humble Servant,
JOHN WESLEY."

The Methodists now visited the Isle of Man; but the preachers did not long enjoy peace. The storm became violent, and Methodism was threatened with a total shipwreck on the island. In the end of May 1777, Mr. Wesley, who always wished to stand foremost in danger, visited the people and was received in a very friendly manner by a few persons of respectability and influence. At Peele-Town, Mr. Corbet said, he would gladly have asked him to preach in his church; but the bishop had forbidden it; and also that his clergy should not admit any Methodist Preacher to the Lord's Supper.

Hitherto the society in London had occupied the old Foundery near Upper-Moorfields, as a place of worship; but were now making preparations to quit it. They had obtained from the city the promise of a lease of a piece of ground in the City-Road, and every thing being prepared, the day was fixed for laying the foundation of a chapel. " The rain," says Mr. Wesley, " befriended us much, by keeping away thousands who proposed to be there. But there were still such multitudes, that it was with great difficulty I got through them to lay the first stone. Upon this was a plate of brass, on which was engraved, " This was laid by John Wesley, on April 1, 1777."

In October 1778, the chapel was finished, and ready to be opened. " November 1," says Mr. Wesley, " was the day appointed for opening the New Chapel in the City-Road. It is pefectly neat, but not fine ; and contains far more than the Foundery ; I believe, together with the morning chapel, as many as the Tabernacle. Many were afraid, that the multitudes crowding from all parts, would have occasioned much disturbance. But they were happily disappointed ; there was none at all : all was quietness, decency, and order. I preached on part of Solomon's prayer at the dedication of the Temple ; and both in the morning and afternoon, God was eminently present in the midst of the congregation."

The year 1780 is distinguished in the British history, by the riots which were excited in consequence of the law that had been passed in favour of the Papists, who could never remove the odium of having in disguise promoted and increased the disgraceful outrages which were then exhibited. The object of the Protestant Association had been strongly defended in a variety of Pamphlets, which their opponents answered. Mr. Wesley in January, published some remarks upon the subject in one of the London newspapers. After premising that persecution was not referred to in the controversy, and that he wished no man to be persecuted for his religious principles; he offers this general proposition, " That no Roman-Catholic does or can give security to a Protestant Government, for his allegiance and peaceable behaviour." His proof was contained in the following arguments.

" It is a Roman-Catholic maxim, established not by private men, but by a public council, that, *No faith is to be kept with heretics.* This has been openly avowed by the Council of Constance; but it never was openly disclaimed. Whether private persons avow or disavow it, it is a fixed maxim of the Church of Rome.

" One branch of the spiritual power of the Pope, is, and has been for ages, the power of granting pardons for all sins past, present, and to come! But those who acknowledge him to have this spiritual power, can give no security for their allegiance.

" The power of dispensing with any promise, oath, or vow, is another branch of the spiritual power of the Pope. And all who acknowledge his spiritual power, must admit this: but whoever acknowledges this dispensing power of the Pope,—nay, not only of the Pope, but even of a Priest who has power to pardon sins! which is an essential doctrine of the Church of Rome, cannot possibly give security for their allegiance to any Government.

" Setting then religion aside, it is plain, that upon principles of reason, no Government ought to tolerate men, who cannot give security to that Government for their allegiance and peaceable behaviour. But this no Romanist can do, not only while he holds that, ' No faith is to be kept with heretics,' but so long as he acknowledges either priestly-absolution, or the spiritual power of the Pope."

"This letter raised him several adversaries. But Mr. O'Leary, a Capuchin friar in Dublin, became the most conspicuous of Mr. Wesley's opponents. He published Remarks upon the letter, to which Mr. Wesley replied. Mr. O'Leary continued his Remarks, and Mr. Wesley again answered him.——The Remarks were afterwards reprinted together in London, with the following title, " Mr. O'Leary's Remarks on the Rev. Mr. Wesley's Letters in defence of the Protestant Association in England, to which are prefixed Mr. Wesley's Letters." This is a most striking proof of Mr. O'Leary's disingenuity and artifice. Mr. Wesley had not written one line in defence of the Protestant Association: his two replies were suppressed, and a spurious letter published as genuine, which Mr. Wesley declared he had never seen, until it appeared in Mr. O'Leary's pamphlet.

Mr. Wesley's second reply, contains the strength of his cause; and will give a full view of the subject.

" Some time ago, in a letter published in London, I observed, ' Roman-Catholics cannot give those whom they account heretics, sufficient security for their peaceable behaviour! Because it has been publickly avowed in one of their general councils, and never publickly disclaimed, That faith is not to be kept with heretics: because they hold the doctrine of priestly-absolution: and the doctrine of Papal Pardons and Dispensations.'

Mr. O'Leary has published remarks on this letter; nine parts in ten of which are quite wide of the mark. Not that they are wide of his mark, which is to introduce a plausible panegyrick upon the Roman-Catholics, mixt with keen invectives against the Protestants; whether true or false it matters not. All this is admirably well calculated to inspire the reader with aversion to these heretics, and to bring them back to the holy, harmless, much injured church of Rome! And I should not wonder, if these six papers should make six thousand converts to her.—Close arguing he does not attempt, but he vapours, and skips to and fro, and rambles to all points of the compass, in a very lively and entertaining manner.

".My argument was, The Council of Constance has openly avowed violation of faith with heretics. But it has never been openly disclaimed. Therefore those who receive this council cannot be trusted by those whom they account heretics—This is my immediate conclusion. And if the premises be admitted, it will infallibly follow.

" On this Mr. O'Leary says, ' A council so often quoted challenges peculiar attention. We shall examine it with all possible precision and impartiality. At a time when the broachers of a new doctrine'—as new as the bible—' were kindling the fire of sedition, and shaking the foundation of thrones and kingdoms'—big words, but entirely void of truth—' was the Council of Constance. To this was cited John Huss, famous for propagating errors tending, to wrest the sceptre from the hand of kings.'—Equally true—' He was obnoxious to the church and state'—To the church of Rome: not to the state in any degree—' Huss strikes at the root of all temporal power and civil authority. He boldly asserts, That all princes, magistrates, &c. in the state of moral sin, are deprived, *ipso facto*, of all power and jurisdiction. And by broaching these doctrines, he makes Bohemia a theatre of intestine war. See the acts of the Council of Constance in L'Abbe's collection of Councils'—I have seen them, and can find nothing of this therein.

' He gave notice that he would stand his trial. But he attempted to escape'—No, never, this is pure invention. ' ' He was arrested at Constance, and confined. His friends plead his safe-conduct. The council declared, no safe-conduct granted by the emperor, or any other princes, to HERETICS, ought to hinder them from being punished as justice shall require. And the person who has promised them security, SHALL NOT BE OBLIGED TO KEEP HIS PROMISE, BY WHATEVER TIE HE MAY BE ENGAGED.'

" And did the Council of Constance declare this? Yes, says Mr. O'Leary. I desire no more. But before I argue upon the point, permit me to give a little fuller account of the whole affair.

" The Council of Constance was called by the emperor Sigismund, and pope John the 23d, in the year 1414. Before it began, the emperor sent some Bohemian gentlemen, to conduct John Huss to Constance, solemnly promising, that he should ' Come and return freely, without fraud or corruption.'

" But before he left Prague, he waited on the bishop of Nazareth, papal inquisitor for that city and diocese, who, in the presence of many witnesses, gave him the following testimonial—' We, Nicholas—do by these presents, make known to all men, that we have often talked with that honourable man, master John Huss, and in all his sayings, doings, and behaviour, have proved him to be a faithful man; finding no manner of evil, sinister, or erroneous doings in him, until the present. Prague, August 30, 1414.

" This was attested by the hand and seal of the public notary, named Michael Pruthatietz.—After this, Conrade, archbishop of Prague, declared before all the barons of Bohemia, that ' He knew not that John Huss was culpable or faulty, in any crime or offence whatever'—So neither the inquisitor, nor the archbishop, knew any thing of ' his making Bohemia a theatre of intestine war.'

"In the seventeenth session, the sentence and condemnation of John Huss, was read and published. The emperor then commanded the duke of Bavaria to deliver him to the executioner ; for which glorious exploit, he was thus addressed by the bishop of Landy, in the name of the council : ' This most holy, and goodly labour, was reserved only for thee, O most noble prince ! Upon thee only doth it lie, to whom the whole rule and ministration of justice is given. Wherefore thou hast established thy praise and renown : even by the mouths of babes and sucklings thy praise shall be celebrated for evermore !

"From the whole of this transaction we may observe; that John Huss was guilty of no crime, either in word or action ; even his enemies, the archbishop of Prague, and the papal inquisitor being judges : that his real fault, and his only one, was opposing the papal usurpations : that this most noble prince, was a bigotted, cruel, perfidious murderer; and that the fathers of the council deserve the same praise, seeing they urged him to embrue his hands in innocent blood, in violation of the public faith, and extolled him to the skies for so doing : and seeing they have laid it down as a maxim that the most solemn promise made to a heretic may be broken.

"But, says Mr. O'Leary, ' This regards the peculiar case of safe-conduct granted by princes to heretics' —But what then ? If the public faith with heretics may be violated in one instance, it may be in a thousand—' But can the rule be extended further ?'—It may ; it must ; we cannot tell where to stop. Away then with your witticisms on so awful a subject. What ! do you sport with human blood ? I take burning men alive to be a very serious thing. I pray spare your jests on the occasion.—Again, ' What more absurd than to insist on a general council's disclaiming a doctrine which they never taught :' they did teach it; and that not by the bye, not incidentally; but they laid it down as a stated rule of action, dictated by the Holy Ghost—and demonstrated their sincerity therein by burning a man alive. And this Mr. O'Leary humourously compares to roasting a piece of beef! With equal tenderness, I suppose, he would compare the ' Singing the beards of heretics! that is thrusting a burning furze-bush, in their face, to the singing a fowl before it is roasted. Now, what security can any Romanist give a Protestant till this doctrine be publickly abjured ? If Mr. O'Leary has any thing more to plead for this council, I shall follow him step by step. But let him keep his word, and ' Give a serious answer to a serious charge.' Drollery may come in, when we are talking of roasting fowls, but not when we talk of ' roasting men.'

" Would I then wish the Roman-Catholics to be persecuted ? I never said or hinted any such thing. I abhor the thought: it is foreign to all I have preached and written for these fifty years. I would wish the Romanists in England to be treated still with the same lenity that they have been these sixty years : to be allowed both civil and religious liberty, but not to be permitted to undermine ours. I wish them to stand just as they did, before the late act was passed : not to be persecuted, or hurt themselves ; but gently restrained from hurting their neighbours."

Notwithstanding the high praises bestowed by some persons on Mr. O'Leary, Mr. Wesley was greatly the superior in point of argument. Mr. O'Leary, allows the charge which Mr. Wesley brought against the council of Constance ; and yet afterwards affects to deny it—Mr. Berrington wrote in defence of the same council ; and observed, " There never was a decision made at Constance tending to shew, that no faith is to be kept with heretics. The words of the canon are not susceptible of such a comment, unless tortured to it. At all events no council, pope, bishop, priest, or layman of our church, ever understood them in the sense of your interpretation,—But every Catholic divine has at all times utterly reprobated the idea of breaking faith with heretics, as contrary to every dictate of reason and religion."—With regard to the council of Constance, if the words of the canon be ambiguous, yet, the burning a man alive, in open violation of the publick faith, was a very plain and unequivocal comment. " Every Catholic divine has at all times utterly reprobated the idea of breaking faith with heretics." The modern rulers of the church of Rome speak in language very different from Mr. Berrington. In 1768, an oath of allegiance was contemplated for the Roman-Catholics of Ireland, which, for the better security of the government, contained a declaration of abhorrence and detestation of the doctrines, " That faith is not to be kept with heretics, and that princes deprived by the Pope may be deposed or murdered by their subjects." The pope's legate at Brussels, Ghilini, archbishop of Rhodes, had then the superintendance of the Romish Church in Ireland. He addressed the titular archbishop of Dublin on this subject, and in his letter treats the above clauses as absolutely intolerable. " Because," says he, " those doctrines are defended, and contended for, by most Catholic nations, and the Holy See has frequently followed them in practice:" and he decides, " That, as the oath is in its whole extent unlawful, so in its nature it is invalid, null, of no effect, and can by no means bind and oblige consciences."

Similar decisions on the validity of oaths which were detrimental to the interests of the holy see, were uniformly made by successive popes, whenever the affairs of the church required them. What has been said fully proves the charge which Mr. Wesley brought—" It is a maxim of the church of Rome that faith is not to be kept with heretics." It has been constantly taught by the first authority, that the Roman-Catholics are not bound to any engagements which they may have made with heretics, though confirmed by the most solemn oath that can possibly be framed, when the good of the church requires that they should break it. This was a doctrine of the Romish church not in the times of great ignorance only; the modern papal rulers maintain it and contend for it. The old spirit of popery is still nourished by the practice of the pope, who once every year, on Maunday-Thursday, excommunicates all heretics in the most awful and terrific manner; and thus feeds that constant spirit of hatred which is rooted in the minds of the Papists against the Protestants. The Romish bishops take an oath at their consecration, totally inimical to every government, and which binds them to use every method in their power to subvert it. —This is a part of the oath: " The Roman papacy, and the royalties of St. Peter, I will, saving my own order, assist the pope and his successors to retain and defend against every man. The rights, honours, privileges, and authority of the holy Roman church, and of our lord the pope, and his successors aforesaid, I will be careful to preserve, defend, enlarge, and promote. All heretics, schismatics, and rebels against our said lord, I will, to the utmost of my power, persecute and oppose, and will never lay down my weapons till they are utterly brought under and rooted out." —The clause, *hereticos pro posse persequar, et expugnabo,* is an obligation to persecute heretics, and to oppose them with temporal weapons; and this clearly appears to be the sense of the church of Rome, both from her decrees and practice, and from late instances of persecuting zeal in the Spanish and Portuguese inquisitions.

From this period there was the same uniformity in Mr. Wesley's life as during the preceding years. His visits were extended to every part of the kingdom, and the success which attended him, was proportioned to his exertions in the Redeemer's cause.

On Thursday, June 12, 1783, he embarked at Harwich; on the following day he arrived at Helvoetsluys, and visited Rotterdam, the Hague, Haerlem, Leyden, Utrecht, and Amsterdam. But nothing material occurred during his journey; and in the beginning of July he returned to London.

During this year at the Bristol conference, Mr. Wesley was so indisposed that neither he nor his friends thought he would recover. From the nature of his complaint, he suspected that a spasm would probably seize his stomach, and occasion sudden death. Under these views of his situation, he said to Mr. Bradford, " I have been reflecting on my past life: I have been wandering up and down between fifty and sixty years, endeavouring in my poor way to do a little good to my fellow creatures : and, now it is probable that there are but a few steps between me and death, and what have I to trust to for salvation? I can see nothing which I have done or suffered, that will bear looking at. I have no other plea than this : I the chief of sinners am: but Jesus died for me." This sentiment, and his reference to it in his last sickness, plainly show how steadily he persevered in the same views of the Gospel, with which he began to preach it.

The deed by which the British Methodist Conference was finally established, is dated February 28th, 1784 : it appoints and nominates one hundred preachers to form that body, under a variety of regulations. They are to assemble once every year: the act of the majority is binding : no business can be transacted unless forty members be present : the session cannot be dissolved within five days from its commencement, nor be continued after twenty-one days: it directs the mode of appointing officers, of filling up vacancies, of admitting preachers, and concludes by declaring the conference extinct, if the number of its members should ever be reduced to less than forty. This is the basis and outlines of the present church government of the British Methodists.

CHAPTER V.

The Methodist doctrines, discipline, and economy; with a view of the progress and present state of Methodism in Great-Britain.

THE regulations of the primitive Methodists, were printed under the title of, *Orders of a religious Society, meeting in Fetter Lane,* in obedience to the command of God by St. James, and by the advice of Peter Bohler. It was determined;

" That they would meet together once a week, to confess their faults one to another, and to pray one for another that they might be healed: that others, of whose sincerity they were well assured, might, if they desired it, meet with them for that purpose.: that the persons desirous of meeting together should be divided into several bands, or little companies, none of which should consist of fewer than five, or more than ten persons: that some person in each band, should be desired to speak to the rest in order, who might be called the leader of that band: that each band should meet twice in a week; once on Monday evening, and the second time when it was most convenient for each band; every meeting to be begun and ended with singing and prayer: that every one in order, should speak as freely, plainly, and concisely as he could, the state of his heart, with his several temptations and deliverances since the last time of meeting: that all the bands should have a conference at eight every Wednesday evening, begun and ended with singing and prayer: that any who desired to be admitted into this society, should be asked, What are your reasons for desiring this? Will you be entirely open, using no kind of reserve? Have you any objection to any of our orders? That when any new member was proposed, every one present should speak clearly and freely whatever objection he had against him : that those against whom no reasonable objection appeared, should be, in order for their trial, formed into one or more distinct bands, and some person agreed on to assist them : that after two months trial, if no objection then appeared, they might be admitted into the society: that every fourth Saturday should be observed as a day of general intercession, which might continue from twelve to two, from three to five, and from six to eight : that on the Sunday seven-night following, there should be a general love-feast, from seven till ten in the evening : that no particular person should be allowed to act in any thing, contrary to any order of this society ; but that every one without distinction should submit to the determination of his brethren ; and that if any person or persons did not, after being thrice admonished, conform to the society, they should no longer be esteemed as members : that any person whom the whole society should approve, might be accounted a corresponding member, and as such be admitted to the general meetings, provided he corresponded with the society, at least once a month."

In the year 1743, when a considerable number of societies had been formed, Mr. Wesley and his brother to preserve order and regularity throughout the whole connection, published *The nature, design and general rules of the United Societies, in London, Bristol, Newcastle-upon-Tyne,* &c.

" Such a society is no other than, " *A company of men, having the form, and seeking the power of godliness ; united in order to pray together, to receive the word of exhortation, and to watch over one another in love, that they may help each other to work out their salvation.*

" That it may the more easily be discerned, whether they are indeed working out their own salvation, each society is divided into smaller companies, called classes, according to their respective places of abode. There are about twelve persons in every class; one of whom is styled the leader. It is his business, to see each person in his class once a week at least, in order to inquire how their souls prosper. To advise, reprove, comfort or exhort, as occasions require: to receive what they are willing to give toward the relief of the poor. To meet the minister, and the stewards of the society once a week, in order to inform the minister of any that are sick; or of any that walk disorderly, and will not be reproved: to pay to the stewards what they have received of their several classes, the week preceding; and, to shew their account of what each person has contributed.

" There is one only condition previously required of those who desire admission into these societies, *A desire to flee from the wrath to come, to be saved from their sins.* But wherever this is really fixed in the soul, it will be shewn by its fruits. It is therefore expected of all who continue therein, that they should continue to evidence their desire of salvation "by doing no harm, by avoiding evil in every kind; especially that which is most generally practised, such as the taking the name of God in vain: the profaning the day of the Lord, either by doing ordinary work thereon, or by buying or selling; drunkenness; fighting, quarrelling, brawling; brother going to law with brother: returning evil for evil, or railing for railing: the using many words in buying or selling: the buying or selling uncustomed goods: the giving or taking things on usury; uncharitable or unprofitable conversation; particularly speaking evil of magistrates or ministers; doing to others as we would not they should do unto us: doing what we know is not for the glory of God: as the putting on gold, or costly apparel : the taking such diversions as cannot be used in the name of the Lord Jesus : the singing those songs, or reading those books, which do not tend to the knowledge or the love of God : softness, or needless self-indulgence : laying up, treasures upon earth : borrowing without a probability of paying ; or taking up goods without a probability of paying for them. It is expected from all who continue in these societies, that they should continue to evince their desire of salvation : by doing good, by being in every kind merciful after their power ; as they have opportunity, doing good of every posssible sort, and as far as is possible to all men : to their bodies, of the ability which God giveth ; by giving food to the hungry, by clothing the naked, by visiting or helping them that are sick, or in prison. To their souls, by instructing, reproving, or exhorting all they have intercourse with ; trampling under foot that enthusiastic doctrine of devils, that, *we are not to do good unless our hearts be free to it :* by doing good especially, to them that are of the household of faith, or groaning so to be ; employing them preferably to others ; buying one of another ; helping each other in business ; and so much the more, because the world will love its own, and them only : diligence and frugality, that the gospel be not blamed : by running with patience the race that is set before them, *denying themselves, and taking up their cross daily.*; submitting to bear the reproach of Christ, to be as the filth and off-scouring of the world : and looking that men should *say all manner of evil of them falsely for the Lord's sake.* It is expected of all who desire to continue in these societies, that they should continue to evidence their desire of salvation : by attending upon all the ordinances of God. Such are, the publick worship of God : the ministry of the word, either read or expounded : the supper of the Lord :

family and private prayer: searching the scriptures; and fasting and abstinence.

" These are the general rules of our societies; all which we are taught of God to observe, even in his written word, the only rule, and the sufficient rule, both of our faith and practice. And all these we know his spirit writes on every truly awakened heart. If there be any among us who observe them not, who habitually break any of them, let it be made known unto them who watch over that soul, as they that must give an account. We will admonish him of the error of his ways: we will bear with him for a season. But if he repent not, he hath no more place with us. We have delivered our own soul.

JOHN WESLEY,
CHARLES WESLEY."

Every member of the society was obliged to meet in class. But those, who had peace with God, were divided into smaller companies, called bands. Each band had a person called the leader, who met the company weekly, and received a small contribution for the poor. At the quarterly visitation, when the tickets were changed, those persons received a ticket with a B. These were called band-tickets, and admitted those who held them into the meetings where the bands alone were assembled.

DIRECTIONS *to the* BAND SOCIETIES.

" You are supposed to have the *faith that overcometh the world*. To you, therefore, it is not grievous: carefully to abstain from doing evil: in particular; neither to buy or sell any thing at all on the Lord's day: to be at a word both in buying and selling: to pawn nothing, no not to save life: not to mention the fault of any behind his back: to wear no needless ornaments, such as rings, ear-rings, necklaces, lace, ruf-

: zealously to maintain good works: in particular:

to give alms of such things as you possess, and that to the utmost of your power: to reprove all that sin in your sight, and that in love, and meekness of wisdom: to be patterns of diligence and frugality, of self-denial, and taking up the cross daily. Constantly to attend on all the ordinances of God: in particular: to be at church, and at the Lord's table every week; and at every publick meeting of the bands: to attend the publick ministry of the word every morning, unless distance, business, or sickness prevent: to use private prayer every day: and family prayer, if you are the head of a family: and to read the scriptures, and meditate therein, at every vacant hour."

The following letter, which Mr. Wesley addressed to Mr. Perronet, details the nature of the Methodist discipline, and assigns the reasons and manner of its introduction.

Some time since you desired an account of the economy of the people called Methodists: but I must premise, that as they had not the least expectation at first, of any thing like what has since followed, so they had no previous design or plan at all, but every thing arose just as the occasion offered.

A few years ago my brother and I were desired to preach in many parts of London. We had no view therein, but so far as we were able, to convince those who would hear, what true Christianity is, and to persuade them to embrace it. Many of those who heard us began to cry out, that we brought strange things to their ears; that this was a doctrine which they never heard before; or at least never regarded. They searched the scriptures, whether these things were so, and acknowledged the truth as it is in Jesus; and their hearts were influenced to follow Christ, and him crucified.

Immediately they were surrounded with difficulties; all the world rose up against them: neighbours, strangers, acquaintances, relations, and friends, began to cry out amain; " be not righteous overmuch: why shouldst thou destroy thyself; let not much religion make thee mad." One and another came to us, asking what they should do? being distressed on every side, as every one strove to weaken, and none to strengthen their hands in God. We advised them, " Strengthen you one another. Talk together as often as you can. And pray earnestly, with and for one another, that you may endure to the end, and be saved." Against this advice, we presumed, there could be no objection; as being grounded on the plainest reason, and on so many scriptures both of the Old and New Testament.

They said, " but we want you likewise to talk with us often, to direct and quicken us in our way, to give us the advices which we need, and to pray with and for us." I asked, ' Which of you desire this?' Let me know your names, and places of abode. They did so. But I soon found they were too many for me to talk with severally so often as they wanted it. So I told them, ' if you will all of you come together, every Thursday in the evening, I will gladly spend some time with you in prayer, and give you the best advice I can." Thus arose, without any previous design on either side, what was afterwards called, " a society." The thing proposed, was to flee from the wrath to come, and by associating themselves together, to assist each other in so doing.

It quickly appeared, that their thus uniting together answered the end proposed. In a few months the far greater part of those who had begun to *fear God, and to work righteousness*, but were not united together, grew faint in their minds, and fell back into what they were before. Mean while the far greater part of those, who were thus united together, continued *striving to enter in at the strait gate*, and to *lay hold on eternal life.*

Upon reflection, I could not but observe, this is the very thing which was from the very beginning of Christianity. In the earliest times, those whom God had sent forth, *preached the gospel to every creature.* And the body of hearers, were mostly either Jews or Heathens. But as soon as any of these were so convinced of the truth, as to forsake sin and seek the gospel-salvation, they immediately joined them together, took an account of their names, advised them to watch over each other, and met these catechumens apart from the great congregation, that they might instruct, rebuke, exhort, and pray with them and for them, according to their several necessities.

But it was not long before an objection was made to this, which had not once entered into my thought. " Is not this making a schism? Is not the joining these people together, *gathering churches out of churches?*" It was easily answered, if you mean only *gathering people out of buildings called churches,* it is. But if you mean, dividing christians from christians, and so destroying christian fellowship, it is not. For, these were not christians before they were thus joined. Most of them were barefaced heathens: neither are they christians, from whom you suppose them to be divided. You will not look me in the face, and say they are. What! Drunken christians? Cursing and swearing christians? Lying christians? Cheating christians? If these are christians at all, they are *devil christians,* as the poor Malabarians term them:—Neither are they divided any more than they were before, even from these wretched *devil christians.* They are as ready as ever to assist them, and to perform every office of real kindness toward them. If it be said, " but there are some true christians in the parish, and you destroy the christian fellowship between these and them." I answer, that which never existed, cannot be destroyed. But the fellowship you speak of, never existed. Therefore it cannot be destroyed. Which of those true christians had any such fellowship with these? Who watched over them in love? Who marked their growth in grace? Who advised and exhorted them from time to time? Who prayed with them and for them as they had need? This, and this alone is christian fellowship: but alas! Where is it to be found? Look east or west, north or south: name what parish you please. Is this christian fellowship there? Rather are not the bulk of the parishoners a mere rope of sand? What christian connexion is there between them? What intercourse in spiritual things? What watching over each other's souls? What bearing of one another's burdens? What a mere jest is it then, to talk so gravely of destroying what never was? The real truth is just the reverse of this: we introduce christian fellowship where it was utterly destroyed. And the fruits have been peace, joy, love, and zeal for every good word and work.

But as much as we endeavoured to watch over each other, we soon found some who did not love the gospel. I do not know that any hypocrites were crept in; for indeed there was no temptation. But several grew cold, and gave way to the sins which had long easily beset them. We quickly perceived, there were many ill consequences of suffering these to remain among us. It was dangerous to others; inasmuch as all sin is of an infectious nature. It brought such a scandal on their brethren, as exposed them to what was not pro-
    he reproach of Christ. It laid a stumbling-block
    y of others, and caused the truth to be evil

We groaned under these inconveniencies long, before a remedy could be found. At length, while we were thinking of quite another thing, we struck upon a method for which we have cause to bless God ever since. I was talking with several of the society in Bristol, concerning the means of paying the debts there; when one stood up and said, " Let every member of the society give a penny a week till all are paid."— Another answered, " but many of them are poor, and cannot afford to do it." " Then," said he, " put eleven of the poorest with me, and if they can give any thing, well. I will call on them weekly, and if they can give nothing, I will give for them as well as myself. And each of you call on eleven of your neighbours weekly: receive what they give, and make up what is wanting." It was done. In a while some of these informed me, " they found such and such a one did not live as he ought." It struck me immediately, " this is the thing; the very thing we have wanted so long." I called together all the leaders of the classes, and desired, that each would make a particular inquiry into the behaviour of those whom they saw weekly: they did so. Many disorderly walkers were detected. Some turned from the evil of their ways. Some were put away from us. Many saw it with fear, and rejoiced unto God, with reverence. As soon as possible the same method was used in London and all other places. Evil men were detected and reproved. They were borne with for a season. If they forsook their sins, we received them gladly: if they obstinately persisted therein, it was openly declared, that they were not of us. The rest mourned and prayed for them, and yet rejoiced, that as far as in us lay, the scandal was rolled away from the society.

At first they visited each person at his own house: but this was soon found inexpedient. It took up more time, than most of the leaders had to spare. Many persons lived with masters, mistresses, or relations, who would not suffer them to be thus visited. At the houses of those who were not so averse, they often had no opportunity of speaking to them but in company : and this did not at all answer the end proposed, of exhorting, comforting or reproving : it frequently happened that one affirmed what another denied : and this could not be cleared up without seeing them together : little misunderstandings and quarrels of various kinds frequently arose among relations or neighbours ; effectually to remove which it was needful to see them all face to face. Upon all these considerations it was agreed, that those of each class should meet altogether, that a more full inquiry might be made into the behaviour of every person. Those who could not be visited at home, or no otherwise than in company, had the same advantage with others. Advice or reproof was given as need required ; quarrels made up, misunderstandings removed : and after an hour or two spent in this labour of love, they concluded with prayer and thanksgiving.

It can scarcely be conceived, what advantages have been reaped from this little prudential regulation. Many now happily experienced that christian fellowship, of which they had not so much as an idea before. They began to *bear one another's burdens*, and *naturally* to *care for each other*. As they had daily a more intimate acquaintance with, so they had a more endeared affection for each other. And *speaking the truth in love, they grew up into him in all things, who is the head, even Christ ; from whom the whole body, fitly joined together, and compacted by that which every joint supplied, according to the effectual working in the measure of every part, increased unto the edifying itself in love.*

About this time, I was informed, that several persons in Kingswood frequently met together at the school, and spent the greater part of the night in prayer, praise and thanksgiving. Some advised me to put an end to this: but upon weighing the thing thoroughly, and comparing it with the practice of the ancient christians, I could see no cause to forbid it. Rather, I believed, it might be made of more general use. So sent them word, "I designed to watch with them, on the Friday nearest the full-moon, that we might have light thither and back again." I gave publick notice of this the Sunday before, and withal, that I intended to preach; desiring, that they and they only would meet me there, who could do it without prejudice to their business or families. On Friday abundance of people came. I began preaching between eight and nine; and we continued till a little beyond midnight, singing, praying, and praising God.

This we have continued to do occasionally ever since, in Bristol, London, and Newcastle, as well as Kingswood. And exceeding great are the blessings we have found therein: it has generally been an extremely solemn season; when the word of God sunk deep into the hearts, even of those who till then knew him not. If it be said, "this was only owing to the novelty of the thing, or perhaps to the awful silence of the night:" I am not careful to answer in this matter. Be it so: however, the impression then made on many souls, has never since been effaced. Now allowing, that God did make use either of the novelty or any other indifferent circumstance, in order to bring sinners to repentance, yet they are brought. And herein let us rejoice together. Nay, may I not put the case farther yet? If I can probably conjecture, that either by the novelty of this ancient custom, or by any other indifferent circumstance, it is in my power to *save a soul from death, and hide a multitude of sins:* am I clear before God, if I do it not? If I do not snatch that brand out of the burning?

As the society increased, I found it required still greater care to separate the precious from the vile. In order to this, I determined, at least once in three months, to talk with every member myself, and to inquire at their own mouths, as well as of their leaders and neighbours, whether they grew in grace and in the knowledge of our lord Jesus Christ? At these seasons I likewise particularly inquire: Whether there be any misunderstanding or differences among them? That every hinderance of peace and brotherly love may be taken out of the way. To each of those, of whose seriousness and good conversation I found no reason to doubt, I gave a testimony under my own hand, by writing their name on a ticket prepared for that purpose: every ticket implying as strong a recommendation of the person to whom it was given, as if I had written at length, "I believe the bearer hereof to be one that fears God and works righteousness." Those, who bore these tickets wherever they came, were acknowledged by their brethren, and received with all cheerfulness. These were likewise of use in other respects. By these it was easily distinguished when the society were to meet apart, who were members of it, and who not. These also supplied us with a quiet and inoffensive method of removing any disorderly member. He has no new ticket at the quarterly visitation; and hereby it is immediately known, that he is no longer of this community.

The thing which I was greatly afraid of all this time, and which I resolved to use every possible method of preventing was, a narrowness of spirit, a party-zeal, a being straitened in our own bowels; that miserable bigotry, which makes so many so unready to believe, that there is any work of God but among themselves. I thought it might be a help against this, frequently to read to all who were willing to hear, the accounts I received from time to time, of the work which God is carrying on in the earth, both in our own and other countries, not among us alone, but among those of various opinions and denominations. For this I allotted one evening in every month. And I find no cause to repent my labour. It is generally a time of strong consolation to those who love God, and all mankind for his sake : as well as of breaking down the partition-walls, which either the craft of the devil, or the folly of man has built up : and of encouraging every child of God to say, *Whosoever doth the will of my Father who is in heaven, the same is my brother and sister and mother.*

By the blessing of God upon their endeavours to help one another, many found the pearl of great price. Being justified by faith, they had *peace with God through our Lord Jesus Christ.* These felt a more tender affection than before, to those who were partakers of like precious faith : and hence arose such a confidence in each other, that they poured out their souls in each other's bosom. Indeed they had great need so to do · for the war was not over as they had supposed. But they had still to wrestle both with flesh and blood, and with principalities and powers : so that temptations were on every side : and often temptations of such kind, as they knew not how to speak of in a class; in which persons of every sort, young and old, men and women, met together. These therefore wanted some means of closer union: they wanted to pour out their hearts without reserve, particularly with regard to the sin which did still easily beset them, and the temptations which were most apt to prevail over them. And they were the more desirous of this, when they observed it was the express advice of an inspired writer, *Confess your faults one to another, and pray one for another that ye may be healed.*

In compliance with their desire, I divided them into smaller companies, putting the married or single men, or married and single women together. The chief rules of these bands, run thus :—In order to *confess our faults one to another, and pray one for another that we may be healed,* we intend, to meet once a week at least: to come punctually at the time appointed: to begin with singing or prayer: to speak, each of us in order, freely and plainly, the true state of our soul, with the faults we had committed in though*t*, word or deed, and the temptations we have felt since our meeting: and, to desire the leader to speak *his* own state first, and then to ask the rest in order, as many and as searching questions as may be, concerning their state, sins and temptations.

In order to increase in them a grateful sense of all the mercies of the Lord, I desired that one evening in a quarter, they should all come together, that we might *eat bread* as the ancient Christians did, *with gladness and singleness of heart.* At these *Love-Feasts* our food is only a little plain cake and water. But we seldom return from them without being fed, not only with the *meat that perisheth,* but with *that which endureth to everlasting life.*

Great and many are the advantages which have ever since flowed, from this closer union of the believers with each other. They prayed one for another, that they might be healed of the faults they had confessed ; and it was so. The chains were broken: the bands were burst in sunder, and sin had no more dominion over them. Many were delivered from the temptations, out of which until then they found no way to escape. They were built up in our most holy faith. They rejoiced in the Lord more abundantly. They were strengthened in love and more effectually provoked to abound in every good work. Most of these who were thus intimately joined together went on daily from faith to faith, yet some fell from it either all at once, by falling into known, wilful sin: or gradually, and almost insensibly, by giving way in what they called little things: by sins of omission, by yielding to heart-sins, or by not watching unto prayer. The exhortations and prayers used among the believers, did no longer profit these.— They wanted advice and instructions suited to their case: which as soon as I observed, I separated them from the rest, and desired them to meet me apart on Saturday evenings. At this meeting all the hymns, exhortations and prayers, are adapted to their circumstances: being wholly suited to those who did see God, but have now lost the light of his countenance, and who mourn after him and refuse to be comforted, until they know he has healed their backsliding. By applying both the threats and promises of God to these real *penitents*, and by crying to God in their behalf, we endeavoured to bring them back to the great Shepherd and Bishop of their souls; and we conformed to the ancient church by dividing the believers from the rest of the society, by separating the *penitents*, and by appointing a peculiar service for them.

The office of the lay-assistants in the absence of the minister, is, to expound every morning and evening: to meet the united society, the bands, and the penitents once a week: to visit the classes once a quarter: to hear and decide all differences; to put the disorderly back on trial, and to receive on trial for the bands or society: to see that the stewards and leaders faithfully discharge their several offices: to meet the leaders of the bands and classes weekly, and the stewards, and to overlook their accounts.

The rules of an assistant are, be diligent ; never be unemployed ; never *while* away time ; never spend any more time in a place than is necessary : be serious ; let your motto be, " holiness unto the Lord :" believe evil of no one ; if you see it done, well ; else do not credit it : put the best construction on every thing ; speak evil of no one ; keep your thoughts within your own breast, till you come to the person concerned : tell every one what you think wrong of him, and that plainly, and as soon as may be ; make haste to cast the fire out of your own bosom : be ashamed of nothing but sin ; be punctual ; do every thing at the time : in all things act, not according to your own will, but as a son in the gospel, and in union with your brethren.

The business of the stewards is ; to manage the temporal things of the society : to receive the subscriptions and contributions : to expend what is needful : to send relief to the poor : to keep an exact account of all receipts and expences : to inform the minister if any of the rules of the society are not punctually observed : and to tell the assistants in love, if they think any thing amiss either in their doctrines or life.

The rules of the stewards are, be frugal ; save every thing that can be saved honestly : spend no more than you receive ; contract no debts : have no long accounts ; pay every thing as soon as possible : give none that ask relief either an ill word or an ill look : expect no thanks from man.

I soon had the pleasure to find, that all these temporal things were done with the utmost faithfulness and exactness so that my cares on this point were at an end : however we still owe some hundred pounds : so much have we *gained* by preaching the gospel !

You now know all of this people ; if I err in any point, you will pray God to shew me his truth. To have a " conscience void of offence toward God and toward man" is the desire of

Your affectionate brother and servant,

JOHN WESLEY."

In June 1747, the fourth conference was held, and the whole minutes were collected and published : this summary includes the Methodist doctrines.

At the first conference, after prayer, the design of the meeting was proposed ; what to teach, how to teach, and what to do ? That is, how to regulate the doctrine, discipline, and practice.

It is desired, that all things be considered as in the immediate presence of God : that we may meet with a single eye; and as little children who have every thing to learn : that every point which is proposed, may be examined to the foundation: that every person may speak freely whatever is in his heart : and that every question which may arise, should be thoroughly debated and settled. Meantime let us all pray for a willingness to receive light ; to know of every doctrine, whether it be of God.

How may the time of this conference, be made more eminently a time of watching unto prayer ?

While we are conversing, let us have a special care to set God always before us : in the intermediate hours, let us visit none but the sick, and spend all the time that remains in retirement: let us give ourselves to prayer for one another, and for a blessing on this our labour.

How far does each of us agree, to submit to the judgment of the majority ?

In speculative things, each can only submit so far as his judgment shall be convinced : in every practical point, each will submit so far as he can without wounding his conscience.

Can a christian submit any further than this, to any man, or number of men upon earth?

It is plain he cannot, either to bishop, convocation, or general council. And this is that general principle of private judgment, on which all the reformers proceeded; ' every man must judge for himself, because every man must give an account of himself to God.'

What is it to be justified?

To be pardoned and received into God's favour; into such a state, that if we continue therein, we shall be finally saved.

Is faith the condition of justification?

Yes; for every one who believeth not is condemned; and every one who believes is justified.

But must not repentance and works meet for repentance go before this faith?

Without doubt: if by repentance you mean conviction of sin; and by works meet for repentance, obeying God as far as you can, forgiving our brother, leaving off from evil, doing good and using his ordinances according to the power we have received.

What is faith?

Faith in general is a divine, supernatural evidence of things not seen; of past, future, or spiritual things: it is a spiritual sight of God and the things of God. A sinner is first convinced by the Holy Ghost, that Christ loved me and gave himself for me.—This is that faith by which he is justified or pardoned, the moment he receives it. Immediately the same spirit bears witness, thou art pardoned: thou hast redemption in his blood.—And this is saving faith, whereby the love of God is shed abroad in his heart.

Have all christians this faith? May not a man be justified and not know it?

That all true christians have such a faith as implies an assurance of God's love, appears from Rom. viii. 15. Eph. iv. 32. 2 Cor. xiii. 5. Heb. viii. 10. 1 John iv. 10. v. 19. And that no man can be justified and not know it, appears further from the nature of the thing. For faith after repentance is ease after pain, rest after toil, light after darkness. It appears also from the immediate, as well as distant fruits thereof.

But may not a man go to heaven without it?

It does not appear from holy writ that a man who hears the gospel, can: Mark xvi. 16. whatever a Heathen may do. Rom. ii. 14.

What are the immediate fruits of justifying faith?

Peace, joy, love, power over all our outward sin, and power to keep down inward sin.

Does any one believe, who has not the witness in himself, or any longer than he sees, loves, and obeys God?

We apprehend not; seeing God being the very essence of faith; love and obedience must be the inseparable properties of it.

What sins are consistent with justifying faith?

No wilful sin. If a believer wilfully sin, he casts away his faith. Neither is it possible he should have justifying faith again, without previously repenting.

Must every believer come into a state of doubt or fear, or darkness? Will he do so, unless by ignorance or unfaithfulness? Does God otherwise withdraw himself?

It is certain, a believer, need never again come into condemnation. It seems, he need not come into a state of doubt or fear, or darkness: and that ordinarily at least, he will not, unless by ignorance or unfaithfulness.

Yet it is true, that the first joy does seldom last long: that it is commonly followed by doubts and fears; and that God frequently permits great heaviness, before any large manifestation of himself.

Are works necessary to the continuance of faith?

Without doubt; for a man may forfeit the free gift of God, either by sins of omission or commission.

Can faith be lost, but for want of works?

It cannot but through disobedience.

How is faith made perfect but by works?

The more we exert our faith, the more it is increased. To him that hath shall be given.

St. Paul says, *Abraham was not justified by works*. St. James, he was *justified by works*. Do they not contradict each other?

No: they do not speak of the same justification. St. Paul speaks of that justification which was when Abraham was seventy-five years old, above twenty years before Isaac was born. St. James of that justification which was when he offered up Isaac on the altar: they do not speak of the same works; St. Paul speaking of works that precede faith: St. James of works that spring from it.

In what sense is Adam's sin imputed to all mankind?

In Adam all died: our bodies then became mortal: Our souls died, were disunited from God: hence we are all born with a sinful devilish nature: we are children of wrath, liable to death eternal. Rom. v. 18. Eph. ii. 3.

In what sense is the righteousness of Christ imputed to all mankind, or to believers?

We do not find it expressly affirmed in scripture, that God imputes the righteousness of Christ to any. Although we do find, that faith is imputed to us for righteousness. That text, *As by one man's disobedience all men were made sinners, so by the obedience of one, all were made righteous,* means, by the merits of Christ, all men are cleared from the guilt of Adam's actual sin. Through the obedience and death of Christ, the bodies of all men become immortal after the resurrection: their souls receive a capacity of spiritual life: an actual spark or seed thereof: all believers become children of grace, are reconciled to God, and made partakers of the divine nature.

What is Antinomianism?

The doctrine which makes void the law through faith.

What are the main pillars thereof?

That Christ abolished the moral law: that therefore christians are not obliged to observe it: that one branch of christian liberty, is liberty from obeying the commandments of God: that it is bondage, to do a thing, because it is commanded, or to forbear it because it is forbidden · that a believer is not obliged to use the ordinances of God or to do good works: That a preacher ought not to exhort to good works: not unbelievers, because it is hurtful; not believers because it is needless.

We affirm faith in Christ is the sole condition of justification. But does not repentance go before that faith? and supposing there be opportunity for them, fruits or works meet for repentance?

Without doubt they do.

How then can we deny them to be conditions of justification? Is not this a mere strife of words?

It seems not, though it has been greviously abused. But so the abuse cease, let the use remain.

Is an assurance of God's pardoning love absolutely necessary to our being in his favour? Or may there possibly be some exempt cases?

We dare not positively say, there are not.

Is such an assurance absolutely necessary to inward and outward holiness?

To inward, we apprehend it is: to outward holiness, we incline to think it is not.

Is it indispensably necessary to final salvation?

Love hopeth all things. We know not how far any may fall under the case of invincible ignorance.

Does a man believe any longer than he sees a reconciled God?

We conceive not. But we allow there may be infinite degrees in seeing God: even as many as there are between him who sees the sun, when it shines on his eye-lids closed, and him who stands with his eyes wide open, in the full blaze of his beams.

Does a man believe any longer than he loves God?

In no wise. For neither circumcision nor uncircumcision avails, without faith working by love.

Have we duly considered the case of Cornelius? Was not he in the favour of God, *when his prayers and alms came up for a memorial before God* before he believed in Christ?

It does seem that he was in some degree. But we speak not of those who have not heard the gospel.

How then can we maintain, that all works done before we have a sense of the pardoning love of God, are sin? And, as such, an abomination to him?

The works of him who has heard the gospel, and does not believe, are not done as God hath *willed and commanded them to be done*. And yet we know not how to say, that they are an abomination to the Lord in him who feareth God, and from that principle, does the best he can.

Seeing there is so much difficulty in this subject, can too tenderly with them that oppose us?

We cannot; unless we were to give up any part of the truth of God.

Is a believer constrained to obey God?

At first he often is. The love of Christ constraineth him. After this, he may obey, or he may not; no constraint being laid upon him.

Can faith be lost, but through disobedience?

It cannot. A believer first inwardly disobeys, inclines to sin with his heart: then his intercourse with God is cut off, his faith is lost. And after this, he may fall into outward sin, being now weak, and like another man.

How can such an one recover faith?

By repenting and doing the first works. Rev. ii. 5.

Whence is it that so great a majority of those who believe fall more or less into doubt or fear?

Chiefly from their own ignorance or unfaithfulness: often from their not watching unto prayer: perhaps sometimes from some defect, or want of the power of God in the preaching which they hear.

Is there not a defect in us? Do we preach as we did at first? Have we not changed our doctrines?

At first we preached almost wholly to unbelievers. To those therefore we spoke almost continually, of remission of sins through the death of Christ, and the nature of faith in his blood. And so we do still, among those who need to be taught the first elements of the gospel of Christ: but those in whom the foundation is already laid, we exhort to go on to perfection; although we occasionally spoke of it from the beginning: we now preach continually faith in Christ, as the prophet, priest, and king, clearly, strongly, and fully.

Do we ordinarily represent a justified state so great and happy as it is?

Perhaps not. A believer, walking in the light, is inexpressibly great and happy.

Should we not have a care of depreciating justification, in order to exalt the state of full sanctification?

Undoubtedly we should beware of this: for one may insensibly slide into it.

How shall we effectually avoid it?

When we are going to speak of entire sanctification, let us first describe the blessings of a justified state, as strongly as possible.

Does not the truth of the gospel lie very near both to Calvinism and Antinomianism?

Indeed it does: as it were, within a hair's breadth. So that it is altogether foolish and sinful, because we do not quite agree either with one or the other, to run from them as far as ever we can.

Wherein may we come to the very edge of Calvinism?

In ascribing all good to the free grace of God: in denying all natural free will and all power antecedent to grace; and in excluding all merit from man; even for what he has or does by the grace of God.

Wherein may we come to the edge of Antinomianism?

In exalting the merits and love of Christ. In rejoicing evermore.

Does faith supersede holiness or good works?

In no wise. So far from it that it implies both, as a cause does its effects.

What is sincerity?

Willingness to know and do the whole will of God. The lowest species thereof seems to be *faithfulness in that which is little.*

Has God any regard to man's sincerity?

So far, that no man in any state can possibly please God without it: nether indeed in any moment wherein he is not sincere.

But can it be conceived that God has any regard to the sincerity of the unbeliever?

Yes, so much, that if he perseveres therein, God will infallibly give him faith.

What regard may we conceive him to have, to the sincerity of a believer?

So much, that in every sincere believer he fulfils all the great and precious promises.

Whom do you term a sincere believer?

One that walks in the light, as God is in the light.

Is not sincerity all in all?

All will follow persevering sincerity. God gives every thing with it; nothing without it.

Are not then sincerity and faith equivalent terms?

By no means. It is as nearly related to works as it is to faith. Who is sincere before he believes? He that then does all he can: he that, according to the power he has received, brings forth *fruits meet for repentance*. Who is sincere after he believes? He that, from a sense of God's love, is zealous of all good works.

Is not sincerity what St. Paul terms a willing mind?

Yes: if that word be taken in a general sense. It is a constant disposition to use all the grace given.

But do we not then set sincerity on a level with faith?

No. For we allow a man may be sincere, and not be justified: but he cannot have faith, and not be justified. The very moment he believes he is justified.

But do we not give up faith, and put sincerity in its place, as the condition of our acceptance with God?

We believe it is one condition of our acceptance, as repentance likewise is. And we believe it a condition of our continuing in a state of acceptance. Yet we do not put it in the place of faith. It is by faith the merits of Christ are applied to my soul. But if I am not sincere, they are not applied.

Is not this that *going about to establish your own righteousness*, whereof St. Paul speaks?

St. Paul there manifestly speaks of unbelievers, who sought to be accepted for the sake of their own righteousness. We do not seek to be accepted for the sake of our sincerity; but through the merits of Christ alone. Indeed, so long as any man believes, he cannot go about to *establish his own righteousness*.

But do you consider, that we are under the covenant of grace? And that the covenant of works is now abolished?

All mankind were under the covenant of grace from the very hour that the original promise was made. If by the covenant of works you mean, that of unsinning obedience made with Adam before the fall; no man, but Adam, was ever under that covenant.

What means then, *to him that believeth, his faith is counted for righteousness?*

That God forgives him that is unrighteous as soon as he believes, accepting his faith instead of perfect righteousness. But then observe, universal righteousness follows, though it did not precede faith.

But is faith thus *counted to us for righteousness*, at whatsoever time we believe?

In whatsoever moment we believe, all our past sins vanish away. They are as though they had never been, and we stand clear in the sight of God.

Are not the assurance of faith, the inspiration of the Holy Ghost, and the revelation of Christ in us, terms nearly of the same import?

He that denies one of them, must deny all; they are so closely connected together.

Is not the whole dispute of salvation by faith, or by works, a mere strife of words?

In asserting salvation by faith, we mean that pardon, salvation begun, is received by faith producing works: that holiness, salvation continued, is faith working by love: that heaven, salvation finished, is the reward of this faith. If those who assert salvation by works, or by faith and works, mean the same thing, we will not strive with them.

May not some degree of the love of God, go before a distinct sense of justification?

We believe it may.

Can any degree of sanctification or holiness?

Many degrees of outward holiness may: yea, and some degree of meekness, and several other tempers which would be branches of christian holiness, but that they do not spring from christian principles. For the abiding love of God cannot spring, but from faith in a pardoning God. And no christian holiness can exist, without that love of God for its foundation.

Is every man, as soon as he believes, a new creature, sanctified, pure in heart? Has he then a new heart? Does Christ dwell therein? And is he a temple of the Holy Ghost?

All these things may be affirmed of every believer, in a true sense.

What is it to be sanctified?

To be renewed in the image of God in righteousness and true holiness.

Is faith the condition, or the instrument of sanctification?

It is both the condition and instrument of it.—When we begin to believe, then sanctification begins. And as faith increases, holiness increases, till we are created anew.

What is implied in being a perfect christian?

The loving the Lord our God with all our heart, and with all our mind, and soul, and strength.

Does this imply that all inward sin is taken away?

Without doubt: or how could he be said to be saved *from all his uncleannesses?*

How much is allowed to our brethren who differ from us, with regard to entire sanctification?

They grant, that every one must be entirely sanctified in the article of death: that till then, a believer daily grows in grace, comes nearer and nearer to perfection: that we ought to be continually pressing after this, and exhort all others so to do.

What do we allow them?

We grant, that many of those who have died in the faith, yea, the greater part of those whom we have known, were not sanctified throughout, not made perfect in love, till a little before death: that the term, " sanctification" is continually applied by St. Paul, to all that were justified, were true believers: that by this term alone, he rarely, if ever means, saved from all sin: that consequently, it is not proper to use it in this sense, without adding the word " wholly, entirely," or the like: that the inspired writers almost continually speak of or to those who were justified; but very rarely, either of or to those, who were wholly sanctified; that consequently, it behoves us to speak in public almost continually of the state of justification: but more rarely, in full and explicit terms, concerning entire sanctification.

What then is the point wherein we divide?

It is this: whether we should expect to be saved from all sin, before the article of death?

Is there any clear scripture promise for this; That God will save us from all sin?

He shall redeem Israel from all his iniquities: then will I sprinkle clean water upon you, and ye shall be clean; from all your filthiness and from all your idols I will cleanse you—I will also save you from all your uncleannesses—Having these promises, let us cleanse ourselves from all filthiness of flesh and spirit, perfecting holiness in the fear of God—The Lord thy God will circumcise thine heart and the heart of thy seed, to love the Lord thy God with all thy heart and with all thy soul.

But does any assertion answerable to this, occur in the New Testament?

For this purpose the Son of God was manifested that he might destroy the works of the devil: the works of the devil, without any limitation or restriction: but all sin is the work of the devil. Parallel to which are those assertions of St. Paul; *Christ loved the church, and gave himself for it—that he might present it to himself a glorious church, not having spot or wrinkle or any such thing, but that it should be holy and without blemish. God sent his son—that the righteousness of the law might be fulfilled in us, who walk not after the flesh but after the spirit.*

Does the New Testament afford any farther ground for expecting to be saved from all sin?

Undoubtedly it does, both in prayers and commands which are equivalent to the strongest assertions.

What prayers do you mean?

Prayers for entire sanctification: which were there no such thing, would be mere mockery of God: *Deliver us from the evil one.* Now when this is done, when we are delivered from all evil, there can be no sin remaining. *Neither pray I for these alone, but for them also who shall believe on me through their word; that they all may be one, as thou, Father, art in me, and I in thee; that they also may be one in us; I in them, and thou in me, that they may be made perfect in one. I bow my knees unto the Father of our Lord Jesus Christ—that he would grant you—that ye being rooted and grounded in love, may be able to comprehend with all saints, what is the breadth, and length, and depth, and height; and to know the love of Christ which passeth knowledge, that ye might be filled with all the fullness of God. The very God of peace sanctify you wholly. And I pray God, your whole spirit and soul and body be preserved blameless unto the coming of our Lord Jesus Christ.*

What commands are there to the same effect?

Be ye perfect as your Father who is in heaven is perfect. Thou shalt love the Lord thy God with all thy heart, and with all thy soul, and with all thy mind. But if the love of God fill all the heart, there can be no sin there.

But how does it appear, that this is to be done before the article of death?

From the very nature of the command, which is not given to the dead, but to the living. Therefore, *thou shalt love God with all thy heart,* cannot mean, Thou shalt do this when thou diest, but while thou livest. From express texts of Scripture: *The grace of God that bringeth salvation hath appeared to all men; teaching us, that having renounced ungodliness and worldly lusts, we should live soberly, righteously and godly in this present world: looking for the glorious appearing of the great God and our Saviour Jesus Christ; who gave himself for us, that he might redeem us from all iniquity, and purify unto himself a peculiar people, zealous of good works. He hath raised up a horn of salvation for us—to perform the mercy promised to our fathers; the oath which he sware to our father Abraham, that he would grant unto us, that we being delivered out of the hands of our enemies, might serve him without fear, in holiness and righteousness before him, all the days of our life.*

Does not the harshly preaching perfection tend to bring believers into a kind of bondage, or slavish fear?

It does. Therefore we should always place it in the most amiable light, so that it may excite hope, joy, and desire.

Why may we not continue in the joy of faith even till we are made perfect?

Why, indeed? Since holy grief does not quench this joy: since even while we are under the cross, while we deeply partake of the sufferings of Christ, we may rejoice with joy unspeakable.

Do we not discourage believers from rejoicing evermore?

We ought not so to do. Let them all their life long, rejoice unto God, so it be with reverence. And then if lightness or pride should mix with their joy, let us not strike at the joy itself, but at that lightness or pride, that the evil may cease and the good remain.

Ought we to be anxiously careful about perfection? Lest we should die before we have attained?

In no wise. We ought to be thus careful for nothing, neither spiritual nor temporal.

But ought we not to be troubled on account of the sinful nature which still remains in us?

It is good for us to have a deep sense of this, and to be much ashamed before the Lord. But this should only incite us, the more earnestly to turn unto Christ every moment, and to draw light, life, and strength from him, that we may go on, conquering and to conquer. Therefore, when the sense of our sin most abounds, the sense of his love should much more abound."

In 1769, Mr. Wesley read the following outlines of a plan for the future union of the Methodist Preachers.

" It has long been my desire, that all those ministers of the church who believe and preach salvation by faith might cordially agree between themselves, and not hinder, but help one another. After occasionally pressing this in private conversation, wherever I had opportunity, I wrote down my thoughts on this head, and sent them to each in a letter. Three only vouchsafed to give me an answer. So I gave this up. I can do no more. They are a rope of sand ; and such they will continue. But it is otherwise with the travelling preachers in our connexion. You are at present one body : you act in concert with each other, and by united counsels. And now is the time to consider what can be done, in order to continue this union ? Indeed, as long as I live, there will be no great difficulty : I am under God, a centre of union to all our travelling as well as local preachers. They all know me, and my communication. They all love me for my work's sake : and therefore, were it out of regard only to me, they will continue connected with each other. But by what means may this connexion be preserved, when God removes me from you ?

I take it for granted, it cannot be preserved by any means, between those who have not a single eye. Those who aim at any thing but the glory of God, and the salvation of souls; who desire, or seek any earthly thing, whether honour, profit, or ease; will not, cannot continue in the connexion: it will not answer their design. Some of them, perhaps a fourth of the whole number, will procure preferment in the church; others will turn Independents, and get separate congregations.—Lay your accounts with this, and be not surprised if some whom you do not suspect, be of this number.

But what method can be taken to preserve a firm union between those who choose to remain together? Can any thing be done now to lay a foundation for this future union? Would it not be well for any that are willing, to sign some articles of agreement, before God calls me hence? Suppose something like these:

"We, whose names are underwritten, being thoroughly convinced of the necessity of a close union between those whom God is pleased to use as instruments in this glorious work, in order to preserve this union between ourselves, are resolved, God being our helper, I. To devote ourselves entirely to God; denying ourselves, taking up our cross daily, steadily aiming at one thing, to save our own souls, and them who hear us. II. To preach the old Methodist doctrines, and no other; contained in the minutes of the conferences. III. To observe and enforce, the whole Methodist discipline, laid down in the said minutes."— These articles were signed by many of the preachers.

In 1770, the larger minutes of conference were printed. The following abstract will complete our view of the economy of the Methodist societies.

"What may we reasonably believe to be God's design, in raising up the preachers called Methodists?

Not to form any new sect; but to reform the nation, particularly the church: and to spread spiritual holiness over the land.

Is it advisable for us to preach in as many places as we can, without forming any societies?

By no means; we have made the trial in various places, and that for a considerable time. But all the seed has fallen as by the highway-side. There is scarcely any fruit remaining.

Where should we endeavour to preach most?

Where there is the greatest number of quiet and willing hearers, and where there is most fruit.

Is field-preaching unlawful?

We conceive not. We do not know that it is contrary to any law either of God or man.

Have we not used it too sparingly?

It seems we have: our call is, to save that which is lost. Now we cannot expect them to seek us.— Therefore we should go and seek them: we are particularly called, by *going into the highways and hedges to compel them to come in*: that reason against it is not good, ' the house will hold all that come.' The house may hold all that come to the house; but not all that would come to the field. Whenever the weather will permit, go out in God's name into the most publick places, and call all to repent and believe the gospel: every Sunday, in particular; especially where there are old societies, lest they settle upon their lees.

Ought we not diligently to observe in what places God is pleased at any time to pour out his spirit more abundantly?

We ought: and at that time to send more labourers than usual into that part of the harvest.

How often shall we permit strangers to be present at the meeting of the society?

At every other meeting of the society in every place, let no stranger be admitted. At other times they may; but the same person not above twice or thrice. In order to this, see that all in every place shew their tickets before they come in. If the stewards and leaders are not exact herein, employ others that have more resolution.

Can any thing further be done, in order to make the meetings of the classes lively and profitable?

Change improper leaders: let the leaders frequently meet each other's classes: let us observe what leaders are the most useful, and let these meet the other classes as often as possible: see that all the leaders be not only men of judgment, but men truly devoted to God.

How can we further assist those under our care?

By meeting the married men and women together, the first Sunday after the visitation; the single men and women apart, on the two following, in all the large societies: by instructing them at their own houses. What unspeakable need is there of this? For personal religion either towards God or man, is amazingly superficial among us. How little faith is there among us? How little communication with God? How little living in heaven, walking in eternity, deadness to every creature? How much love of the world? Desire of pleasure, of ease, of getting money? How little brotherly-love? What continual judging one another? What gossipping, evil-speaking, tale-bearing? What want of moral honesty? Who does as he would be done by, in buying and selling? Particularly in selling horses? Family religion is shamefully wanting, almost in every branch: and the Methodists will be little the better, till we take quite another course with them. For what avails publick preaching alone, though we could preach like angels? We must, yea every travelling preacher must instruct them from house to house. Let every preacher, having a catalogue of those in each society, go to each house. Deal gently with them, that the report of it may move others to desire your coming. Give the children, " the instructions for children," and encourage them to get them by heart. Great scholars may think this work beneath them. But they should consider, the laying the foundation skilfully, as it is of the greatest importance, so it is the master-piece of the wisest builder. And let the wisest of us all try, whenever we please, we shall find, that to lay this ground-work rightly, to make the ignorant understand the grounds of religion, will put us to the trial of all our skill. Perhaps in doing this it may be well; after a few loving words spoken to all in the house, to take each person singly into another room, where you may deal closely with him, about his sin, and misery, and duty. Set these home, or you lose all your labour: do this in earnest, and you will soon find what a work you take in hand, in undertaking to be a travelling preacher.

How shall we prevent improper persons from insinuating themselves into the society?

Give tickets to none till they are recommended by a leader, with whom they have met at least two months on trial. Give notes to none but those who are recommended by one whom you know, or till they have met three or four times in a class. Give them the rules the first time they meet.

Should we insist on the band-rules? Particularly with regard to dress?

By all means. This is no time to give any encouragement to superfluity of apparel. Therefore give no band-tickets to any, till they have left off superfluous ornaments. Let every assistant read the thoughts upon dress, at least once a year, in every large society. In visiting the classes, be very mild, but very strict.— Allow no exempt case, not even of a married woman.

Better one suffer than many. To encourage meeting in band, in every large society, have a love-feast quarterly for the bands only. Never fail to meet them once a week. Exhort every believer to embrace the advantage. Give a band-ticket to none till they have met a quarter on trial.

Do not sabbath-breaking, dram-drinking, evil-speaking, unprofitable conversation, lightness, expensiveness or gaiety of apparel, and contracting debts without due care to discharge them, still prevail in several places? How may these evils be remedied?

Let us preach expressly on each of these heads.— Read in every society the sermon on evil-speaking. Let the leaders closely examine and exhort every person to put away the accursed thing. Let the preacher warn every society, that none who is guilty herein can remain with us. Extirpate smuggling, and buying or selling uncustomed goods out of every society. Let none remain with us, who will not totally abstain from every kind and degree of it. Speak tenderly, but earnestly and frequently of it, in every society near the coasts. Extirpate bribery, receiving any thing directly or indirectly for voting in any election. Shew no respect of persons herein. Largely shew, both in publick and private, the wickedness of thus selling our country.

What shall we do to prevent scandal, when any of our members become bankrupt?

Let the assistant talk with him at large. And if he have not kept fair accounts, or have been concerned in raising money by coining notes, let him be expelled immediately.

What is the office of a christian minister?

To watch over souls, as he that must give account.

In what view may we and our helpers be considered?

As extraordinary messengers designed to provoke the regular ministers to jealousy; and to supply their want of service, toward those who are perishing for lack of knowledge.

What power is this, which you exercise over the preachers and societies?

In November 1738, two or three persons who desired to flee from the wrath to come, and then a few more came to me in London, and desired me to advise, and pray with them. I said, ' If you will meet me on Thursday night, I will help you as well as I can.'— More and more then desired to meet with them, till they were increased to many hundreds. The case was afterwards the same at Bristol, Kingswood, Newcastle, and in many other parts of England, Scotland, and Ireland. Here commenced my power; namely, a power to appoint when, and where, and how they should meet; and to remove those whose lives shewed that they had not a desire to flee from the wrath to come. And this power remained the same, whether the people meeting together were twelve, or twelve hundred, or twelve thousand. In a few days some of them said, ' Sir, we will not sit under you for nothing : we will subscribe quarterly.' I said, ' I will have nothing ; for I want nothing. My fellowship supplies me with all I want.' One replied, ' Nay, but you want an hundred and fifteen pounds to pay for the lease of the foundery : and likewise a large sum of money, to put it into repair.' On this consideration I suffered them to subscribe. 'And when the society met, I asked, ' Who will take the trouble of receiving this money, and paying it where it is needful ?' One said, ' I will do it, and keep the account for you.' So here was the first steward. Afterwards I desired one or two more to help me as stewards, and in process of time, a greater number. Let it be remembered, it was I, not the people, who chose these stewards, and appointed to each the distinct work wherein he was to help me. And herein I began to exercise another sort of power, namely, that of appointing and removing stewards. After a time a young man named Thomas Maxfield, came and desired to help me as a son in the gospel. Soon after came a second, Thomas Richards, and then a third, Thomas Westall. These severally desired to serve me as sons, and to labour when and where I should direct. And here commenced my power, to appoint each of these when and where and how to labour, while he chose to continue with me. For each had a power to go away when he pleased : as I had also to go away from them. The case continued the same, when the number of preachers increased. I had just the same power still, to appoint when, and where, and how each should help me ; and to tell any ' I do not desire your help any longer.' On these terms, and no other, we joined at first : on these we continue joined. In 1744, I wrote to several clergymen, and to all who then served me as sons in the gospel ; desiring them to meet me in London, and to give me their advice, concerning the best method of carrying on the work of God. And when their number increased, so that it was not convenient to invite them all, for several years I wrote to those with whom I desired to confer, and they only met me at London, or elsewhere. I sent for them to advise, not to govern me. Neither did I at any time divest myself of any part of the power above described, which the Providence of God had cast upon me, without any design or choice of mine. What is that power ? It is a power of admitting into and excluding from the societies under my care : of choosing and removing stewards : of receiving or not receiving helpers : of appointing them when, where, and how to help me, and of desiring any of them to confer with me when I see good. But 'several gentlemen are offended at your having so much power.' I did not seek any part of it. But when it was come, I used it to the best of my judgment. Yet I never was fond of it. I always did, and do now, bear it as my burden; the burden which God lays upon me, and therefore I dare not lay it down. But if you can tell me any one, or any five men, to whom I may transfer this burden, who can and will do just what I do now, I will heartily thank both them and you.

What general method of employing our time would you advise us to?

We advise you, as often as possible to rise at four. From four to five in the morning, and from five to six in the evening, to meditate, pray, and read, partly the scripture with the notes, partly the closely-practical parts of what we have published. From six in the morning till twelve to read in order, with much prayer, the Christian library, the other books which we have published in prose and verse, and then those which we recommended in our rules of Kingswood-School.

Should our helpers follow trades?

The question is not, Whether they may occasionally work with their hands, as St. Paul did: but whether it be proper for them to keep shop or follow merchandize? After long consideration, it was agreed by all our brethren, that no preacher who will not relinquish his trade of buying and selling, shall be considered as a travelling preacher any longer.

Why is it that the people under our care are no better?

Because we are not more knowing and more holy.

But why are we not more knowing?

Because we are idle. We forget our first rule. There is altogether a fault in this matter, few of us are clear. Who of you spends as many hours a day in God's work, as you did formerly in man's work? We talk, talk,—or read history, or what comes next to hand. We absolutely must cure this evil, or betray the cause of God. But how? Read the most useful books, regularly and constantly. Steadily spend all the morning in this employ, or at least five hours in four and twenty. 'But I read only the bible.' Then you ought to teach others to read only the bible, and by parity of reason, to hear only the bible; but if so, you need preach no more. Just so said George Bell. And what is the fruit? Why, now he neither reads the bible, nor any thing else. This is rank enthusiasm. If you need no book but the bible, you are got above St. Paul. He wanted others too. Bring the books, says he, but especially the parchments. In the afternoon, follow Mr. Baxter's plan. Then you will have no time to spare: you will have work enough for all your time. And you will have need of all the knowledge you have or can procure. Go into every house in course, and teach every one young and old, if they belong to us, to be christians, inwardly and outwardly: make every particular plain to their understanding; fix it in their memory; write it in their heart.

In what particular method should we instruct them?

You may as you have time, read, explain, enforce, the rules of the society: instructions for children: the fourth volume of sermons, and Philip Henry's method of family prayer. We must needs do this, were it only to avoid idleness: no idleness can consist with growth in grace. Nay without exactness in redeeming time, we cannot retain the grace which we received in justification. But what shall we do for the rising generation? Unless we take care of this, the present revival will last only the age of a man: let him that is zealous for God and the souls of men begin now. Where there are ten children in a society, meet them at least an hour every week: talk with them every time you see any at home: pray in earnest for them: diligently instruct and vehemently exhort all parents at their own houses: preach expressly on education, particularly at midsummer, when you speak of Kingswood.—Study the instructions and lessons for children.

Why are not we more holy? Why do not we live in eternity? Walk with God all the day long? Why are we not all devoted to God? Breathing the whole spirit of missionaries?

Chiefly because we are looking for the end, without using the means. Who of you rises at four in summer? Or even at five, when he does not preach? Do you recommend to all your societies, the five o'clock hour for private prayer? Do you observe it? Or any other fixt time? Do not you find by experience, that any time is no time?

What is the best general method of preaching?

To invite: to convince: to offer Christ: and to build up in every sermon.

Have not some of us been led off from practical preaching?

We have. The most effectual way of preaching Christ, is to preach him in all his offices, and to declare his law as well as his gospel, both to believers and unbelievers. Let us strongly and closely insist upon inward and outward holiness, in all its branches.

How shall we guard against formality in publick worship? Particularly in singing?

By preaching frequently on this head: taking care to speak only what we feel: by choosing such hymns as are proper for the congregation; by not singing too much at once; seldom more than five or six verses: by suiting the tune to the words.

Who is the assistant?

That preacher in each circuit, who is appointed from time to time to take charge of the societies, and the other preachers therein.

How should an assistant be qualified for his charge?

By walking closely with God, by having his work greatly at heart: and by understanding and loving our discipline.

What is the business of an assistant?

To see that the other preachers in his circuit behave well, and want nothing: to visit the classes quarterly, regulate the bands, and deliver tickets: to take in, or put out of the society or the bands: to keep watch-nights and love-feasts: to hold quarterly meetings, and therein diligently to inquire both into the temporal and spiritual state of each society: to take care that every society be duly supplied with books: to send from every quarterly-meeting a circumstantial account of every remarkable conversion, and remarkable death: to take exact lists of his societies every quarter, and send them up to London: to meet the married men and women, and the single men and women in the large societies once a quarter: to overlook the accounts of all the stewards.

Are there any other advices, which you would give the assistants?

Take a regular catalogue of your societies: leave your successor a particular account of the state of the circuit: see that every band-leader has the rules of the bands: vigorously, but calmly enforce the rules concerning needless ornaments, &c. As soon as there are four men or women believers in any place, put them into a band: suffer no love-feast to last above an hour and a half: and instantly stop all breaking the cake with another: warn all from time to time, that none are to remove from one society to another, without a certificate from the assistant: every where recommend decency and cleanliness. Cleanliness is next to godliness.

Do we sufficiently watch over our helpers?

We might consider those that are with us as our pupils: into whose behaviour and studies we should inquire every day. Should we not frequently ask each, Do you walk closely with God? Have you now fellowship with the Father, and the Son? At what hour do you rise? Do you punctually observe the morning and evening hour of retirement? Do you spend the day in the manner which we advise? Do you converse seriously, usefully and closely? Do you use all the means of grace yourself, and enforce the use of them on all other persons?

What can be done, to form a closer union among our helpers?

Let them be deeply convinced of the want and absolute necessity of it: let them pray for a desire of union: let them speak freely to each other: when they meet, let them never part without prayer: let them beware how they despise each other's gifts: let them never speak slightly of each other in any kind: let them defend one another's characters in every thing, so far as consists with truth; and let them labour in honour each to prefer the other before himself.

How shall we try those who think they are moved by the Holy Ghost to preach?

Inquire, Do they know God as a pardoning God? Have they the love of God abiding in them? Do they desire and seek nothing but God? And, are they holy, in all manner of conversation? Have they gifts for the work? Have they a clear, sound understanding? Have they a right judgment in the things of God? Have they a just conception of salvation by faith? And has God given them any degree of utterance? Do they speak justly, readily, clearly? Have they fruit? Are any truly convinced of sin, and converted to God by their preaching? As long as these three marks concur in any one, we believe he is called of God to preach. These we receive as sufficient proof that he is moved thereto by the Holy Ghost.

What method may we use in receiving a new helper?

A proper time, for doing this, is at a conference after solemn fasting and prayer. Every person proposed is then to be present; each of them may be asked; Have you faith in Christ? Are you going on to perfection? Do you expect to be perfected in love in this life? Are you groaning after it! Are you resolved to devote yourself wholly to God and to his work? Do you know the Methodist plan? Have you read the plain account? The appeals? Do you know the rules of the society? Of the bands? Do you keep them? Have you read the minutes of the conference? Are you willing to conform to them? Have you considered the rules of an helper? Will you keep them for conscience-sake? Are you determined to employ all your time in the work of God? Will you preach every morning and evening: endeavouring not to speak too long, or too loud? Will you diligently instruct the children in every place? Will you visit from house to house? Will you recommend fasting, both by precept and example? We may then receive him as a probationer by giving him the minutes of the conference inscribed thus : ' You think it your duty to call sinners to repentance. Make full proof hereof, and we shall rejoice to receive you as a fellow labourer.' When he has been on trial four years, if recommended by the assistant, he may be received into full connexion, by giving him the minutes inscribed thus : ' As long as you freely consent to, and earnestly endeavour to walk by these rules, we shall rejoice to acknowledge you as a fellow-labourer.'

What is the method wherein we usually proceed in our conferences ?

We inquire, What preachers are admitted ? Who remain on trial ? Who are admitted on trial ? Who desist from travelling ? Are there any objections to any of the preachers ? How are the preachers stationed this year ? What numbers are in the society ? What is the Kingswood collection ? What boys are received this year ? What girls are assisted ? What is contributed for the contingent expences ? How was this expended ? What is contributed toward the fund, for superannuated and supernumerary preachers ? What demands are there upon it ? How many preachers' wives are to be provided for ? By what societies ? Where, and when, may our next conference begin ?

How can we provide for superannuated, and supernumerary preachers ?

Those who can preach four or five times a week, are supernumerary preachers. As for those who cannot, let every travelling preacher contribute half a guinea yearly at the conference : let every one when first admitted as a travelling preacher pay a guinea : let this be lodged in the hands of the stewards : out of this let provision be made first for the worn-out preachers, and then for the widows and children of those who are dead : let an exact account of all receipts and disbursements be produced at the conference : let every assistant bring to the conference, the contribution of every preacher in his circuit.

What can be done, to revive the work of God where it is decayed?

Let every preacher read carefully over the life of David Brainerd. Let us be *followers of him, as he was of Christ,* in absolute self-devotion, in total deadness to the world, and in fervent love to God and man. Let us but secure this point, and the world and the devil must fall under our feet: let both assistants and preachers be conscientiously exact in the whole Methodist discipline: see that no circuit be at any time without preachers. Therefore let no preacher, who does not attend the conference, leave the circuit, at that time, on any pretence whatever: let not all the preachers in any circuit come to the conference: let those who do come, set out as late and return as soon as possible: wherever you can, appoint prayer-meetings; let a fast be observed in all our societies, the last Friday in August, November, February, and May: be more active in dispersing the books: strongly and explicitly exhort all believers, to go on to perfection. That we may all speak the same thing; Shall we defend this perfection, or give it up? You all agree to defend it, meaning salvation from all sin, by the love of God and man filling our heart. But, as to the circumstance, is the change gradual or instantaneous? It is both the one and the other. From the moment we are justified, there may be a gradual sanctification, a growing in grace, a daily advance in the knowledge and love of God. And if sin cease before death, there must, in the nature of the thing, be an instantaneous change. There must be a last moment wherein it does not exist. ' But should we in preaching insist both on one, and the other?' Certainly we must insist on the gradual change; and that earnestly and continually. And are there not reasons why we should insist on the instantaneous also? If there be such a blessed change

G g

before death, should we not encourage all the believers to expect it ? And the rather, because constant experience shews, the more earnestly they expect this, the more swiftly and steadily does the gradual work of God go on in their soul : the more watchful they are against all sin ; the more careful to grow in grace, the more zealous of good works, and the more punctual in their attendance on all the ordinances of God.

How may we raise a general fund for carrying on the whole work of God?

By a yearly subscription to be proposed by every assistant when he visits the classes at Christmas, and received at the visitation following.

We said in 1744, "We have leaned too much to Calvinism." Wherein ?

With regard to *man's faithfulness*. Our Lord himself taught us to use the expression, therefore we ought never to be ashamed of it. We ought steadily to assert upon His authority, that if a man be not *faithful in the unrighteous mammon, God will not give him the true riches :* With regard to *working for life*, which our Lord expressly commands us to do; *Labour* literally, *work for that meat that endureth to everlasting life.* And in fact, every believer, till he comes to glory, works *for* as well as *from* life. We have received it as a maxim, That " a man is to do nothing, *in order to justification.*"

Nothing can be more false. Whoever desires to find favour with God should *cease from evil and learn to do well:* So God himself teaches by the prophet Isaiah. Whoever repents should *do works meet for repentance.* And if this is not *in order* to find favour, what does he do them for ? Once more review the whole affair : Who of us is *now* accepted of God ? He that now believes in Christ, with a loving obedient heart. But who among those that never heard of Christ ? He that according to the light that he has, *feareth God and worketh righteousness*. Is this the same with he that is sincere? Nearly, if not quite: is not this salvation by works? Not by the merit of works, but by works as a condition: What have we then been disputing about for these thirty years? About words: as to merit itself, of which we have been so dreadfully afraid: we are rewarded according to our works, yea, because of our works? And how differs this from as our works deserve? Can you split this hair? I cannot. The grand objection to one of the preceding propositions, is drawn from matter of fact. God does in fact justify those, who by their own confession neither feared God, nor wrought righteousness. Is this an exception to the general rule? It is a doubt, whether God makes any exception at all. But how are we sure that the person in question never did fear God and work righteousness? His own thinking so is no proof. For we know how all that are convinced of sin, undervalue themselves in every respect. Does not talking, without the proper caution, of a justified state, tend to mislead men? Almost naturally leading them to trust in what was done in one moment? Whereas we are every moment pleasing or displeasing to God, according to our works; according to the whole of our present inward tempers, and outward behaviour."

After the enrollment of the deed of declaration, ordination was introduced into the society: and to avoid the repetition of insults which had been experienced by some of the worshipping assemblies in consequence of their not being under the protection of the law, the Methodist ministers and chapels, were all licensed according to the requisitions of the toleration act. That no improper use might be made by the conference of the authority which Mr. Wesley had delegated to them by this deed of declaration, he wrote to them this letter which

Mr. Bradford delivered soon after the opening of the first conference subsequent to his death.

My dear Brethren,

" Some of our travelling preachers have expressed a fear, that after my decease you would exclude them either from preaching in connexion with you, or from some other privileges which they now enjoy. I know no other way to prevent any such inconvenience, than to leave these my last words with you. I beseech you by the mercies of God, that you never avail yourselves of the deed of declaration, to assume any superiority over your brethren : but let all things go on, among those itinerants who choose to remain together, exactly in the same manner as when I was with you, so far as circumstances will permit. In particular I beseech you, if you ever loved me, and if you now love God and your brethren, to have no respect to persons, in stationing the preachers, in chusing children for Kingswood-school, in disposing of the yearly contribution and the preachers' fund, or any other publick money. But do all things with a single eye, as I have done from the beginning. Go on thus, doing all things without prejudice or partiality, and God will be with you even to the end.

JOHN WESLEY."

The conference immediately and unanimously resolved, that all the preachers in the connection should enjoy every privilege which they possessed.

In the year 1793, permission was given to any of the societies who desired it, to celebrate the dying love of the Redeemer in their own chapels, which duty they had before performed in the established church only.——This is the economy of the British Methodists at this time.

The minutes of the conference have been printed every year : but it was not till 1765, that the stations of the preachers were inserted in them. And no regular account of the number of members in the societies through the three kingdoms was obtained until 1767. The following table shews the increase of the itinerant preachers and of the Methodist societies, till the last conference in 1806.

Years.	No. of Itinerant Preachers.	People in the Societies.
1765	92	
1767	104	25,911.
1770	122	29,046.
1775	138	38,150.
1780	172	43,830.
1785	206	52,433.
1790	293	71,568.
1795	357	83,368.
1800	417	109,961.
1802	475	118,732.
1806	558	134,576.

In the year 1802, there were 738 Methodist chapels in England, 26 in Wales, 20 in Scotland, 130 in Ireland, 19 in the Isle of Man, 3 in the Isle of Wight, 3 in the Norman Isles, 1 in Berwick-upon-Tweed, and 1 in the Isles of Scilly, amounting to 941 houses for divine worship.

CHAPTER VI.

From the year 1784 until his death.

THE work of God increased yearly: and new societies were formed, in all of which the same rules were observed. Though now declining in the vale of years, Mr. Wesley rose at four in the morning, preached two, three or four times daily, travelled between four and five thousand miles yearly, making a tour once in two years through Great Britain and Ireland.

The following letter written to a travelling preacher in 1786, shews us Mr. Wesley's fatherly care of the preachers; and gives us an example of his delicate manner of conveying reproof where he saw it necessary.—" Dear S——, you know I love you; ever since I knew you, I have neglected no way of shewing it that was in my power. And you know I esteem you for your zeal and activity, for your love of discipline, and for your gifts which God has given you: particularly, quickness of apprehension, and readiness of utterance, especially in preaching and prayer. Therefore I am jealous over you, lest you should lose any of the things you have gained, and not receive a full reward: and the more so, because I fear you are wanting in other respects. And who will venture to tell you so? You will scarce know how to bear it from me, unless you lift up your heart to God—If you do this, I may venture to tell you what I fear, without any further preface. I fear you think of yourself more highly than you ought to think. Do you not think too highly of your own understanding? of your gifts? particularly in preaching! as if you were the very best preacher in the connection? of your own importance? as if the work of God here or there, depended wholly or mainly on you? and of your popularity? which I have found to my surprise far less than I expected. May not this be much owing to your want of brotherly-love? With what measure you mete, men will measure to you again. I fear there is something unloving in your spirit: something not only of roughness, but of harshness, yea of sourness! Are you not likewise extremely open to prejudice, and not easy to be cured of it? So that whenever you are prejudiced, you become bitter, implacable, unmerciful? If so, that people are prejudiced against you, is both the natural and judicial consequence. I am afraid lest your want of love to your neighbours, should spring from your want of love to God: from your want of thankfulness. I have sometimes heard you speak, in a manner that made me tremble: indeed, in terms that not only a weak christian, but even a serious deist would scruple to use. I fear you greatly want evenness of temper. Are you not generally too high, or too low? Are not all your passions too lively? your anger, in particular? Is it not too soon raised: and is it not often too impetuous? causing you to be violent, boisterous—bearing down all before you! Now lift up your heart to God, or you will be angry at me. But I must go a little further. I fear you are greatly wanting in the government of your tongue. You are not exact in relating facts. I have observed it myself. You are apt to amplify: to enlarge a little beyond the truth. You cannot imagine, if others observe this, how it will affect your reputation. But I fear you are more wanting in another respect. That you give a loose to your tongue when you are angry: that your language then, is not only sharp, but coarse, and ill-bred—If this be so, the people will not bear it. They will not take it, either from you, or me."

On his birth-day in 1788, he makes the following observations, " I this day enter on my eighty-fifth year. And what cause have I to praise God, as for a thousand spiritual blessings, so for bodily blessings also? How little have I suffered yet, by the rush of numerous years! It is true, I am not so agile as I was in times past : I do not run or walk so fast as I did. My sight is a little decayed. I find likewise some decay in my memory, with regard to names and things lately past : but not at all with regard to what I have read or heard, twenty, forty, or sixty years ago. Neither do I find any decay in my hearing, smell, taste, or appetite, nor do I feel any such thing as weariness, either in travelling or preaching. And I am not conscious of any decay in writing sermons, which I do as readily, and I believe, as correctly as ever.

" To what cause can I impute this, that I am as I am ? First, doubtless to the power of God, fitting me for the work to which I am called, as long as he pleases to continue me therein : and next, subordinately to this, to the prayers of his children—May we not impute it, as inferior means, to my constant exercise and change of air ? To my never having lost a night's sleep, sick or well, at land or sea, since I was born ? To my having sleep at command, so that whenever I feel myself almost worn out, I call it, and it comes day or night ? To my having constantly, for above sixty years, risen at four in the morning ? To my constant preaching at five in the morning, for above fifty years ? To my having had so little pain in my life, and so little sorrow or anxious care ?—Even now, though I find pain daily in my eye, temple, or arm, yet it is never violent, and seldom lasts many minutes at a time.

" Whether or not this is sent to give me warning, that I am shortly to quit this tabernacle, I do not know: but be it one way or the other, I have only to say,

"My remnant of days
I spend to his praise,
Who died the whole world to redeem:
Be they many or few,
My days are his due,
And they all are devoted to him!"

Dr. Johnson desired Mrs. Hall to procure him an interview with her brother. She made known his desire to Mr. Wesley, and a day was accordingly appointed for him to dine with the doctor. The doctor conformed to Mr. Wesley's hours, and appointed two o'clock: the dinner however was not ready till three. They conversed till that time. Mr. Wesley had devoted two hours to his learned host. He rose as soon as dinner was ended, and departed. The Doctor was extremely disappointed, and could not conceal his chagrin. Mrs. Hall said, "Why, Doctor, my Brother has been with you two hours!" He replied, "Two hours, Madam! I could converse all night with your Brother."

A letter from Alexander Knox of Londonderry, introduces the philanthropist, John Howard. "In the course of his tour through Ireland in the year 1787, he remained a few days in Londonderry. I earnestly wished to see him; but bad health confined me to the house, and I thought I could not be gratified, when I was told that a gentleman had called to see me. It was Mr. Howard! I was most delightfully surprised. I acknowledge it was one of the happiest moments of my life. He came to see me, because he understood that I was Mr. Wesley's friend. He began immediately to speak of him. He told me he had seen him shortly before, in Dublin: that he had spent some hours with him, and was greatly edified by his conversation. "I was," said he, "encouraged by him to go on vigorously with my own designs. I saw in him how much

H h

a single man might atchieve by zeal and perseverance. And I thought, why may not I do as much in my way, as Mr. Wesley has done in his, if I am only as assiduous and persevering? And I determined I would pursue my work with more alacrity than ever."

In the beginning of the year 1789, Mr. Howard called at Mr. Wesley's house to bid him adieu, as he was again flying to the continent at the call of mercy. He carried his last quarto upon the jails under his arm, to present it to his friend. But Mr. Wesley had departed for Ireland. " I have," said he, " but one thing to do, and I strive to do it with all my might. The Lord has taken away whatsoever might be an incumbrance. All places are alike to me, for I find misery in all. He gives me continual health. I have no need to be careful for any thing. I eat no animal food; and can have all I want in the most inconvenient situation. Present my respects and love to Mr. Wesley. Tell him I hoped to have seen him once more. Perhaps we may meet again in this world; but if not, we shall meet, I trust, in a better. I have gained, I think, a little knowledge concerning the plague. I shall therefore, after visiting the Russian camp, pass into the Turkish, and thence by Constantinople to Egypt." So he purposed; but on the journey, God said, it is enough: Come up hither: enter thou into the joy of thy Lord!

Mr. Wesley began now to feel the infirmities of age increase fast upon him. In January 1790, he observes, " I am now an old man, decayed from head to foot. My eyes are dim: my right-hand shakes much: my mouth is hot and dry every morning: I have a lingering fever almost every day: and my motion is weak and slow. However, blessed be God, I do not slack my labour. I can preach and write still." And on his birth-day, he remarks, " This day I enter into my eighty-eighth year. For above eighty-six years, I found none of the infirmities of old age; my eyes did not wax dim, neither was my natural strength abated. But last August, I found almost a sudden change; my eyes were so dim, that no glasses could help me: my strength likewise quite forsook me, and probably will not return in this world. But I feel no pain from head to foot, only it seems nature is exhausted, and humanly speaking, will sink more and more, till,

"The weary springs of life stand still at last."

This was the case; the death of Mr. Wesley, like that of his brother Charles, was one of those rare instances, in which nature drooping under the load of years, sunk by a gentle decay. For several years preceding his death, this was more visible to others than to himself; particularly by a more frequent disposition to sleep during the day; by a growing defect in his memory, and by a general diminution of the vigour and agility which he had so long enjoyed. His labours, however, suffered little interruption: and when the summons came, it found him occupied in his Master's work!

Thursday, the 17th of February 1791, Mr. Wesley preached at Lambeth: but on his return home, felt much indisposed, and supposed that he had taken cold. The next day, he read and wrote as usual; and in the evening preached at Chelsea with some difficulty, having a high degree of fever. On Saturday he still persevered in his usual employments, though to those about him, his complaints seemed evidently increasing. He dined at Islington, and desired a friend to read to him from the fourth to the seventh chapter of Job inclusive. On Sunday he rose early according to custom, but totally unfit for the exercises of the day. He was obliged to lie down about seven o'clock in the morning, and slept several hours. When he awoke, he said, " I have not had such a comfortable sleep this fortnight past:" but the effects were soon gone, and he slept two hours after dinner. In the course of the day, two of his own discourses on the sermon on the mount, were read to him; and in the evening he walked down to supper. Monday, he seemed much revived, and visited a friend at Twickenham. Tuesday, he continued his usual work, preached at the City-Road, and appeared better than he had been for some days. Wednesday, he visited Leatherhead, where he delivered his *last* sermon, from *Seek ye the Lord while he may be found; call ye upon him while he is near.*—Thursday, he rode to Mr. Wolff's at Balaam, whence he returned on Friday the 25th, extremely ill His friends were struck with the manner of his alighting from the carriage, and still more when he ascended the stairs, and sat down up in his chair. He sent every one out of the room, and desired not to be interrupted for half an hour. When that time was expired, some mulled wine was carried him, of which he drank a little. In a few minutes he vomited and said, " I must lie down." His friends were now alarmed, and Dr. Whitehead was summoned to attend him. On entering the room, he said in a cheerful voice, " Doctor, they are more afraid than hurt." Much of this day he continued in bed, with a quick pulse, and a considerable degree of fever and stupor. Saturday, the 25th, he continued nearly in the same state; taking very little, either of medicine or nourishment. Sunday morning, he was refreshed, arose and drank a cup of tea. Sitting in his chair, he looked very cheerful, and repeated those words of his brother Charles,

 " Till glad I lay this body down,
  Thy servant, Lord, attend;
  And O! my life of mercy crown
  With a triumphant end."

Soon after he most emphatically said, " Our friend *Lazarus* sleepeth." Exerting himself to converse with some friends, he was soon fatigued, and obliged to lie down. After being some time quiet, he looked up, and said, " Speak to me, I cannot speak." The persons present kneeled down to pray with him, and his hearty *Amen*, proved that he was perfectly sensible of what was said. Some time after he said, " There is no need of more; when at Bristol, in 1783, my words were,

"I the chief of sinners am,
But Jesus died for me."

Dr. Whitehead said, " Is this the present language of your heart and do you now feel as you then did?" He replied, " Yes." When he added

" Bold I approach th' eternal throne,
And claim the crown through Christ my own,"

" Tis enough. *He*, our precious Immanuel has purchased, has promised all ;" Mr. Wesley earnestly replied, " He is all !" and then said, " I will go."

Monday the 28th, his weakness increased. He slept most of the day, and spoke but little; yet that little testified how much his whole heart was engaged in the care of the societies, the glory of God, and the promotion of the things pertaining to that kingdom, to which he was hastening. Once he said, in a low but distinct manner, " There is no way into the holiest, but by the blood of Jesus." He asked what the words were, from which he had preached a little before at Hampstead. Being told they were these; *Brethren, ye know the grace of our Lord Jesus Christ, who, though he was rich, yet for your sakes became poor, that ye through his poverty might become rich :* He replied, " That is the foundation, the only foundation, and there is no other." This day he was asked, if he would have any other physician called to attend ? but this he refused. He suffered little, never complaining of any pain during his illness, but once in his breast. Tuesday morning, he sang two verses of an hymn : then lying still, as if to recover strength, he called for pen and ink; but when it was brought he could not write. Dr. Whitehead said, " Let me write for you, Sir: tell me what you would say." He replied, " Nothing, but that God is with us." In the forenoon he wished to rise. While his clothes were preparing, he sang,

> " I'll praise my Maker while I've breath,
> And when my voice is lost in death,
>   Praise shall employ my nobler powers:
> My days of praise shall ne'er be past,
> While life, and thought, and being last,
>   Or immortality endures!"

Having seated him in his chair, his friends observed him change for death. But he, regardless of his dying body, said with a weak voice, " Lord, Thou givest strength to those who can speak, and to those who cannot. Speak, Lord, to all our hearts, and let them know that Thou loosest tongues." He then sung,

> "To Father, Son, and Holy Ghost,
>   Who sweetly all agree,".

Here his voice failed. After gasping for breath, he said, " Now we have done all." He was then laid on the bed, whence he rose no more. After resting a little, he called to those who were with him, " To pray and praise." Presently he added, " Let me be buried in nothing but what is woollen, and let my corpse be carried in my coffin, into the Chapel." He again called upon them to "pray and praise," and taking each by the hand, and affectionately saluting them, bade them farewell. Attempting afterwards to say something which they could not understand, he paused a little, and then with all the remaining strength which he had, said, " The best of all is, God is with us." And, lifting his hand, he repeated the same words in a holy triumph, " The best of all is, God is with us." Something being given him to moisten his lips, he said, " It will not do; we must take the consequence. Never mind the poor carcase:"

Being told that his brother's widow was come, he said, " He giveth his servants rest ;" thanked her as she pressed his hand, and affectionately endeavoured to kiss her. His lips being again moistened, he repeated his usual address after a meal ; " We thank Thee, O Lord, for these and all thy mercies : grant us truth and peace, through Jesus Christ our Lord." After some pause he said, " The clouds drop fatness. The Lord is with us; the God of Jacob is our refuge." He again called them to prayer, and appeared fervently to join in their petitions.

During the following night, he often attempted to repeat the psalm before mentioned ; but could only utter, " I'll praise, I'll praise." On Wednesday morning, his end drew near. Mr. Bradford, his old and faithful friend, who, with the affection of a son, had attended him many years, now prayed with him; and the last word which he was heard to articulate, was " Farewell."—A few minutes before ten, on the second day of March, 1791, while a number of his friends were kneeling around his bed, died Mr. John Wesley, without a groan, in the eighty-eighth year of his age, and entered into the joy of his Lord.

March the 9th was the day appointed for his interment. The intention was to carry the corpse into the chapel, and place it in a raised situation before the pulpit during the service. But the crowds who visited the body while it laid in the coffin, both in the private house, and especially in the chapel on the day before the funeral, were so great, that his friends were apprehensive of a tumult. It was therefore resolved to bury him between five and six in the morning. Though the time of notice to his friends was short, and the design itself was spoken of with great caution, yet a considerable number of persons attended at that early hour. The late Mr. Richardson, who now lies with him in the same vault, read the funeral service. When he came to that part, " For as much as it hath pleased Almighty God to take unto himself the soul of our dear brother, &c." he substituted, with the most tender emphasis, the epithet *father* instead of brother; which had so powerful an effect on the congregation, that from silent tears, they seemed universally to burst into loud weeping. The discourse was delivered in the chapel at the hour appointed in the forenoon, to an astonishing multitude of auditors; among whom were many ministers of the gospel, both of the Establishment, and Dissenters.

The following Inscription has since his Interment been placed on the Tomb.

To the Memory of
THE VENERABLE JOHN WESLEY, A M.
Late Fellow of LINCOLN College, OXFORD.
This GREAT LIGHT arose
By the singular Providence of God,
To enlighten THESE NATIONS,
And to *revive*, *enforce*, and *defend*,
The Pure, Apostolical DOCTRINES and PRACTICES of
THE PRIMITIVE CHURCH:
Which he continued to do, by his WRITINGS and his
LABOURS,
For more than HALF A CENTURY:
And, to his inexpressible Joy,
Not only, beheld their INFLUENCE extending,
And their EFFICACY witnessed,
In the Hearts and Lives of MANY THOUSAND
As well in the WESTERN WORLD, as in these
KINGDOMS:
But also, far above all human Power or Expectation,
Liv'd to see PROVISION made, by the singular Grace
of GOD,
For their CONTINUANCE and ESTABLISHMENT,

To the Joy of future Generations!
Reader, If thou art constrained to bless the Instrument, Give God the 'Glory!
After having languished a few days, he at length finished his Course *and his* Life *together: gloriously triumphing over* Death, *March 2, An. Dom. 1791, in the Eighty-Eighth Year of his Age.*

Mr. John Wesley's WILL.
" *In the Name of God.* Amen!

I John Wesley, Clerk, some time fellow of Lincoln-College, Oxford, revoking all others, appoint this to be my last will and testament. I give all my books now on sale, and the copies of them, subject to a rent charge only of 85l. a year to the widow and children of my brother, to my faithful friends, John Horton, merchant, George Wolff, merchant, and William Marriott, stock-broker, all of London, in trust for the general fund of the Methodist conference in carrying on the work of God, by itinerant preachers, on condition that they permit the following committee, Thomas Coke, James Creighton, Peard Dickenson, Thomas Rankin, George Whitefield, and the London assistant for the time being, still to superintend the printing-press, and to employ Hannah Paramore and George Paramore, as heretofore, unless four of the committee judge a change to be needful. I give the books, furniture, and whatever else belongs to me in the three houses at Kingswood, in trust to Thomas Coke, Alexander Mather, and Henry Moore, to be still employed in teaching and maintaining the children of poor travelling preachers. I give to Thomas Coke, doctor John Whitehead, and Henry Moore, all the books which are in my study and bed-chamber at London, and in my studies elsewhere, in trust for the use of the preachers who shall labour there from time to time. I give the coins, and whatever else is found in the drawer of my bureau at London, to my dear grand daughters Mary and Jane Smith. I give all my manuscripts to Thomas Coke, Doctor Whitehead, and Henry Moore, to be burnt or published as they see good I give whatever money remains in my bureau and pockets at my decease to be equally divided between Thomas Briscoe, William Collins, John Easton, and Isaac Brown. I desire my gowns, cassocks, shoes, and bands may remain at the chapel for the use of the clergymen attending there. I desire the London assistant for the time being to divide the rest of my wearing apparel between those four of the travelling preachers that want it most ; only my pellise I give to the Rev. Mr. Creighton ; my watch to my friend Joseph Bradford : my gold seal to Elizabeth Ritchie. I give my chaise and horses to James Ward and Charles Wheeler, in trust, to be sold, and the money to be divided, one half to Hannah Abbott, and the other to the poor members of the select society. Out of the first money which arises from the sale of books, I bequeath to my dear sister Martha Hall, if alive, 40l. to Mr. Creighton aforesaid 40l. and to the Rev. Mr. Heath 60l. And whereas I am empowered by a late deed to name the persons who are to preach in the new chapel at London, the clergymen for a continuance, and by another deed to name a committe for appointing preachers in the new chapel at Bath, I do hereby appoint John Richardson, Thomas Coke, James Creighton, Peard Dickinson, clerks, Alexander Mather, William Thompson, Henry Moore, Andrew Blair, John Valton, Joseph Bradford, James Rogers, and William Myles, to preach in the new chapel at London, and to be the committee for appointing preachers in the new chapel at Bath. I likewise appoint Henry Brooke painter, Arthur Keen, gent. and William Whitestone, stationer, all of Dublin, to receive the annuity of 5l. English, left to Kingswood School by the late Roger Shiel, Esq. I give 6l. to be divided among the six poor men, named by the assistant, who shall carry my body to the grave; for I particularly desire there may be no hearse, no coach, no escutcheon, no pomp, except the tears of them that loved me, and are following me to Abraham's bosom. I solemnly adjure my executors in the name of God, punctually to observe this. Lastly, I give to each of those travelling preachers who shall remain in the connexion six months after my decease, as a little token of my love, the eight volumes of sermons. I appoint John Horton, George Wolff, and William Marriott, aforesaid, to be executors of this my last will and testament, for which trouble they will receive no recompence till the resurrection of the just. Witness my hand and seal the 20th day of February 1789.

JOHN WESLEY. (Seal.)

Signed, sealed, and delivered, by the said testator as and for his last will and testament, in the presence of us,

WILLIAM CLULOW,
ELIZABETH CLULOW.

Should there be any part of my personal estate undisposed of by my last will: I give the same unto my two nieces E. Ellison, and S. Collet, equally.

JOHN WESLEY.

WILLIAM CLULOW,
ELIZABETH CLULOW.

February 25, 1789.

I give my types, printing-presses, and every thing pertaining thereto, to Mr. Thomas Rankin, and Mr. George Whitefield, in trust for the use of the conference.

JOHN WESLEY."

CHAPTER VII.

A Review of Mr. Wesley's Character and Writings.

IT is not some particular circumstances or a few occasional acts in a man's life, but the general tenour of his conduct; that fixed principle which uniformly operates upon him, that forms his character. And when a long, virtuous, and useful life is crowned with an end suitable to it, death stamps his virtues, as genuine.

Some persons have unjustly insinuated that Mr. Wesley was a man of slender capacity. His apprehension was clear, his penetration quick, and his judgment discriminative and sound: of which his controversial writings, and his celebrity at Oxford are sufficient proofs. In governing a large body of preachers and people, of various habits, interests, and principles, with astonishing calmness and regularity for many years; he shewed a strong capacious mind, which could comprehend and combine together a vast variety of circumstances, and direct their influence through the great body which he governed. As a scholar, he was conspicuous, being a critic in the Latin and Greek classics; he was also acquainted with the Hebrew, and with most of the European languages. But the Greek was his favourite, in which his knowledge was extensive and accurate—At college, he had studied with much care, Euclid, Keil, Sir Isaac Newton's Optics, &c. &c. but he never advanced to the higher branches of the mathematics, as they would have diverted his mind from the more important objects of his own profession. He was not a friend to metaphysical disquisitions: and a most determined opposer of those systems of natural philosophy, which represent the power of matter as the efficient cause of all the phenomena of nature ; by which the superintending Providence of God is banished from the world, and all things even the actions of men, are supposed to be determined by laws unalterably fixed. He doubted the truth of the calculations of the planetary distances, and some other parts of modern astronomy. Natural history was a field which he contemplated with infinite pleasure; learning from it the wisdom, the power, and the goodness of God, in the structure of natural bodies, and in the various instincts and habits of the animal creation.

Mr. Wesley's attitude in the pulpit was graceful and easy ; his action was calm and natural, yet pleasing and expressive : his voice not loud, but clear and manly ; his style neat, simple, and perspicuous ; and admirably adapted to the capacity of his hearers. His discourses, in point of composition, were extremely dissimilar on different occasions. When he studied, he succeeded ; otherwise he frequently failed.—It was indeed manifest to his friends many years previous to his death, that his employments were too many, and that he preached too often, to appear with the same advantage at all times in the pulpit. His sermons were always short : he seldom occupied more than half an hour in delivering a discourse, sometimes not so long. His subjects were judiciously chosen, instructive and interesting to the audience, and adapted to gain the attention and to warm the heart.

During fifty years Mr. Wesley travelled, four thousand five hundred miles yearly : it would have been impossible for him to have performed this excessive labour, without great punctuality and care in the management of his time. He had stated hours for every purpose : and his sole relaxation was a change of employment. His rules were like the laws of the Medes and Persians, absolute and irrevocable. He felt a peculiar pleasure in reading and study ; and highly relished polite conversation, with pious, learned, and sensible men ; but whenever the hour arrived that he was to commence a journey, he instantly quitted any subject or any company in which he might be engaged, without any apparent reluctance. For fifty-two years or upwards, he generally delivered two, frequently three or four sermons daily. But calculating at two* sermons, and allowing fifty annually for extraordinary occasions, the whole number will be, forty thousand five hundred and sixty. To these may be added an infinite number of exhortations to the societies after preaching, and in other occasional meetings at which he assisted.

In social life, Mr. Wesley was lively and conversible. He had most exquisite talents to render himself agreeable in company : and having been much accustomed to society, the rules of good breeding were habitual to him. The abstraction of a scholar did not appear in his behaviour ; he was attentive and polite. He talked much when he saw it was expected, which was almost always the case. Having seen much of the world, and read more ; his mind was stored with an infinite number of anecdotes and observations ; and the manner in which he related them, was no inconsiderable addition to the entertainment which they afforded. In private life among his friends, his manner was equally sprightly and pleasant ; and it was impossible to be long in his company, without partaking of his placid cheerfulness; which was not abated by the infirmities of age, or the approach of death ; being equally conspicuous at fourscore and seven, as at twenty.

A remarkable feature in Mr. Wesley's character, was his placability. Having an active penetrating mind, his temper was naturally quick ; but the influence of religion, and his constant habit of close thinking, had in a great measure corrected this disposition. In general he preserved an air of sedateness and tranquillity, which formed a striking contrast with the vivacity apparent in all his actions. Persecution, abuse, or injury he bore from strangers, not only without anger, but without any visible emotion. What he said of himself was strictly true: that he had a great facility in forgiving injuries. Submission on the part of the offender immediately disarmed his resentment, and he would treat him with great kindness and cordiality. No man was ever more free from jealousy or suspicion, or more liable to the impositions of others.

One peculiar trait in Mr. Wesley was his openness—he could not avoid relating every thing which he knew—Mr. Charles Wesley said of him in a letter to their mutual friend; "You expect he will keep his own secrets; let me tell you, he never could do it since he was born; it is a gift which God has not given him."

The temperance of Mr. Wesley was extraordinary. He was remarkable in the article of sleep. "Healthy men," says he, "require above six hours sleep: healthy women, a little above seven, in four and twenty. If any one desires to know exactly what quantity of sleep his own constitution requires, he may easily make the experiment, which I made about sixty years go. I then waked every night about twelve or one, and lay awake for some time. I readily concluded, that this arose from my being in bed longer than nature required. To be satisfied, I procured an alarum, which waked me the next morning at seven, yet I lay awake again at night. The second morning I rose at six; but notwithstanding this, I lay awake the second night. The third morning I rose at five: but nevertheless I lay awake the third night. The fourth morning I rose at four, as, by the grace of God, I have done ever since: and I lay awake no more. And

I do not now lie awake, taking the year round, a quarter of an hour together in a month. By the same experiment, rising earlier and earlier every morning, may any one find how much sleep he wants." Nevertheless for many years before his death, Mr. Wesley slept every day. And his great readiness to fall asleep at any time when fatigued, was a considerable means of preserving his strength, and enabling him to perform so much labour. He would come to the place where he had to preach at noon after a long wearisome ride in a hot day, and without any refreshment immediately sleep. After reposing ten minutes or a quarter of an hour, he would rise refreshed and fitted for his work—He never could endure to sleep on a soft bed: even in the latter part of life, when the infirmities of age pressed upon him, his whole conduct was at the greatest distance from effeminacy.

Perhaps Mr. Wesley was the most charitable man in England. His liberality to the poor, knew no bounds but an empty pocket. He gave away, not merely a certain part of his income, but all that he had; his own wants provided for, he devoted all the rest to the necessities of others. He entered upon this good work at a very early period. When he possessed thirty pounds a year, he expended twenty-eight, and gave away forty shillings. The next year, receiving sixty pounds, he gave away two and thirty. The third year he received ninety pounds, and gave away sixty-two. The fourth year he received one hundred and twenty pounds. Still he lived on twenty-eight, and gave to the poor ninety-two." In this ratio he proceeded during the rest of his life: and in the course of fifty years, he gave away between twenty and thirty thousand pounds.

In the distribution of his money, Mr. Wesley was as disinterested as he was charitable. He had no regard to family connexions, or even to the wants of the preachers who laboured with him, in preference to strangers. He knew that these had some friends; and he thought the poor destitute stranger might have none, and therefore first claimed his liberality. When a trifling legacy has been paid him, he has been known charitably to dispose of it before he slept, that it might not remain his own property for one night. He declared, that if he died worth more than ten pounds, independent of his books, and the arrears of his fellowship which he then held, he would give the world leave to call him, " A thief and a robber." His chaise and horses, his clothes, and a few trifles were all, his books excepted, which he left at his death. His books, were placed in the hands of trustees that the profits arising from the sale of them might be applied to the use and benefit of the conference; reserving a few legacies only, and a rent-charge of eighty-five pounds yearly, payable to his brother's widow; as a consideration for the copyright of the hymns.

During the time that Mr. Wesley ruled the societies, his power was absolute. There were no rights, no privileges, no offices of power or influence, which were not created or sanctioned by him: nor could any persons hold them, but during his pleasure. The whole system of Methodism, like a great and complicated machine, was formed under his direction; and his will gave motion to all its parts, and turned it as he thought proper. Yet no man ever used his power with more moderation. He never sought his own ease or advantage; the societies experienced no inconvenience, but prospered under his government: and they derived this benefit from his authority, that if any were injured, they obtained immediate redress by an application to him.

These three sketches of Mr. Wesley's character, written soon after his death, will be acceptable.

"Now that Mr. John Wesley has finished his course upon earth, I may be allowed to estimate his character, and the loss which the world has sustained by his death. Upon a fair account, it appears to be such as not only annihilates all the reproaches that have been cast upon him; but such as does honour to mankind, at the same time that it reproaches them. His natural and acquired abilities were both of the highest rank. His apprehension was lively and distinct; his learning extensive. His judgment, though not infallible, was in most cases excellent. His mind was stedfast and resolute. His elocution was ready and clear, graceful and easy, accurate and unaffected. As a writer, his style, though unstudied and flowing with natural ease, for accuracy and perspicuity, was such as may vie with the best writers in the English language. Though his temper was naturally warm, his manners were gentle, simple, and uniform. Never were such happy talents better seconded by an unrelenting perseverance in those courses, which his singular endowments and his zealous love to the interests of mankind marked out for him. His constitution was excellent; and never was a constitution less abused, less spared, or more excellently applied, in an exact subservience to the faculties of his mind. His labours and studies were wonderful. The latter were not confined to theology only, but extended to every subject that tended either to the improvement, or the rational entertainment of the mind. If we consider the reading which he discovers by itself, his writings, and his other labours by themselves, any one of them will appear sufficient to have kept a person of ordinary application, busy during his whole life. In short, the transactions of his life could never have been performed, without the utmost exertion of two qualities; which depended, not upon his capacity, but on the uniform stedfastness of his resolution. These were, inflexible temperance and unexampled economy of time. In these he was a pattern to the age in which he lived; and an example, to what a surprizing extent a man may render himself useful in his generation, by temperance and punctuality. His friends and followers have no reason to be ashamed of the name Methodist, which he has entailed upon them: as, for an uninterrupted course of years, he has given the world an instance of the possibility of living without wasting a single hour; and of the advantage of a regular distribution of time, in discharging the important duties and purposes of life. Few ages have more needed such a publick testimony to the value of time; and perhaps none have had a more conspicuous example of the perfection, to which the improvement of it may be carried. As a minister his labours were unparalleled, and such as nothing could have supported him under, but the warmest zeal for the doctrine which he taught, and for the eternal interests of mankind. He studied to be gentle, yet vigilant and faithful towards all. He possessed himself in patience, and preserved himself unprovoked, nay, even unruffled in the midst of persecution, reproach, and all manner of abuse, both of his person and name. But let his own works praise him. He now enjoys the fruit of his labours, and that praise which he sought, not of men, but of God. Examine the general tenour of his life, and it will be found self-evidently inconsistent with his being a slave to any one passion or pursuit, that can fix a blemish on his character. Of what use were the accumulation of wealth to him, who, through his whole course, never allowed himself to taste the repose of indolence, or even of the common indulgences in the use of the necessaries of life. Free from the attachment of any party, the writer of this character, with a tear, pays it as a just tribute to the memory of a great and good man, who, when alive, was his friend."

Mr. Knox says, " Very lately I had an opportunity, for some days together, of observing Mr. Wesley with attention. I endeavoured to consider him, not so much with the eye of a friend, as with the impartiality of a philosopher: and I must declare, every hour I spent in his company afforded me fresh reasons for esteem and veneration. So fine an old man I never saw. The happiness of his mind, beamed forth in his countenance. Every look shewed how fully he enjoyed ' The gay remembrance of a life well spent :' and wherever he went, he diffused a portion of his own felicity. Easy and affable in his demeanour, he accommodated himself to every sort of company, and shewed how happily the most finished courtesy may be blended with the most perfect piety. In his conversation, we might be at a loss whether to admire most, his fine classical taste, his extensive knowledge of men and things, or his overflowing goodness of heart. While the grave and serious were charmed with his wisdom, his sportive sallies of innocent mirth delighted even the young and thoughtless; and both saw in his uninterrupted cheerfulness, the excellency of true religion. No cynical remarks on the levity of youth embittered his discourse: no applausive retrospect to past times marked his present discontent. In him, even old age appeared delightful, like an evening without a cloud; and it was impossible to observe him without wishing fervently, ' May my latter end be like his!' But I find myself unequal to the task of delineating such a character. What I have said, may to some appear as panegyrick; but there are numbers, and those of taste and discernment too, who can bear witness to the truth, though by no means to the perfectness of the sketch which I have attempted. With such I have been frequently in his company; and every one of them, I am persuaded, would subscribe to all I have said. For my own part, I never was so happy as while with him, and scarcely ever felt more poignant regret than at parting from him; for well I knew, " I never should look upon his like again."

This portrait of Mr. Wesley was inserted in Woodfall's Diary.

" His indefatigable zeal in the discharge of his duty has been long witnessed by the world; but as mankind are not always inclined to put a generous construction on the exertion of singular talents, his motives were imputed to the love of popularity, ambition, and lucre. It now appears that he was actuated by a disinterested regard to the immortal interests of mankind. He laboured, and studied, and preached, and wrote, to propagate what he believed to be the gospel of Christ. The intervals of these engagements were employed in governing and regulating the concerns of his numerous societies; in assisting the necessities, solving the difficulties, and soothing the afflictions of his hearers. He observed so rigid a temperance, and allowed himself so little repose, that he seemed to be above the infirmities of nature, and to act independent of the earthly tenement which he occupied. The recital of the occurrences of every day of his life would be the greatest encomium.

Had he loved wealth, he might have accumulated it without bounds. Had he been fond of power, his influence would have been worth courting by any party. I do not say he was without ambition; he had that which Christianity need not blush at, and which virtue is proud to confess. I do not mean, that which is gratified by splendour and large possessions; but that which commands the hearts and affections, the homage and gratitude of thousands. For him they felt sentiments of veneration, inferior to those only which they paid to heaven: to him they looked as their father, their benefactor, their guide to glory and immortality: for him they fell prostrate before God, with prayers and tears, to spare his doom, and to prolong his stay. Such a recompence as this, is sufficient to repay the toils of the longest life. Short of this, greatness is contemptible impotence. Before this, lofty prelates bow, and princes hide their diminished heads.

His zeal was not a transient blaze, but a steady and constant flame. The ardour of his spirit was neither damped by difficulty, nor subdued by age. This was ascribed by himself to the power of Divine Grace; by the world to Enthusiasm. Be it what it will, it is what philosophers must envy and infidels respect; it is that which gives energy to the soul, and without which there can be no greatness or heroism.

Why should we condemn that in religion, which we applaud in every other profession and pursuit? He had a vigour and elevation of mind, which nothing but the belief of the Divine favour and presence could inspire. This threw a lustre round his infirmities, changed his bed of sickness into a triumphal car, and made his exit resemble an Apotheosis rather than a dissolution.

He was qualified to excel in every branch of literature: he was well versed in the learned tongues, in metaphysics, in oratory, in logic, in criticism, and in every requisite of a christian minister. His style was nervous, clear, and manly; his preaching was pathetic and persuasive; his journals are artless and interesting; and his compositions and compilations to promote knowledge and piety were almost innumerable.

I do not say he was without faults, or above mistakes; but they were lost in the multitude of his excellencies and virtues.

To gain the admiration of an ignorant and superstitious age, requires a little artifice and address only; to stand the test of these times, when all pretensions to sanctity are stigmatized as hypocrisy, is a proof of genuine piety, and real usefulness. His great object was to revive the obsolete doctrines, and the extinguished spirit of the church of England; and they who are its friends, cannot be his enemies. Yet for this he was treated as a fanatick and an impostor, and exposed to every species of slander and persecution. Even bishops and dignitaries entered the lists against him; but he never declined the combat, and generally proved victorious. He appealed to the scriptures, as vouchers for his doctrine; and they who could not decide upon the merits of the controversy, were witnesses of the effects of his labours; and they judged of the tree by its fruit. It is true, he did not succeed much in the higher walks of life: but that impeached his cause no more, than it did the first planters of the gospel. However, if he had been capable of assuming vanity on that score, he might rank among his friends some persons of the first distinction, who would have done honour to any party. After surviving almost all his adversaries, and acquiring respect among those who were the most distant from his principles, he lived to see the plant which he had reared, spreading its branches far and wide, and inviting not these kingdoms only, but the Western world to repose under its shade.—No sect, since the first ages of Christianity, could boast a founder of such extensive talents and endowments. If he had been a candidate for literary fame, he might have succeeded to his utmost wishes; but he sought not the praise of man; he regarded learning as the instrument of usefulness only. The great purpose of his life was to do good. For this he relinquished all honour and preferment; to this he dedicated all his powers of body and mind; at all times and in all places, in season and out of season, by gentleness, by terror, by argument, by persuasion, by reason, by interest, by every motive and every inducement, he strove with unwearied assiduity, to turn men from the error of their ways, and to awaken them to virtue and religion. To the bed of sickness, or the couch of prosperity; to the prison, the hospital, the house of mourning, or the house of feasting; wherever there was a friend to serve, or a soul to save, he readily repaired to administer assistance or advice, reproof or consolation. He thought no office too humiliating, no condescension too low, no undertaking too arduous, to reclaim the meanest of God's offspring. The souls of all men were equally precious in his sight, and the value of an immortal creature beyond all estimation. He penetrated the abodes of wretchedness and ignorance to rescue the profligate from perdition; and communicated the light of life to those who sat in darkness and the shadow of death. He changed the outcasts of society, into useful members; civilized even savages, and filled those lips with prayer and praise, which had been accustomed only to oaths and imprecations. But as the strongest religious impressions are apt to become languid without discipline and practice, he divided his people into classes and bands, according to their attainments. He appointed frequent meetings for prayer and conversation, where they gave an account of their experience, their hopes and fears, their joys and troubles: by which means they were united to each other, and to their common profession. They became centinels upon each other's conduct, and securities for each other's character.—Thus the seeds which he sowed sprang up and flourished, bearing the rich fruits of every grace and virtue. Thus he governed and preserved his numerous societies, watching their improvement with a paternal care, and encouraging them to be faithful to the end. But I will not attempt to draw his full character, nor to estimate the extent of his labours and services They will be best known when he shall deliver up his commission into the hands of his great Master."

"The figure of Mr. Wesley was remarkable. His stature was low: and his habit of body in every period of life was the reverse of corpulent, indicating strict temperance, and continual exercise: and notwithstanding his small size, his step was firm, and his appearance, till within a few years of his death, vigorous and muscular. His face was very fine. A clear, smooth forehead, an aquiline nose, an eye bright and piercing, and a freshness of complexion scarcely ever to be found at his years, and expressive of the most perfect health, conspired to render him truly venerable and interesting. Few have seen him without being struck with his appearance: and many, who had been greatly prejudiced against him, have been known to change their opinion, upon being introduced into his presence. In his countenance and demeanour, there was a cheerfulness mingled with gravity; a sprightliness, that was the natural result of an unusual flow of spirits, and which was accompanied with every mark of the most serene tranquillity. His aspect, particularly in profile, had a strong character of acuteness and penetration. In dress, he was a pattern of neatness and simplicity. A narrow plated stock, a coat with a small upright collar, no buckles at his knees, no silk or velvet in any part of his apparel, and a head as white as snow, gave an idea of a man primitive and apostolick: while an air of neatness and cleanliness was diffused over his whole person."

As a writer, Mr. Wesley possessed talents both from nature and education, which were sufficient to procure him considerable reputation. But content with doing good, he never wrote for fame or to amass money. His objects constantly were to inform the understanding, to mend the heart, to discourage vice ; to promote virtue ; and to instruct and benefit that numerous class of people, who have a plain understanding, with plain common sense, little learning, little money, and but a small portion of time to devote to reading. A great degree of candour and liberality runs through all his publications ; and in matters of mere speculation, he endeavoured to shew the necessity of christian love, and mutual forbearance among those who differ in opinion. He thought that we ought to contend for this christian temper and practice, much more earnestly, than for any speculative notions, not essentially necessary to obtain them.

In all his writings these circumstances governed him: the distinguishing characters of his style being brevity and perspicuity. Mr. Wesley's notes on the New Testament are briefly explanatory and practical ; but judicious and pertinent.——His sermons in eight volumes were written with the same spirit, and with the same design as the notes. The first four volumes were published in the earlier part of Methodism ; several of the sermons having been preached before the university of Oxford, while he held his fellowship. The subjects are important, and the discourses written with great animation and strength of language. The last four volumes were composed for the Arminian Magazine. These are generally more practical than the others ; and have been admired for their composition, and for the simpicity, accuracy, and ease of style in which they are written.

His "appeals to men of reason and religion," have great merit. Mr. Wesley wrote them in the fullness of his heart, viewing and lamenting the wretched state of the world with regard to religion and morality.

The treatise on "Original Sin," is his most laboured performance. He knew and respected the abilities and character of Dr. Taylor, his opponent. He bestowed much time and attention in a careful investigation of the subject; but avoided minute metaphysical disquisitions. He knew that nothing could be affirmed in this way of reasoning, however true, but what another might deny with some degree of plausibility. His treatise therefore is an animated defence of the orthodox doctrine, in a deduction from the actual state of morality in all ages, and under every kind of restraint from evil that has been imposed on mankind; or as he expresses it, "From scripture, reason, and experience."

In none of his publications, are instruction and entertainment more happily combined, than in the work entitled, "A survey of the Wisdom and goodness of God in the creation." This was first issued in two volumes; it was afterwards enlarged, and published in five volumes, in 1784. In the fourth volume is a translation of a considerable part of Bonnet's "Contemplations de la Nature," a work highly elegant and instructive. In the fifth volume, Mr. Wesley has given an abstract of Mr. Deuten's "Inquiry into the origin of the discoveries attributed to the Moderns." This survey of the wisdom of God in the Creation, was not intended as a history of the present state of philosophy; but as a general view of the most useful and remarkable things in natural history, and an illustration, for common use, of the wisdom and goodness of the creator. Considered in this light, it is well entitled to public approbation: and the moral reflections which it contains, are distinguished as much by their justness and elegance, as by their utility.

He wrote a very great number of pamphlets on various subjects: among the rest, one entitled "Thoughts on Slavery." He was one of the earliest writers on this subject, and has treated it, in a moral and religious view; but with great spirit and impartiality.

In controversy, Mr. Wesley certainly excelled; he wrote like a christian, a gentleman and a scholar. Few have equalled him, either in skill, freedom from logomachy, or in the moderation which appeared on these occasions. It does not seem, that he was fond of controversy, at least for more than thirty years before his death. He calls it "Heavy work, yet sometimes necessary to be done." Among his controversial pieces, his "Predestination calmly considered," is of distinguished excellence. It is clear and cogent; concise and argumentative; and the more convincing, because the spirit in which it is written, is as amiable as the reasoning is irrefutable.

As an author, Mr. Wesley has been blamed for his numerous extracts from the writings of others. But he presumed that the works from which he selected were the property of the publick; and that the abridgements might be useful to the Methodists, who would probably never see the originals. And we can excuse it when we reflect that all the profits of his printing business were applied to the relief of the poor. His works have been published in thirty-two volumes. He was a laborious writer: and if usefulness be excellence; if universal good be the chief object of attention in publick characters; and if the greatest benefactors to mankind be the most estimable, Mr. Wesley will long be remembered as one of the best, most diligent and most indefatigable of men.

A DISCOURSE

DELIVERED

AT THE NEW CHAPEL IN THE CITY-ROAD, LONDON,

ON THE NINTH OF MARCH, 1791;

AT THE FUNERAL

OF THE

REVEREND JOHN WESLEY.

And I heard a voice from heaven, saying unto me, Write, Blessed are the dead which die in the Lord from henceforth; Yea, saith the Spirit, that they may rest from their labours; and their works follow them.—Rev. xiv. 13.

BY JOHN WHITEHEAD.

II SAMUEL iii. 38.

Know ye not that there is a Prince, and a great man fallen this day in Israel?

I SHALL observe only on this passage of scripture, that the Hebrew word which is rendered prince, sometimes signifies a leader, and sometimes a person of superior or princely qualities. In this general sense the passage may be applied to that eminent servant of God, of whose character I am now to speak. This is all the use that I shall make of the words; I consider them as a motto only to the discourse which I intend to deliver.

When we consider the public character of the late Rev. Mr. WESLEY; the various opinions which have been entertained concerning him; the extent of his labours; the influence which he had over a large body of people ; and the prevalence of his sentiments, not in these only, but in other nations ; it becomes a matter of some importance to inquire the leading features of his character, both as a man, and as a minister of the gospel.

I. Although the acquisition of human learning has been little esteemed by some religious people ; yet it is of very considerable service to a minister of the gospel. The knowledge of the languages, and of the arts and sciences is not only an ornament to the mind, but it enlarges the human faculties ; it improves the understanding, gives a habit of thinking closely and reasoning justly ; and prepares the mind, when under a proper direction, for great attainments even in religion. These advantages Mr. Wesley possessed in a high degree, and he knew well how to improve them to the most useful purposes in his ministerial labours. His mind was richly furnished with literature in its various branches: he was well read in the ancient, and several modern tongues. In the learned languages he was a critic; and must have studied them with peculiar pleasure in his youth, or he could not have made that progress in classical learning, which so justly raised him to a distinguished rank as a scholar. It has been acknowledged by men who were good judges, and no great friends to Mr. Wesley, that when at college he gave proofs of a fine classical taste : and there are some poems which he wrote at that time, that shew that he had formed his taste on the best models of antiquity. Those who were much in his company, and who heard his apt and pointed quotations from the Greek and Roman classics, on the various occasions which occurred in travelling and conversation, could not but be sensible that he read them as a critic, that he admired their style, and entered into their spirit, and was delighted with their beauties.—He has selected some pieces from the Roman classics; and as he travelled, he would sometimes read them for his amusement.

But he did not confine his studies of this kind to profane literature: sacred learning likewise occupied much of his time and attention. He was well read in the Hebrew scriptures; and in the original language of the New Testament he was an able critic, and so conversant with it, that sometimes when he has evidently been at a loss to repeat a passage out of the New Testament in the words of our common translation, he was never at a loss to repeat it in the original Greek; the words seemed to flow without the least difficulty or hesitation, and he was always correct in reciting them; which made it evident, that the words and phrases of the original were more familiar to him than the words of any translation.

The works of God in the creation, afford another fruitful source of instruction and pleasure to an inquiring mind; and the five volumes which he published on *Natural Philosophy*, shew how well he had studied that branch of knowledge. He did not study the higher branches of the mathematicks; but he esteemed the knowledge of this science of great importance in the improvement of the mind. It forms a person to a habit of close attention to a subject, and of thinking and reasoning justly upon it. And he applied himself to the study of it in his youth, so far as to make himself master of Sir Isaac Newton's Principia, and his theory of light and colours.

The *Art of Logic* was another branch of science, which he had cultivated with the utmost attention and care. It has been universally acknowledged that he was a master in it. But logic in his view of it, is not what has been commonly so called in the schools: it is not the art of wrangling, nor of making frivolous distinctions, often without a difference. Logic, according to him, is common sense improved by art ; or in his own words, " The art of good sense ; the art of comprehending things clearly ; of judging truly ; and of reasoning conscientiously : or, in another view of it, the art of learning and teaching."

If we take a view of his conduct in the early part of life, we shall find that he paid a strict attention to religion : his character was moral from early youth ; he always reverenced God and his sacred word : he was attentive to the forms of religion, and so far as he at that time understood it, he was conscientious and regular in the practice of all its duties.

If we consider his qualifications for inquiring after truth, we shall find that he possessed every requisite to examine a subject, that we could expect or wish a man to have : a strong natural understanding highly cultivated, and well stored with the knowledge of languages, and of the various arts and sciences; he had a reverence for God : he was conscientious in all his ways, and intent upon discovering the truth in every thing that became the subject of his inquiries. And he had firmness and resolution to embrace truth wherever he found it, however unfashionable it might appear. This is not the case with all men of learning : many persuade themselves that they are searching after truth ; but if they meet with it dressed in a different form to that under which they have been accustomed to consider it, they are ashamed of it. This cannot be said of Mr. Wesley ; cautious in his inquiries, he sought truth from the love of it, and whenever he found it, had firmness to embrace it, and publickly to avow it. These are evidences of a strong and liberal mind, possessed of every requisite to prosecute inquiries after truth.

This is a just representation of him ; for, notwithstanding the extent of his knowledge, the seriousness of his devotion, and the regularity of his conduct; and although at this time he gave all he had to feed and to clothe the poor, and was not only blameless in the eye of the world, but in many things excelled; yet, after a diligent and patient examination of the scriptures, he became sensible that all he knew and all he did, was insufficient to reconcile him to God: he became sensible that all he could do, could never atone for one sin. I will give you his own words; which he wrote, not by way of ostentation, but of humiliation; and to awaken reflection, if possible, in the minds of those who might think of themselves as he had formerly thought of himself.

" Are they read in philosophy? so was I. In ancient or modern tongues? so was I also. Are they versed in the science of Divinity? I too have studied it many years. Can they talk fluently on spiritual things? the very same could I do. Are they plenteous in alms? Behold! I gave all my goods to feed the poor. Do they give their labour as well as their substance? I have laboured more abundantly than they all. Are they willing to suffer for their brethren? I have thrown up my friends, reputation, and ease. I have put my life in my hand. I have given my body to be parched up with heat, consumed with toil and weariness, or whatever God should please to bring upon me. But does this make me acceptable to God? Does all I ever did or can *know*, *say*, *give*, *do*, or *suffer*, justify me in his sight? by no means. If the oracles of God are true; if we are still to abide by the law and the testimony; all these things, though when enabled by faith in Christ, they are holy, just, and good; yet without it are dung and dross. This then I have learned, that, having nothing in or of myself to plead, I have no hope but that if I seek I shall find Christ, and be found in him, not having my own righteousness, but that

M m

which is through the faith of Christ, the righteousness which is of God by faith."

These were the thoughts he had of himself, when his understanding was opened to the view of gospel truths; when he began to see the purity and holiness of God and his own sinfulness; notwithstanding all the excellencies he had to plead in the opinion of others.

This opinion was not taken up rashly: no doubt many of his friends when they heard him speak in this manner, thought him beside himself: when they considered his former manner of life, and his regularity in every part of his conduct, and heard him say that he was a sinner, a sinner under the wrath of God, a sinner that stood in need of mercy; they looked upon him as almost insane. But this opinion of himself was the result of the most mature inquiry; it was not an enthusiastic notion, the effect of an heated imagination; it was a conviction of his mind founded on a scriptural and rational view of the nature of God, and of his own state. Consider, what I have been observing of his qualifications to inquire after truth: a man of a strong understanding, of a cultivated mind, accustomed to the habit of reasoning, accustomed to investigate every thing in the most cautious manner before he drew his conclusions: and tell me if this be the conduct of an enthusiast? If it be the character of one that takes up things rashly; that follows the dictates of a wild imagination? Will any man calmly affirm this? We must say, that this opinion of himself was not formed in any such way. He tells us, that after conversing with people of experience, he sat down and read his Greek Testament over, with a view to the grand and leading doctrines of justification: he could not be satisfied with any thing less than this: he proceeded upon conviction in every step that he took. And could any man proceed with more caution, or take wiser methods to guard against error, in a matter of such importance to his own comfort and happiness, and to the peace and comfort of others? And here we may again trace the marks of a great and liberal mind; when he saw the truth he embraced it, though it condemned himself. This is not the case with all: how many see the truth and shrink from it? He on the contrary embraced it though it condemned him; and though he knew the profession of it would expose him to ridicule, and contempt, and reproach. Is it possible for any man to give a stronger proof than this, that he acts from conviction; and from a love of what he conceives to be the truth? Had all those who have read Mr. Wesley's writings, or heard him preach, acted with the same sincerity and firmness that he did, the number of converts would have been much more numerous.

II. We shall now take a view of his religious sentiments. He made up his mind upon the doctrines which he taught in the most cautious manner, examining the scriptures continually, never adopting any opinion without evidence from scripture and reason. So far was he from following an heated imagination, or taking up opinions as an enthusiast, that he maintained we ought to use our understanding, compare one thing with another, and draw just conclusions from such comparisons, as well in matters of religion as in other things. It is in this sense he uses the word reason when he says, "There are many that utterly decry the use of reason in religion, nay, that condemn all reasoning concerning the things of God, as utterly destructive of true religion; but we can in no wise agree with this. We find no authority for it in holy writ So far from it, that we find there both our Lord and his apostles reasoning continually with their opposers. Neither do we know in all the productions of ancient and modern times such a chain of reasoning and argumentation, so close, so solid, so regularly connected, as the epistle to the Hebrews. And the strongest reasoner whom we have ever observed excepting Jesus Christ of Nazareth only, was that Paul of Tarsus; the same who has left this plain direction for all christians, "In malice or wickedness be ye children; but in understanding, or reason, be ye men."

Hence it is evident, that Mr. Wesley deemed it necessary to use his reason in searching into the things of God. He read the Scriptures, and used his understanding in the best manner he could, to comprehend their meaning. He formed his religious principles in this way; he examined every step he took, and admitted no doctrine, nor any interpretation of Scripture, but what appeared to him to be agreeable to reason.

How absurd is it to suppose, that we must lay aside our reason in matters of religion. What has a man to guide him, if he lay aside the use of his reason? You will say, the scriptures are the rule of our faith and practice: but, can a man apply the rule without using his reason? What has he to shew him that he applies it right rather than wrong? A man that gives up his reason in matters of religion, or of experience; in matters that concern the internal state of his own mind, abandons himself to imagination, and is liable to be carried away by his passions, he knows not whither; like a ship at sea without a rudder, and without a compass, he has nothing to direct him how to steer his course, and he cannot tell whither he is going. How justly then did Mr. Wesley adopt this principle, that we ought to use our reason to guard our minds from error; and to enable us to form a true judgment both of scripture and experience.

Speaking to one who required a religion agreeable to reason, he says, "We join with you, in desiring a religion founded on reason, and every way agreeable thereto. But one question remains to be asked, what do you mean by reason? I suppose you mean the eternal reason, or the nature of things: the nature of God, and the nature of man, with the relations necessarily subsisting between them. This is the very religion we preach: a religion evidently founded on, and every way agreeable to eternal reason, to the essential nature of things. Its foundation stands on the nature of God, and the nature of man, with their mutual relations."

We have here his general view of religion; and he publicly avows that the Gospel which he preached is agreeable to this view; that it is agreeable to the nature of God and the nature of man, with their mutual relations. He was indeed at the utmost distance from the supposition, that the Gospel, as a system, is inconsistent with reason. And he explained and illustrated, on some occasions, the general doctrines which he taught, in such a way as to shew that they are conformable to the general principle which he has here laid down. The outcry then which has been raised against him, and the whole body with whom he was connected, as enthusiasts and fanatics, is wholly unfounded; it proceeds from the workings of a prejudiced mind, and a want of attention to the things spoken.

The Gospel, considered as a general plan of salvation, he viewed as a display of the divine perfections, in a way agreeable to the nature of God; in which all the divine attributes harmonize, and shine forth with peculiar lustre. Divine love in the gift of a Redeemer; divine wisdom conspicuous in the plan of redemption: divine justice tempered with mercy to man, in the death of the Saviour; and divine energy and power in making the whole effectual to raise a fallen creature from a state of sin and misery, to a state of holiness and happiness, and from a state of death, to immortal life and glory. All these are conspicuous in the gospel, as a general plan of salvation; and shine forth in the face of Jesus Christ, with peculiar glory. Thus far then the gospel, in his view of it, is worthy of God, and coincides with our notions of the harmony and unity of the divine attributes.

The gospel, considered as a means to attain an end, discovers as great fitness in the means to the end, as can possibly be discovered in the structure of natural bodies, or in the various operations of nature, from a view of which we draw our arguments for the existence of God. How often have you heard this excellent man enlarge on these things? How often has he shewn you, that the gospel affords as clear a display of the moral perfections of God, as the works of nature do of his existence? This certainly was not an irrational view of the gospel; but shewed a mind enlarged, capacious, capable of comprehending great things, of investigating every part of the gospel, and of harmonizing the whole.

Considering the gospel as holding forth benefits to man, those benefits are suited to the nature and state of man. How often have you heard him explain this? Man is blind, ignorant, wandering out of the way; his mind being estranged from God, he lives without God in the world. But the gospel, as a system of moral truths, is adapted to enlighten the understanding and to direct the judgment. Experience and observation may convince us, as well as scripture, that a man may contemplate moral truths, and learn to discourse well of them, without acquiring a practical moral principle of sufficient strength to reform his conduct. It is conscience that judges of the right or wrong of a man's motives and actions. And till conscience interpose its authority, and pass sentence on him, the man remains insensible of his own state and condition, however well he may discourse on morality in general. He is, in the language of scripture, dead in trespasses and sins. The gospel then, being the power of God to salvation, must be more than a mere system of morals.

It promises, and God actually gives the spirit of promise, which convinces the world of sin. The Spirit of God accompanies the word of the gospel, and the other means of grace, and makes them effectual to awaken conscience to the exercise of its offices, to pass the sentence of condemnation for what has been done wrong; and the speculative truths of the understanding being thus combined with the dictates of conscience, a practical principle is formed of sufficient strength to restrain the passions and reform the conduct. This our Rev. Father used to call repentance, and often conviction for sin. And was he irrational in this? Is not this blessing of the gospel agreeable to the state, and to the natural faculties of man?

He considered the gospel as a dispensation of mercy to men, holding forth pardon, a free pardon of sin to all who repent and believe in Christ Jesus. That this is a scriptural doctrine no man can doubt who reads the New Testament: it is interwoven with every part of scripture. It will bear the test of reason also. It is suited to the state and wants of men, as they stand related to an holy God. It is suited to the wants of every man living: every man has sinned and comes short of the glory of God; every man therefore stands in need of mercy. It was not then irrational in our minister, to hold forth the rich display of divine grace in Christ Jesus to penitent sinners, in the most free manner. His doctrine is founded on a general view of the scriptures; on the peculiar promises of the gospel; and it is suited to the present condition and wants of men, as they stand related to God and to the prospects of another world.

The gospel enjoins universal holiness both in heart and the conduct of life. The design of it is to regulate our affections and govern our actions. It requires us to be dead to the world and alive to God: to love the Lord our God with all our heart, and our neighbour as ourselves : to do unto others as we would wish they should do unto us. And God has promised in the gospel, the continual aid and assistance of his holy Spirit, to strengthen us with all might in the inner man : Christ is a Saviour that is able to save to the uttermost all them that come unto God by him ; and there is a throne of grace, at which we may obtain, not only mercy, but grace to help in time of need. To him who rightly believes the gospel, it is a means adequate to the end intended by it : to him it is a quickening spirit, a purifying and cleansing word, the power of God to his salvation : it influences every faculty of his mind, and regulates every action of his life : to his mind it exhibits such views of paternal love in every part of the plan of redemption, and of a superintending Providence, directing all things with unerring wisdom, to promote his holiness here, and his happiness and glory hreafter, that he is continnally animated to the practice of every christian virtue, and strengthened with patience to run the race that is set before him.

The gospel then, considered as a large comprehensive plan of redemption, holds forth blessings suited to our present state of necessities : wisdom to instruct us, grace to justify or pardon, and to sanctify and cleanse us from evil ; with promises of protection and help through the snares and difficulties of life. It operates upon us in a way that is suited to our faculties : it enlightens the understanding, awakens the conscience, governs the will, and regulates the affections. Nor are its benefits confined to the present life, they extend to the regions of the dead, and expand our views to the prospects of eternity. What a glorious view does the gospel give us of a resurrection from the dead ! Our Lord hath died and risen again, that he might be Lord both of the dead and of the living. They that die in the Lord are still under his protection and guidance. Death cannot separate any from the love of Christ. The gospel therefore presents blessings suited to our necessities, comprehensive as our wants, and adapted to our state in life and death, and the enjoyments of a glorious and happy eternity.

But in explaining the order in which the blessings of the gospel are promised to man, he shewed a mind well instructed in the oracles of God, and well acquainted with human nature. There is not perhaps greater confusion in any part of the system of religion, or in the common explanations given of the gospel than in this; the order in which the blessings of the gospel are promised to us, and in which we ought to expect them. Our Father, who is gone to his reward, had an excellent introduction to this part of his ministerial office : he himself had entered in at the right door. When a minister is awakened in his own heart, when he is truly sensible of his sin and of the want of a Saviour ; and comes to God for mercy as a poor sinner, and accepts it as the free gift of God through Jesus Christ ; being sensible that he must be justified by faith, without the deeds of the law ; he is well prepared to instruct others ; and to instruct them not in the right way only, but also in the right order in which we ought to expect the benefits of the gospel. How accurate was Mr. Wesley in shewing that the first step to be a christian, is to repent ; that till the conscience be awakened to a sense of the evil of sin, a man cannot enter into a state of justification : it would totally subvert the design of the gospel, were it possible that an unawakened person could be justified. The very supposition frustrates every intention of the coming of the Son of God ; which was to deliver us from sin, to reconcile us to God, and to prepare us for heaven. He has carefully and properly distinguished these matters in his preaching and writings: how often has he told you that the awakening of conscience is the first step in supernatural religion: and that till a man is convinced of the evil of sin and is determined to depart from it; till he is convinced that there is a beauty in holiness, and something truly desirable in being reconciled to God; he is not prepared to receive Christ. It would be well if all the ministers of the gospel laid this true foundation of christian experience; and did not confound the order in which the blessings of the gospel are given to the soul. It has been a singular blessing to you, and to the Methodists at large, that your ministers have so accurately distinguished these things, and guarded you against error in a matter that so nearly concerns your peace and your progress in the divine life. You have by these distinctions been enabled to judge with more certainty of your state of mind, and to what degree of experience you have already attained in the things of God: you have been enabled to see more distinctly and clearly the benefits of the gospel which are still before you, and have been animated in the pursuit of them, by an assurance of success, if you persevere in the way which God has appointed.

In marking so distinctly the order in which we experience the benefits of the gospel, Mr. Wesley has followed the example of our Lord and his Apostles. Our Lord began his preaching, by saying, *Repent, for the kingdom of heaven is at hand.* Peter, preaching to the Jews at Jerusalem, says, *Repent ye, and be converted.* Paul has made this distinction in the most pointed manner: " I kept back nothing," says he, " that was profitable unto you, but have shewed you, and have taught you, publickly and from house to house; testifying both to the Jews and also to the Greeks, *repentance toward God, and faith toward our Lord Jesus*

Christ." He has not followed the scripture only in observing this order, but also reason and the natural order of things. Does not the natural order of things require, that a man be first convinced of his faults, before he can be reclaimed from them ? Must not a man be conscious of his condemnation before he will apply to God for pardon ? Our progress in Christian experience bears a striking analogy to our progress in any art or science. A man must first be instructed in the fundamental principles of an art or science, before he can proceed to the higher branches of it. The first step prepares him for the second, and so on through the whole of his progress. The same order is observable in christian experience. The first step in it prepares the mind for the second ; and so on till we come to the measure of the stature of the fulness of Christ.

The second important and necessary step in christian experience, is, faith in the Lord Jesus Christ arising from a scriptural view of his priestly office. When the mind is duly prepared to receive Christ in this character, pardon is held forth in the gospel as a free gift, without money and without price ; Christ is here proposed to us as the atonement for our sins. How often has he set him forth as crucified before your eyes ? He has exhibited him to your view in his priestly character as the atonement for the sins of the world. He has often shewn you that the atonement which he has made is complete ; that the most vile helpless sinner who repents and turns from his sins, may come and freely receive pardon as the gift of God in and through Christ, and have free admittance to this throne of grace. How gloriously has he often explained this truth, and with what good effect to many of you ! You have been blessed and strengthened under his word, God has born witness to the truth of it, and sealed its evidence upon your hearts.

In explaining sanctification he has accurately distinguished it from justification, or the pardon of sin. Justification admits us into a state of grace and favour with God, into the family of heaven; into a state of fellowship with the Father and with his Son Jesus Christ, and lays the foundation of sanctification or christian holiness in all its extent. He has shewn you that the tendency and end of your justification, is holiness of heart and holiness in all manner of conversation: that being justified by faith your relation to God is altered; your sins are forgiven; you are now become children of God and heirs of all the promises of the gospel, and are quickened and animated with the spirit of it. In this stage of christian experience, faith realizes the truths of the gospel to the mind; it becomes a practical principle of sufficient strength not only to restrain the passions, but to purify the heart, to influence every faculty of the soul, and every action in life, and to transform the man as a moral agent into the image of God. What a glorious view of the gospel has he afforded you; and how often has he instructed you that Christ, as the living head of his church, and acting upon it, in and by the means of every part of the gospel, is sufficient to accomplish the end of his coming; to change the heart, write his laws upon our mind, and make us like himself! He has urged these views of the gospel upon you again and again, and roused you to an ardent pursuit of universal holiness and purity. But a great clamour has been raised against him on this subject, because he called his view of sanctification by the word perfection; many even of the professors of religion have thought him very absurd in this matter: he has often explained to you what he meant by that term; and, that he did not mean to differ with any one about a word, though it be Scriptural. That he meant by the word perfection such a degree of the love of God and the love of man ; such a degree of the love of justice, truth, holiness and purity as will remove from the heart every contrary disposition towards God or man: and that this should be our state of mind in every situation, and in every circumstance of life. Oh! what a paradise would this earth be, were all christians sanctified in this degree! Can there be a more amiable picture of the gospel than this? Is it irrational to tell us that God sent his Son into the world to make us new creatures? To give us true views of God and of ourselves : of his love, mercy, truth and goodness : of his providential care, and his all-sufficiency to bless us with every blessing in heavenly things in Christ Jesus; to give us true views of life, death, and eternity, and hereby to arm us with divine strength to resist and overcome the world, the flesh and the devil ; and to give us those dispositions of mind which prepare us to worship, love, reverence and serve God, and to be just, true, and helpful to one another in this wilderness, as a preparation for the enjoyment of God, and the society of heaven? And is this, to talk irrationally? as an enthusiast? as one, who is doing an injury to the world? How rashly do men judge and speak when their passions are inflamed ! but candour must acknowledge that in this he excelled, and that though his doctrine is contrary to the lives of the professors of religion in general, it is agreeable to the oracles of God.

There is another point relative to his religious opinions, that has been strangely misunderstood, and a great outcry raised against it ; not indeed by the bulk of religious people, but by men of abilities, and of learning, who make pretensions to reason and calm discussion : that all the blessings of the gospel are to be obtained by faith. He has told us expressly, that we are saved by faith : he has told us also, what he means by salvation ; the being put in possession of the blessings of the gospel; the being justified by the grace of God through the redemption that is in Christ; the being sanctified, or made holy in heart, and holy in all manner of conversation; he has taught you that all these things are to be obtained by faith: and you can hardly open your Testament in any part but you will find this doctrine taught: you can hardly read a chapter in St. Paul's Epistles but you find it inculcated again and again. It will bear the test of reason also, and will be found upon the strictest inquiry, to be agreeable to our state and condition in this life. Is it unreasonable, that we should believe in God? that we should believe in him who made us, who upholds us, and who governs all things; in him, who conducts the whole machine of nature in all its vast extent, and in all its complicated operations; who comprehends every thing as it were in one grasp; in whom all things live, and move, and have their being? Is it unreasonable that a poor mortal that knows not what is just coming upon him, not even what shall happen to him the next moment, should trust in God? That he should confide in the goodness and providence of him, who sees all things at one view, past, present, and to come; and who sees man at one glance, in every period of his existence, with every surrounding circumstance? Is not this agreeable to the nature of God, and the state of man?

The gospel promiseth to us a state of intercourse and fellowship with God, in the present enjoyment of spiritual blessings in Jesus Christ. Faith is made a necessary condition of entering into this state of intercourse and enjoyment. In this, God has dealt with us in a way suitable to our faculties, and our state of intercourse with one another. For you have no kind of connection with each other, without faith; all must acknowledge that faith is the bond of human society. Can you transact any kind of business without it? You can have no enjoyment of the things of this life without an act of faith preceding it. All your expectations and future prospects in life are founded on faith. You will find, upon examination, that in every branch of business, in every social intercourse, you must first believe, and then you will obtain the thing you expected, provided your faith be rightly placed. You cannot engage a servant, without faith in him. A merchant cannot transact business with any one, without first having faith in the person with whom he transacts that business. When the husbandman ploughs his land and sows his seed, faith is the principle from which he acts. Unless then we act from faith, we can have no fellowship with one another, nor enjoy the comforts of life. And, if the mind be sufficiently furnished with knowledge and prudence, our success will be in proportion to the degree of faith, and the exertions that are made in consequence of it. This great man then, has shewn himself well acquainted both with scripture and human nature, in explaining this important article of christian experience.

How does faith operate on the mind in Christian experience? In repentance, the first step towards the christian life is, a man must believe that there is a God, who is holy, just, and good: he must believe the word of God; that there is a judgment to come, when every thought and action will be examined, and when the wicked will be condemned to punishment, and the righteous will inherit eternal life. He must believe also that God is merciful, that pardon may be obtained through Jesus Christ: for a view of the holiness of God and of his own sinfulness, would, without this, produce despair, which is not gospel repentance. When, by the grace of God, these things are impressed upon the mind of a man, with full conviction of their truth, they awaken the conscience, and excite him to attention and self-examination, and gradually prepare him to receive Christ in his mediatorial character. With respect to pardon, when the mind is rightly prepared for it, the gospel has made faith the express condition of it. How ably has our aged minister established this truth, and defended it against all opposition. Pardon of sins is obtained for us by the blood of Christ, it is promised to us by the word of God; but must be received by faith; we must believe in the word of promise, in order to receive it. And he that believeth is justified: he is justified now, the moment he receives Christ as his mediator, as his saviour, as his atonement. His faith is counted to him for righteousness; it gives him a title to the promise of pardon, and to the blessings connected with it.

If we examine how faith purifies the heart, we shall find nothing irrational in the doctrine. There is nothing better adapted to remove every evil from the human heart than faith in Christ; there is nothing more efficacious, to preserve us from evil through life, than faith rightly explained and rightly exercised; faith as it unites us to Christ our living head, gives us a principle of divine life; we begin to live unto God, from a principle of love in the heart; to live a life that is given by him who is the resurrection and the life, and who raiseth the soul to an union with God. When this has taken place, old things are done away, all things are become new; the views, the purposes and the affections of the man are changed: he no longer acts from the same motives, nor by the same rule as before; a new principle of action is formed in the heart, which directly leads to holiness and to God.

Faith, as a practical principle, is called by Paul, *the substance of things hoped for, and the evidence of things not seen.* It gives the things hoped for a present subsistence in the mind, in that degree which is suited to our present state. It is the evidence of things not seen; it realizes the truths of the gospel to the mind, and enables it to view them with as much certainty as we have of the existence of corporeal objects, when we feel their influence on our senses. A man who acts under the influence of this faith, who has gospel truths full in his view, with all the certainty that his senses can give him of the existence of external objects, will undoubtedly find his heart powerfully affected by them. This faith will work by love, it will purify the heart from every thing contrary to the mind that was in Christ. It will enable him to acknowledge God in all his ways, to set him continually before his eyes, to live as in his presence, with a view to his glory, and resigned to his will. Let us instance in one thing only at present. Suppose a man believe that there is a Providence which superintends human affairs: if he be assured that divine love can intend nothing but good in every thing that happens to him, and that Infinite Wisdom cannot err in adapting the means to the end intended: if he be as fully assured of these truths as he is of the existence of the things which he sees or hears; will not this faith lead him to a reverential fear of God, and to a perfect resignation to his will in every occurrence of life? It will make him cautious in his conduct, and attentive to every part of his duty. He will be anxiously careful for nothing, but living under a deep sense of the Divine Presence and care, his mind will be kept in perfect peace, because it is stayed upon God. In this, then, our Father in Christ spoke agreeably to scripture and to reason.

Let us now notice his notions of the universality of the gospel blessings. Here he shone with peculiar lustre; here he did honour to God and to the Divine attributes; he maintained that God is a God of love, not to a part of his creatures only, but to all; that he who is the Father of all, who made all, who stands in the same relation to all his creatures; loves them all: that he loved the world and gave his son a ransom for all without distinction of persons; that there is no respect of persons with God. This is an amiable character of the Deity. It always appeared to him, that to represent God as partial, as confining his love to a few, was unworthy our notions of the Deity. He therefore explained the gospel in the most glorious and extensive point of view. He maintained that Christ died for all men, that he is to be offered to all; all are to be invited to come to him; and whosoever comes in the way which God has appointed may partake of his blessings. He maintained, that sufficient grace is given to all, in that way and manner which is best adapted to influence the mind. And may we not appeal to every man's experience for the truth of this? How often has he appealed to the consciences of men? Have not your hearts reproved you? Have you not at times trembled for your sins? Have you not been ashamed of yourselves, have you not detested your own conduct in secret, when none has seen you but God, and none has been privy to your actions but your own heart? Whence does this arise? Certainly not from man but from God. It is an evidence that there is salvation for thee, O man, who art in this state; God is not willing that thou shouldst perish; he is calling thee, inviting thee, to turn from thy sins, and to turn to God. He has thus stated the truths of the gospel with convincing evidence. The expressions of scripture are positive in favour of this doctrine: there are passages which so positively declare it, that it is impossible to give any other construction to them without the greatest violence; but there is not a single passage in the New Testament, which seems to favour the doctrine that Christ died for a part of mankind only, which will not easily admit of a different construction.

He raised some enemies by this doctrine. He has been called an Arminian; and perhaps many who have used the term have annexed an idea to it by no means just. How often has he wished, and it is devoutly to be wished by all the friends of true religion, that the names of Calvinist and Arminian were buried in oblivion; they have tended to keep up strife and discord only, amongst those who ought to love one another as brethren, however they have differed on some points of doctrine. But some have supposed that to be an Arminian is to maintain salvation by works; that it is to degrade Christ: and to throw the lustre of redemption by Christ into a cloud at any rate, if not to overturn it. Was this the case with our minister of the gospel? Did he not preach free grace as much as any Calvinist? Did he not assert that pardon is the free gift of God, without money and without price? Did he not assert that repentance itself only prepares the heart to receive the gift of God, that it does not give any kind of merit to the man? How often has he declared to you that the best works any man can perform need atonement? So far was he from putting works in the place of the blood of Christ, that he gave them their just value only; he placed them in the order of christian experience where the gospel places them; as the fruits of a living operative faith, and as the measure of our future reward; for every man will be rewarded, not for his works, but according to the measure of them. This is undoubtedly a scriptural representation of this matter, and it would be well if all christians were to attend to this distinction more than they do. It is to be feared that some may have cried out against works, not from the very best motives, at least from some inclination to relax in holiness. The way in which some have preached faith, has done no honour to the gospel; and may probably have encouraged some persons to pay less attention to christian duties than they ought to do. But while he insisted on good works, as the necessary fruits of faith, he gave the whole glory of salvation to God, from first to last; not in the general plan of it only, but in the order of communicating the benefits of Christ to the mind. He believed that man would never turn to God, if God did not begin the work: nay, how often has he told you, that the first approaches of grace to the mind are irresistible; that a man cannot avoid being convinced that he is a sinner; that God by various means awakens his conscience; and whether the man will or no, these convictions approach him. He gave all the glory of the work of salvation in the heart to the grace of God, he ascribes no merit to works; he tells you indeed that in proportion as you improve the grace given, you shall have more, and be rewarded according to your works, with grace here as well as glory hereafter.

There is one subject more, which I must touch upon, christian experience. It is well known that this able minister of the gospel, together with his brother Charles, and the Rev. Mr. Whitefield, have been the principal instruments in the hands of God, of diffusing the knowledge of this important article of the christian religion, amongst the bulk of the people of this country. And in this respect only, they have been a blessing to every class and order of men. For though all have not believed their report, yet many have believed it in every station of life, and born a happy testimony to the truth of it. How ably has our beloved Father illustrated and defended this part of christianity? Many indeed have supposed that what we call experience is mere imagination: that it is nothing more than the working up of our own minds into a fancy of something which can have no foundation in truth or reason. But christian experience is something real and not imaginary; it rests upon as solid a foundation as the evidence of our external senses. We have no more reason to doubt the reality of our experience, when it is scriptural, than we have to doubt of the existence, of an object which we see with our eyes, or of a sound which we hear, when these organs are in the most sound and healthy state. But what is christian experience, and what degree of certainty is there in it?

Christian experience is the present possession of the benefits of the Gospel which relate to this life, and which prepare us for the enjoyment of God in glory. If we use the word in the most extensive sense, so as to include the preparation of the mind to receive Christ in his mediatorial character, it will imply repentance toward God, faith in the Lord Jesus Christ, and the fruits of the Spirit, so admirably described by Paul; love, joy, peace, long-suffering, gentleness, goodness, fidelity, meekness and temperance, with all the privileges of the Christian state here. In the gospel we are commanded to repent and return to God; to believe in the Lord Jesus Christ, and to be filled with the fruits of the Spirit. The Gospel promises every necessary aid and assistance to put us in possession of these benefits; and we read also in the New Testament of many persons who professed to have experience of these things. If indeed the Gospel be a fable, then the things of which it speaks and the promises which it makes, signify nothing real, they are purely imaginary, and to profess any experience of them must be delusion. But, as we have the most certain evidence that the Gospel is of God: that it gives a true account of what God has done and is now doing for the salvation of men, and of the means by which he is accomplishing this great purpose, the promises it gives us must signify something real, and they must be as certain as the existence and truth of God himself. It is evident then, that we may experience the blessings which it promises to us, if we seek them in the way which God hath appointed.

If we inquire into the evidence which a man has that he does experience the things which we here speak of, we shall find that it is of the strongest kind possible. If a man's understanding be enlightened with Gospel truths; if his conscience be awakened to decide justly on his motives and actions, as they are related to God and his law ; if in consequence of this, he turns from his sins, and is humbled, abased and ashamed before God for them, and prays for mercy : how is it possible for such a change as this is to take place in the dictates of his conscience and in the opinion he has had of himself, and he not know it? The very supposition is absurd; he must be as conscious of it as he is of his own existence, or of any thing that happens to him. In like manner, when a person in the state I have now described, is enabled to believe in Jesus Christ to the saving of his soul; to rely fully upon him for pardon and acceptance with God ; must not such a person be conscious of this act of his mind, and of the change in his views of God, and in the feelings of his mind that are subsequent to it? Will he not be as conscious and certain of these things as he is when he sees an object before him, or feels pleasure or pain ? If he that believeth be filled with love, joy, peace, and the other fruits of the Spirit just mentioned, must he not be certain of this ? Our internal consciousness carries the same conviction of reality with it, as our external senses. Would it not appear exceedingly absurd to you, if you heard a person say in the common affairs of life, that he loved an object dearly, but that he was not conscious of any love ; that he rejoiced exceedingly in a thing, but that he did not feel any joy ? It is just the same in christian experience. If from proper views of the Gospel and faith in Christ, I feel peace, I cannot be ignorant of it ; if I look up to God through Jesus Christ with holy confidence, and feel pleasure and delight, I must be conscious and certain of it.

Christian experience then, has certainty in it; if a man has it he cannot be ignorant of it. How is it possible for any man who has not felt the peace of God to form a just notion of it? Its evidence stands on the same ground as the evidence of our external senses. For if a man had never seen colours, he could not form any true idea of them; if a man had never felt pain or pleasure, he could not be taught to understand what they are: however perfect his rational faculties might be, he must feel them to know them. So it is with Christian experience, you must enter into it and feel it, and then you will know what it is; and will as easily distinguish it from the feelings or consciousness arising from other things, as you distinguish seeing from hearing, or the touch from the smell.

III. Having considered the character of the Rev. Mr. Wesley as a man of learning, and well qualified to examine a subject and to discover the truth; and having taken a view of his principal and leading opinions in religion: my intention is, very briefly to consider his labours as a minister of the Gospel, and the effects of them.

Mr. Wesley was a man of industry from his youth, and employed his time to the greatest advantage in pursuit of literary knowledge. After he was convinced of the pure doctrines of the Gospel, he was assiduous in declaring them to others. How few possess the necessary qualifications for useful studies and for active life! These were united in him in a very high degree. His leading doctrines discover a diligent and patient examination of the scriptures, great strength of judgment, and closeness of reasoning: and he was not less remarkable for his zeal, activity and steadiness in propagating them among the people, for which many thousands have had reason to thank God in their dying moments. At first he preached in the churches wherever an opportunity offered; but his doctrines giving offence to some, and the crouds that attended him raising envy in others, the churches were by degrees shut against him. If we consider his firm attachment to the church of England, and his fondness for regularity and order in church government, it will appear surprising that this circumstance did not damp his zeal, and shake the firmness of his mind. It is happy that it did not. Being convinced of the importance of the doctrines of the Gospel to the people at large, and that it was his duty to preach the glad tidings of peace and salvation to all; knowing also that God loves mercy rather than sacrifice, he thought it would be criminal in him to sacrifice his views of the gospel, and his opportunities of doing good, to the prejudices of others. He therefore went out into the highways and hedges, to invite sinners to repentance and to make them partakers of gospel blessings. He must have foreseen, that in taking this step mankind would put different constructions on his conduct; and, that, to attempt a thing so new in the world would raise many enemies against him, and expose him to many difficulties. Whatever prospect his former situation had offered him, of ease, honour or wealth, these he left behind him; and nothing could at this time present itself to his view, but labour and weariness, accompanied with reproach, persecution and contempt from men. Is it possible to suppose for a moment, that a man of calm reflection as Mr. Wesley was, who never took any step of importance without mature deliberation, would have acted as he did at this time, without a full conviction that he was doing his duty? That the doctrines which he taught were the truths of the gospel, and of the utmost importance to the happiness of men? He must have had more than a bare conviction of these truths; he must have been animated with an ardent desire to glorify God in the propagation of his truth, and to be instrumental of good to his fellow creatures.

The regularity and steadiness with which Mr. Wesley pursued his labours, and the extent to which he carried them, are almost beyond conception, and sufficient to awaken astonishment in the mind of any man who reflects upon them. When he first went out to preach in the different parts of the kingdom, and to carry the light of the gospel to those who sat in darkness and in the shadow of death, he was surrounded with difficulties on every side. In many places he had scarcely food to eat, or a place in which to lie down. In some places, he was considered as an enemy to his country; in others, that he had private and interested views in what he did; for few could at first imagine that any man would undergo the labour and fatigue which he underwent, purely for the good of others. But none of these things ever moved him; he still continued to travel from place to place to do good to those who reviled and persecuted him. He laboured day and night for the good of the people. This he did through persecution, reproach, and every difficulty that lay in his way: nothing turned him aside from the grand object of his preaching the gospel to the poor. Here we cannot but admire the strength and firmness of his resolution, and his love of God and man, which enabled him to persevere in this arduous and difficult undertaking. O what a glorious influence would the gospel soon acquire over the minds of men, if those who are true ministers of it, had the bold, the firm, the intrepid spirit which Mr. Wesley has shewn: Did they, like him give up their ease, their pleasure, and every thing which is counted dear in this world, to do good unto men, to glorify God, and to bring men to the obedience of Christ! There are many ministers of the gospel who wish well to experimental religion, and many who truly preach

P p

it, but their preaching is limited to a few persons comparatively speaking: his mind expanded to larger views of public good: his arms would have embraced, if possible, all mankind, and as far as his strength would carry him, he spread the knowledge of gospel truth into every part of these kingdoms.

But Mr. Wesley was not proof against labour, persecution and reproach only; but against the softer and finer feelings of human nature also, when they stood in the way of the great work in which he was engaged: those feelings which are apt to effeminate the mind, or to warp a man from a uniform and steady attention to his duty. He had a peculiar pleasure in reading and study; and every literary man knows the force of this passion, and how apt it is to make him encroach on the time which ought to be employed in other duties. But Mr. Wesley had the resolution to lay aside any subject, whenever the hour came that he was to set out on his journey, or was to preach, or visit the sick. He had a high relish for rational and polite conversation; but whatever company might happen to come where he was, to converse with him during supper, he would constantly retire to rest at his usual hour, that he might rise at four o'clock in the morning, which was his constant practice winter and summer for more than sixty years together. He was far from being insensible to the feelings of friendship; but whenever any friendship he had formed, interfered with the good of the work he was called to, he could immediately break it off. The work to which God had called him occupied all his time and attention: he considered it as the business of his life, and sacrificed every pleasure and gratification to it. How much do all of you owe him, who has sacrificed every thing dear to flesh and blood for so many years together to benefit you. It appears astonishing, to see a man pursuing the publick good with so much ardour and steadiness for so long a time, denying himself every gratification and pleasure, except that of doing good. This was his general character for the number of years during which he was engaged in this work.

The industry of Mr. Wesley was almost incredible. From four o'clock in the morning till eight at night his time was employed in reading, writing, preaching, meeting the people, visiting the sick or travelling. Before the infirmities of age came upon him, he usually travelled on horse-back, and would sometimes ride thirty, forty, or fifty miles in a day, and preach two, three, or sometimes four times. He had a constant correspondence with some persons in the different societies all over the three kingdoms, and with the preachers in every part, and would answer his letters with great punctuality. He knew the state of the societies in general, and of many individuals in each of them. He read most publications that were deemed valuable, if they related to religion or natural philosophy, and often made extracts from them. If we consider the whole of his labours, and compare them with what most men of industry have done, we may say that he has lived two or three lives.

The effects of Mr. Wesley's labours have been much more extensive than any person would at first imagine. He was at the head of the little company first formed at Oxford. And if we consider the state of these kingdoms when the two Mr. Wesleys and Mr. Whitefield first went out to preach publickly, we must acknowledge that experimental religion was almost lost, at least among the common people. Without being censorious, religion was little more than loose opinions, and modes and forms of worship among the people in general. The preaching of these three men of God has had a very extensive influence on all denominations of religious people ; it has been the means of awakening their attention to the grand and leading principles of the gospel: and of making them consider the experimental part of it. Their labours also have had a happy influence on the ministers of the gospel of every denomination, although some may have been ashamed to own it. With respect to the whole body of the people commonly called Methodists, they have been the means of raising them up. What were you, before you heard these three servants of God, and those associated with them, declare the glad tidings of peace and salvation: but you that were not a people, are now become the people of God, by their instrumentality. And what shall I say to you my brethren, who have been more immediately connected with him who is now no more with us? You have been knit together by him in the bonds of christian fellowship: you have been growing up under his paternal care for many years. He has nourished and cherished you as a tender father: he has watched over you with anxious care, as a faithful shepherd over his flock. Consider the effects of his labours on different bodies of people who have no immediate connection with us; the numerous societies spread over the three kingdoms in connection with him, and over whom he exercised the care of a father; extend your views to America, and consider the thousands and ten thousands, who have felt the influence of his labours in the course of sixty years; and it seems an extent of usefulness beyond that of which we could imagine any one man capable. But the hand of God has been in it; the Providence of God has been over it: and it is evident that he was raised up of God for this great work.

The effects of Mr. Wesley's labours on civil society have been, and still will be, very considerable. Not particular parts only of the kingdom have received benefit from the preaching of the Methodists, but society in general must feel some beneficial influence from it. If you consider the whole body of people usually called Methodists, and the immense numbers who attend their places of worship and are benefited by them, they will amount to several hundred thousands. These are dispersed through the three kingdoms, and occupy almost every situation in life: they are become more conscientious in all their ways; more sober and regular in their behaviour; more true to their word, and more attentive to every social duty than they were before. They are better husbands and wives, better masters and servants, and better neighbours and friends, than before they heard the preaching of the Methodists. Society in general therefore has received benefit from them.

There is another view in which we may consider his usefulness; a view which I should not have noticed but for the sake of a pamphlet just now published; in which it is observed, that the Methodists are become so large a body of people, that they ought to attract the notice of government. The Rev. Mr. Wesley was a warm and steady friend to the government; you know that he enforced these principles as far as he could, on the minds of all that heard him. The Methodists then, are not only made better citizens, but also better subjects. It is a rule in the society, that all the members of it shall submit themselves to the laws. If it be known that any one acts contrary to this rule, he is put away from the society. Now if you consider a large body of people, increasing on every side, spreading themselves through the whole kingdom, who are friends to the government, friends in every point of view, and from principle; you will acknowledge, that whatever influence these people may have upon government, it must be friendly and have a tendency to peace and good order. And if all the people were Methodists, no times of difficulty could come; but if such times should arrive, the more numerous this body of people is, the better it will be for the country.

Thus our dear and aged father in Christ spent nearly sixty years in the labour and work of the Lord, going about from place to place, convincing gainsayers, comforting mourners, building up and strengthening those that believed : and the church of God increased daily under his paternal care. Thus he spent his life: and his labours lasted very near to the close of it. Oh how happy a life to be spent in doing good ; to have no attachment but to God and his work ; to forsake all for it ! And his conduct in private life was conformable to his publick character. How many persons have been ready to say, that Mr. Wesley had private ends in view : that he was accumulating money and would die rich. All that knew him, knew how false these assertions were; but all did not know him ; thousands however did, who have been witnesses of his integrity and disinterestedness : and thousands of poor have experienced his benevolence. He constantly made a rule of giving all that he had to the poor: this was a favourite practice with him. He attended to the words of Christ ; *For as much as ye have done it unto these, ye have done it unto me.* He considered the poor as left upon earth, that the followers of Christ might shew their benevolence to them as they would to the person of Christ himself, were he upon earth. How many have said, how gladly would I have entertained Christ, had I lived in that country where he appeared, and at the time of his appearance. But he has left the poor behind him, that you may exercise your benevolence towards them, as you would have done to him. Mr. Wesley took a pleasure and delight in doing this, and sometimes left himself so destitute, that he had hardly sufficient to defray his travelling expences.

I was asked the other day, whether Mr. Wesley had not many meeting-houses and chapels that were his property, and whether he did not die rich? I answered, Sir, Mr. Wesley had not one house of his own in the three kingdoms, neither a private house nor a preaching house; therefore he did not die rich. What money he had, which was the produce of his books, and what charitable persons gave him to distribute to the poor, he constantly gave away: and he observes, it only went through his hands, but none of it remained with him.

We must naturally suppose that a person so devoted to the work and service of God, and for so long a time, must be an object of divine approbation; and God shewed marks of it to him even in his last moments; which was a great comfort both to him and to his numerous friends.

IV. I was called to Mr. Wesley on Friday the 25th of February. When I entered the room he cheerfully said, " Doctor, they are more afraid than hurt." I found great oppression on the brain, a universal tremor, great debility of the whole nervous system, and a fever, which I considered as symptomatic, depending wholly on the state of debility. I wrote for him; but he neither took medicine nor nourishment in a quantity sufficient to be of any use. Friday night and Saturday forenoon, the lethargic symptoms increased. It now appeared to me that the powers of nature were exhausted; and I was so certain of his approaching dissolution, that I desired Mr. Bradford to ask him if he had any affairs which he wished to settle; or if there were any person either in London or in the country, whom he desired to see. To these questions he gave no answer. We were all extremely anxious that the lethargy might be removed before his departure hence; and on Saturday evening the means made use of were successful the lethargic symptoms abated, and on Sunday morning he seemed quite in possession of his faculties, and to feel his situation. His debility however increased, and the fever continued with alternate changes of flushings and paleness. On Monday the 28th, I desired he might be asked if he would have any other physician called in to attend him: but this he absolutely refused. On Tuesday it appeared to me that death was approaching, and in the evening it was very evident. I was with him till past twelve o'clock that night. I asked him, before I left the room, if he knew me: he answered yes, and pressed my hand with all the little strength he had. From this time he gradually sunk, and about twenty minutes before ten on Wednesday morning, the 2d of March, he died without a struggle, or groan, and went to receive the glorious reward of his labours.

From these outlines of the illustrious character of Mr. Wesley, it appears that he did not follow cunningly devised fables, but the evidence of gospel truth. And the candid will perceive, that we have not adopted these opinions merely because Mr. Wesley taught them, but because they appear to us to be true. Let us then, my brethren, hold fast the beginning of our confidence stedfast to the end; and prove to the world that our doctrines are true, not by reason and argument only, but by our tempers and conduct. Let us be careful to act worthy of our holy vocation, and to persevere to the end in well doing, we shall then receive with him who is now gone before us, the promised reward: Which may God of his infinite mercy grant, through Jesus Christ our Lord. Amen.

A COMPREHENSIVE HISTORY

OF

AMERICAN METHODISM.

NO part of the Ecclesiastical History of the New World is more interesting than that which details the rise, progress, and present state of the Methodist Episcopal Church. From a grain of mustard seed, it is become in a few years a large spreading tree!

Although Mr. Whitefield extended his labours through almost all the Atlantic States, it does not appear that he introduced the Methodist economy among his disciples. Great success attended him, and multitudes were converted to God by the energy of his ministrations.—The fruit which was produced by his efforts was scattered from New-England to Georgia; the people were without a leader, and lived according to no certain discipline; hence by death, and through the influence of a worldly spirit, the number of his friends daily diminished, and many of the survivors exhibited nothing of the power of vital godliness.—From the year 1760, a few persons belonging to the Methodist societies in England and Ireland, annually emigrated to this country. Their distance from their native land, their harmony in religious opinions, and the influence of Christian love united them together in very affectionate bonds. So few however were their numbers, and so depressed their situation, that they never assembled for publick worship as a distinct body. But

Q q

the Providence of God had determined that beginning, from this little company, the truths of the glorious Gospel should be disseminated through every civilized part of this Continent.—In the latter part of the year 1766, Mr Philip Embury, from Ireland, began to publish " salvation by Christ," in his own house in New-York, until the increased number of his hearers forced him to procure a larger room; and those who had formerly belonged to the society in Europe united themselves together upon the same plan. Early in the spring of 1767 captain Webb visited New-York, and his appearance and manners attracted a large congregation; which induced them to remove to a more convenient house for divine worship.—The little society continued to augment their numbers, upon which Mr. Embury formed two classes according to the discipline established by Mr. Wesley.

At this period Mr. Strawbridge, a local preacher from Ireland, settled in Frederick county, Maryland, and formed several societies. It has long been a question with the curious who are anxious to know every circumstance which is connected with the commencement of Methodism in the United States; whether the first society was established, and whether the first house of worship was erected in Maryland or in New-York; whether the old log house in which Mr. Strawbridge preached on Pipe Creek, was not antecedent to the building which was used by captain Webb and Mr. Embury? After the most accurate research, the information which I have procured induces me to believe, that a Methodist society was formed at New-York at least nine or twelve months previous to the first which was collected by Mr. Strawbridge; and there can be no doubt, that the room, and even the rigging house were devoted to the publick worship of God in New-York, prior to the use of the log house on Pipe Creek.

The following letters will afford additional intelligence upon the subject, as it relates to New-York; and are doubly valuable as exhibiting a view of its religious situation, and of that of Charleston. The former was addressed to Mr. Wesley, and was discovered among Mr. Hopper's papers; the latter was communicated by Mr. Cussons who received it: they corroborate this narrative, and more minutely describe the circumstances which occurred in the erection of the first chapel in Mr. Wesley's connection in America.

NEW-YORK, 11th April 1768.

" Rev. and very dear Sir,

I intended writing to you for several weeks past; but a few of us had a very material transaction in view: the purchasing of ground for building a preaching-house upon, which by the blessing of God we have now concluded; but before I proceed, I shall give you a short account of the state of religion in this city. By the best intelligence I can collect there was little either of the form or power of it till Mr. WHITEFIELD came over thirty years ago; and even after his first and second visit there appeared but little fruit of his labours. But during his visit fourteen or fifteen years ago, there was a considerable shaking among the dry bones. Divers were savingly converted, and this work was much increased in his last journey, when his words were really as a hammer and as a fire. Most part of the adults were stirred up: great numbers were pricked to the heart and by the judgment of charity several found peace and joy in believing. The consequence of this work was, the churches were crouded, and subscriptions raised for building new ones. Mr. Whitefield's example provoked most of the ministers to a much greater degree of earnestness. And by the multitudes of people, young and old, rich and poor, flocking to the churches, religion became an honourable profession;

there was no outward cross to be taken up therein. Nay, a person who could not speak about the grace of God and the new birth was esteemed unfit for company. But in a while, instead of pressing forward and growing in grace, the generality were pleading for the remains of sin and the necessity of being in darkness. They esteemed their opinions as the very essentials of christianity, and regarded not holiness either of heart or of life.

The above appears to me to be a genuine account of the state of religion in New-York eighteen months ago, when it pleased God to raise up Mr. Embury to employ his talent, which for several years had been hid in a napkin, in calling sinners to repentance, and in exhorting believers to let their light shine before men. He spoke at first in his own house only. A few soon collected together, and joined in a little society; chiefly his own countrymen, Irish. In about three months after, Brothers White and Sause from Dublin joined them. They then rented an empty room in the neighbourhood, which was in the most infamous street in the city, adjoining the barracks: for some time few thought it worth while to hear: but God so ordered it by his Providence, that about fourteen months ago, captain Webb, barrack master at Albany, who was converted about three years ago at Bristol, found them out and preached in his regimentals. The novelty of a man preaching in a scarlet coat, soon brought greater numbers to hear than the room could contain. But his doctrines were quite new to the hearers; for he told them plainly, " that all their knowledge and profession of religion was not worth a rush, unless their sins were forgiven, and unless they had the witness of God's spirit with theirs, that they were the children of God." This doctrine, with some peculiarities in his person, caused him soon to be noticed; and obliged the little society to look out for a larger house to preach in. They found a place that had been built for a rigging house, sixty feet in length, and eighteen feet in breadth.

About this period, Mr. Webb took a house near Jamaica on Long-Island, and began to preach in his own dwelling, and in several other places on the Island: within six months about twenty-four persons received justifying grace; nearly half of them were whites, the rest were negros. While Mr. Webb, to borrow his own phrase, was "felling the trees on Long-Island," brother Embury was exhorting all who attended on Thursday evenings, and Sunday morning and evenings, at the rigging house, to flee from the wrath to come. His hearers began to increase, and some gave heed to his report, about the time the gracious providence of God brought me safe to New-York, after a very favourable passage of six weeks from Plymouth. It was the 26th day of October last when I arrived, recommended to a person for a lodging. I inquired of my host, who was a very religious man, if any Methodists were in New-York; he informed me that there was one captain Webb, a strange sort of a man, who lived on Long-Island, and who sometimes preached at one Embury's at the rigging house. In a few days I found out Embury. I soon discovered what spirit he was of, and that he was personally acquainted with you, and your doctrines, having been a helper in Ireland. He had formed two classes, one of the men and another of the women, but had never met the society apart from the congregation, although there were six or seven men, and about the same number of women who had a clear sense of their acceptance in the beloved.

You will not wonder at my being agreeably surprized to meet with a few here who have been, and desire again to be in connection with you.

Mr. Embury has lately been more zealous than formerly; the consequence of which is, that he is more lively in his preaching; and his gifts as well as his graces are much increased. Great numbers of serious people came to hear God's word as for their lives. And their numbers increased so fast, that our house for these six weeks past would not contain the half of the people.

We have had some consultations how to remedy this inconvenience, and Mr. Embury proposed to rent a lot of ground for twenty-one years, and to exert our utmost endeavours to collect as much money as would build a wooden tabernacle. A piece of ground was proposed: the ground rent was agreed for, and the house was to be erected in a few days. We however, in the mean time, had two several days for fasting and prayer, for the direction of God, and for his blessing upon our proceedings: and Providence opened such a door as we had no expectation of. A young man, a sincere Christian, and constant hearer, though not joined in society, would not give any thing towards this house, but offered ten pounds to buy a lot of ground, and went of his own accord to a lady who had two lots to sell, on one of which there is a house that rents for eighteen pounds per annum. He found the purchase money of the two lots was six hundred pounds, which she was willing should remain in the purchaser's hands on good security. We called once more upon God for his direction and resolved to purchase the whole. There are eight of us, who are joint purchasers; among whom Mr. Webb and Mr. Lupton are men of property. I was determined the house should be upon the same footing as the Orphan House at Newcastle, and others in England; but as we were ignorant how to draw the deeds, we purchased for us and our heirs, until a copy of the writings from England was sent us, which we desire may be sent by the first opportunity.

Before we began to talk of building, the devil and his children were very peaceable: but since this affair took place, many ministers have cursed us in the name of the Lord and laboured with all their might to shut up their congregations from assisting us. But he that sitteth in Heaven laughed them to scorn. Many have broken through and given their friendly assistance. We have collected above one hundred pounds more than our own contributions; and have reason to hope in the whole we shall have two hundred pounds more, so that unless God is pleased to raise up friends we shall yet be at a loss. I believe Mr. Webb and Mr. Lupton will borrow or advance two hundred pounds rather than the building should not go forward. Some of our brethren proposed writing to you for a collection in England: but I was averse to this, as I well knew our friends there are over burdened already. Yet so far I would earnestly beg; if you would intimate our circumsances to particular persons of ability, perhaps God would open their hearts to assist this infant society, and contribute to the first preaching house on the original Methodist plan in all America.

There is another point far more material, and in which I must importune your assistance not in my own name only, but in the name of the whole society. We want an able experienced preacher; one who has both gifts and graces necessary for the work. God has not despised the day of small things. There is a real work in many hearts by the preaching of Mr. Webb and Mr. Embury: but although they are both useful, and their hearts are in the work, they want many qualifications necessary for such an undertaking, where they have none to direct them: and the progress of the gospel here depends much upon the qualifications of the preachers.

I have thought of Mr. Helton; for we must have a man of wisdom, of sound faith and a good disciplinarian; one whose heart and soul are in the work: and I doubt not, by the goodness of God, such a flame would be soon kindled as would never stop, until it reached the South Sea. We may make many shifts to evade temporal inconveniences; but we cannot purchase such a preacher as I have described. I intreat you for the good of thousands, to use your utmost endeavours to send one over. I would advise him to take shipping in July or early in August; by embarking at this season, he will have fine weather, and probably arrive here in September. He will himself see what progress the gospel has made before winter. With respect to the money for the payment of a preacher's passage over, if he could not procure it, we would sell our coats and shirts to pay for it.

I must earnestly beg an interest in your prayers, and trust that you and our brethren will not forget the church in this wilderness. T. T——."

CHARLESTON, May 1, 1769.

"When I came to London, I went on board a vessel bound for New-York, to stay in America. We had Mr. Whitaker, a Presbyterian minister on board who came to England with the Indian preacher: he was a great satisfaction to me, for we had prayers twice a day, while he was on board of the vessel. When I came to New-York I found that our business was not very plentiful for strangers. Though there is a good deal of business in the town, it is entirely overstocked with trades-people; but what added most to my satisfaction was, I found a few of the dear people of God in it. There is Mr. Embury one of our preachers, who came from Ireland nine years ago. Lately, there was two who came from Dublin. They have met together and their number has increased; and they have built a large new house which cost them 600l. sterling. They are very poor in this world. They expect assistance from England; but I often used to tell them they need not; for many of the people of England were very poor themselves; and they, that had of this world's goods, did not care to part with them. There is another of our preachers Mr. Webb, who was a captain in the army: he was convinced of the truth before he left England: God has been pleased to open his mouth. So, the Lord carries on a very great work by these two men. They were, however sore put to it in building their house; they made several collections about the town for it; and they went to Philadelphia, where they procured part of the money. I wrought upon it six days.

New-York is a large town; in it are three places of worship of the church of England, two of the church of Scotland, three of the Dutch church, one Baptist meeting, one Moravian chapel, one Quaker's meeting, one Jews' synagogue, and one French reformed chapel. Amongst all these, there are very few who like the Methodists. The Dutch Calvinist has preached against them. Many of the people of America have been at times stirred up to seek the Lord by Mr. Whitefield, but I do not believe that he ever formed them into classes.

In all the places of America, where I have been, there is as much need of the Methodists preachers, as in any town in England. Mr. Wesley says, the first message of the preachers is, to the lost sheep of the church of England: and are there none in America? They have strayed from England into the wild woods here, and are running wild after this world. They are drinking their wine in bowls; and are jumping and dancing, and serving the devil in the groves and under the green trees. And are not these lost sheep, and will none of the preachers come here? No, they will not come? Well! But I shall never give over crying, "Oh, my Saviour, send some who are not ashamed of thy gospel; that they may go into the highways and hedges, and compel them to come in, that thy house may be filled.

"But my business would not suit me to stay in New-York; and I was obliged to leave these few happy people: I was there but one quarter of a year: so I came to Charleston, South-Carolina. This town stands on a sandy bay, with Ashley river on one side, and Cooper river upon the other, upon low land. There are here, two chapels of the church of England, one of the church of Scotland, one Independent meeting, two Baptist meetings, one Dutch church, and one French reformed chapel; but amongst all these, I cannot find the gospel preached as my conscience dictates to me. O! I often think, if our preachers would only come, what a harvest there might be in this place, and in many other places in America. May the Lord, in his own good time, lay it before them!" T. B.

At the British Conference in 1769, Mr. Boardman and Mr. Pilmoor were sent to this country, in conformity to the request of captain Webb and the brethren. A few days after their landing they wrote to Mr. Wesley:

Mr. Pilmoor says, "I have preached several times, and the people flock to hear in multitudes. Sunday evening I went out upon the common. I had the stage appointed for the horse-race, for my pulpit, and I think between four and five hundred hearers, who heard with attention still as night. Here seems to be a great and effectual door opening in this country, and I hope many souls will be gathered in. The people in general like to hear the word, and seem to have some ideas of salvation by grace."

Mr. Boardman observes, "Our house contains about seventeen hundred hearers. About a third part of those who attend the preaching get in; the rest are glad to hear without. There appears a great willingness in the Americans to hear the word. They have no preaching in some part of the back settlements. I doubt not but an effectual door will be opened among them."

At the conference at Bristol in August 1771, a proposition was made that more of the itinerant preachers should visit America—Mr. Asbury and Mr. Wright offered themselves for the work, and were accepted; in October following they landed in this country. The work of God in the United States in its commencement was much hindered by the laxity of discipline which prevailed among the people, who had not been used to maintain the strictness of the regulations which governed the British societies; Mr. Asbury had great difficulty to enforce order and to preserve regularity. The first attempt to introduce the discipline with firmness, that I have been able to discover was by bishop Asbury in New-York, in 1772, where after much disquietude, he established regular preaching, and obliged the society meetings to be held privately, whereas the doors had formerly been opened; but in many points he was so strongly opposed that he was obliged to consent.

The following extract from bishop Asbury's Journal will shew the nature of the opposition which the ministers of the establishment have always made to the spread of evangelical piety.

Friday, Dec. 12. Went 12 miles into Kent county, and had a great many people to hear me. But before preaching, one Mr. R. a church minister, came to me and desired to know who I was, and whether I was licenced. I told him who I was. He spoke great swelling words, and told me he had authority over the people, and was charged with the care of their souls. He also told me that I could not and should not preach; and if I did, he would proceed against me according to law. I let him know that I came to preach, and preach I would; and farther asked him if he had authority to bind the consciences of the people, or if he was a justice of the peace; and told him I thought he had nothing to do with me. He charged me with making schism. I told him I did not draw the people from the church; and asked him if his church was then open? He told me that I hindered people from their work; but I asked him if fairs and horse-races did not hinder them? And farther told him that I came to help him. He said he had not hired me for an assistant, and did not want my help. I told him, if there were no swearers or other sinners, *he* was sufficient. But, said he, what did you come for? I replied, to turn sinners to God. He said, cannot I do that as well as you? I told him that I had authority from God. He then laughed at me, and said you are a fine fellow indeed! I told him I did not do this to invalidate his authority, and also gave him to understand that I did not wish to dispute with him, but he said he had business with me, and came into the house in a great rage. I began to preach, and urged the people to repent and turn from all their transgressions, so iniquity should not prove their ruin. After preaching the parson went out and told the people, they did wrong in coming to hear me; and said I spoke against learning. Whereas, I only spoke to this purpose,—when a man turneth from all sin, he will adorn every character in life, both in church and state."

In the latter end of the year 1772, bishop Asbury endeavoured to establish order among the societies in Maryland. After preaching at a quarterly meeting he says, " We proceeded to our temporal business, and considered the following propositions.

1. What are our collections? We found them sufficient to defray our expences.

2. How are the preachers stationed?

3. Shall we be strict in our society meetings, and not admit strangers? Agreed.

4. Shall we drop preaching in the day-time through the week? Not agreed to.

5. Will the people be contented without our administering the sacraments? J. K. was neuter; brother S. pleaded much for the ordinances; and so did the people, who appeared to be much biassed by him. I told them I would not agree to it at that time, and insisted on our abiding by our rules. But Mr. B. had given them their way at the quarterly meeting held here before, and I was obliged to connive at some things for the sake of peace."

6. Shall we make collections weekly, to pay the preachers' board and expences? This was not agreed to; we then inquired into the moral characters of the preachers and exhorters. Only one exhorter was found any way doubtful, and we have great hopes of him. Great love subsisted among us in this meeting, and we parted in peace."

At a quarterly meeting held on the thirtieth of March, the discipline was still further introduced, after preaching, says bishop Asbury, " the following questions were propounded, viz.

1. Are there no disorderly persons in our classes? It was thought not.

2. Does not dram-drinking too much prevail among our people?

3. Do none contract debts without due care to pay them? We found that this evil is much avoided among our people.

4. Are the band-meetings kept up?

5. Is there nothing immoral in any of our preachers?

6. What preachers travel now, and where are they

stationed? It was then urged that none must break our rules, under the penalty of being excluded from our connexion. All was settled in the most amicable manner."

During the spring of year 1773, Mr. Rankin, and Mr. Shadford, arrived in this country, having been appointed by Mr. Wesley to support and aid their brethren. Not long after their arrival the first conference of the American Methodist ministers was held at Philadelphia: the introduction of general regularity and order now took place: the following rules were established by the consent and authority of the conference.

1. The old Methodist doctrine and discipline shall be enforced and maintained, amongst all our societies in America.

2. Any preacher who acts otherwise, cannot be retained amongst us as a fellow-labourer in the vineyard.

3. No preacher in our connexion shall be permitted to administer the ordinances at this time; except Mr. S. and he under the peculiar direction of the assistant.

4. No person shall be admitted, more than once or twice, to our love feasts or society-meetings—without becoming a member.

5. No preacher shall be permitted to re-print our books, without the approbation of Mr. Wesley, and the consent of his brethren.

6. Every assistant is to send an account of the work of God in his circuit, to the general assistant."

Monday, April 18th, 1774. " This day," says bishop Asbury, " the foundation of our house in Baltimore was laid. Who could have expected that two men, once amongst the chief of sinners, would have engaged in so great an undertaking for the cause of the blessed Jesus? He hath touched and changed their hearts. He hath moved them to this acceptable undertaking ; he will surely complete it; and raise up a people to serve him in this place."

The Revolutionary contest impeded the progress of the gospel exceedingly ; and some imprudencies in a few of the ministers who publickly espoused the British cause, excited a suspicion with regard to the whole body of the Methodists and particularly the preachers. At the conference near Dear Creek in 1777, the English missionaries generally declared their determination to leave America : and during the following months when the war had become general and there was no safety for those preachers who had interfered with the political concerns of the states ; they all returned to England. Bishop Asbury alone remained, to fulfil the duties of the mission to which the Providence of God had called him : and although he never expressed his opinion respecting the propriety of the separation, he was partially confined during the spring of the year 1778. The following extract from his diary shews the variety of those mental exercises which he must have experienced. April 11th. " I was at a loss to know what to do: my time was useless in respect to others ; though I carefully improved it for my own spiritual advantage, which, for some years past, had been in a degree neglected, on account of my great attention to the souls of others. And I know not what to determine, whether to deliver myself into the hands of men, to embrace the first opportunity to depart, or to wait till Providence shall farther direct. The reason of this retirement was as follows. From March 10, 1778, on conscientious principles I was a non-juror, and could not preach in the state of Maryland ; and therefore withdrew to the Delaware state, where the clergy were not required to take the state oath : though with a clear conscience, I could have taken the oath of the Delaware state, had it been required ; and would have done it, had I not been prevented by a tender fear of hurting the scrupulous consciences of others." During his seclusion in the state of Delaware the conference was held in 1779, at which he was appointed general assistant of the Methodist church in America, which choice was ratified by the conference held in Virginia in 1782. At this period, the societies were destitute of the sacraments, except in two or three of the cities; and they were so grieved on this account, and so influenced the minds of the preachers by their incessant complaints, that a considerable number of them earnestly importuned Mr. Asbury to take proper measures, that the people might enjoy the privileges of all other churches, and no longer be deprived of the christian sacraments. Mr. Asbury's situation and opinions induced him to refuse them any redress: the majority of the preachers therefore withdrew and chose from themselves three senior brethren who ordained others by the imposition of their hands. The preachers thus set apart, administered the sacraments to those whom they judged proper to receive it. However, through the labour and attention of Mr. Asbury, a perfect union took place.

After the lapse of some time Mr. Asbury was permitted again to travel in safety through the states: through the influence of a letter of recommendation from John Dickinson.

Amidst all the hurry, confusion and distress which many of the states experienced from the conflicting troops, the gospel was propagated, its truths were more widely diffused, and after that the Virginia division had been healed, the societies received large and constant additions.

Peace having been established between the United States, and Great-Britain, the intercourse was opened betwixt the Methodist societies of both countries. Mr. Wesley received from Mr. Asbury a full account of the progress of the gospel during the war. He informed

Mr. Wesley that the people were extremely uneasy for want of the sacraments: that thousands of their children were unbaptized, and that the members of the societies in general had not partaken of the Lord's supper during many years.

Having considered the subject, Mr. Wesley, at the conference held in Leeds in 1784, declared his intention of sending Dr. Coke and some other preachers to America. Mr. Whatcoat and Mr. Vasey offered themselves as missionaries for that purpose, and were accepted. Before they sailed, Mr. Wesley abridged the Common Prayer-book of the Church of England, and wrote to Dr. Coke, then in London, desiring him to meet him in Bristol, when he ordained Mr. Whatcoat and Mr. Vasey presbyters for America: and, afterwards ordained Dr. Coke a superintendent, giving him the following letter to be printed, and circulated in the United States.

BRISTOL, September 10, 1784.

To Dr. Coke, Mr. Asbury and our Brethren in North America.

"By a very uncommon train of Providences, many of the provinces of North-America are totally disjoined from their mother country, and erected into independent states. The English government has no authority over them either civil or ecclesiastical, any more than over the states of Holland. A civil authority is exercised over them, partly by congress and by the provincial assemblies. But no one either exercises or claims any ecclesiastical authority at all. In this peculiar situation some thousands of the inhabitants of these states desire my advice; and in compliance with their desire, I have drawn up a little sketch.

"Lord King's account of the primitive church convinced me many years ago, that bishops and presbyters are the same order, and consequently have the same right to ordain. For many years I have been importuned from time to time, to exercise this right, by ordaining part of our travelling preachers. But I have still refused: not only for peace sake; but because I was determined, as little as possible to violate the established order of the national church to which I belonged.

"But the case is widely different between England and America. Here there are bishops who have a legal jurisdiction. In America there are none, neither any parish ministers. So that for some hundred miles together there is none either to baptize or to administer the Lord's supper. Here therefore my scruples are at end: and I conceive myself at liberty, to appoint and send labourers into the harvest.

"I have accordingly appointed Dr. Coke and Mr. Francis Asbury, as joint superintendents over our brethren in North-America: as also Richard Whatcoat and Thomas Vasey, to act as elders among them, by baptizing and administering the Lord's supper. And I have prepared a liturgy, little differing from that of the Church of England, I think the best constituted national church in the world, which I advise all the travelling preachers to use on the Lord's day, in all the congregations, reading the Litany only on Wednesdays and Fridays, and praying extempore on all other days. I also advise the elders to administer the supper of the Lord on every Lord's day.

"If any one will point out a more rational and scriptural way, of feeding and guiding those poor sheep in the wilderness, I will gladly embrace it. At present, I cannot see any better method than that I have taken.

"It has indeed been proposed, to desire the English bishops, to ordain part of our preachers for America. But to this I object, 1. I desired the bishop of London to ordain only one; but could not prevail: 2. If they consented, we know the slowness of their proceedings; but the matter admits of no delay. 3. If they would ordain them *now*, they would likewise expect to govern them. And how grievously would this entangle us? 4. As our American brethren are now totally disentangled both from the state, and from the English hierarchy, we dare not entangle them again, either with the one or the other. They are now at full liberty, simply to follow the scriptures and the primitive church. And we judge it best that they should stand fast in that liberty, wherewith God has so strangely made them free.

JOHN WESLEY."

Doctor Coke arrived in this country in December 1784, and early in January 1785, a general conference was held in Baltimore, when the mode of church government which was recommended by Mr. Wesley, was adopted by the Methodist preachers and the ministers who arrived from England were consequently received. At that conference Mr. Asbury was *elected* jointly with Dr. Coke to superintend all the Methodist societies, but as the latter's engagements precluded him from residing in this country, the general conference in the year 1800, elected the late Mr. Whatcoat, to supply the deficiency which was occasioned by the Doctor's non-residence and to ease Mr. Asbury of part of the augmented fatigue and burden arising from the prodigious increase of the societies and the gradually extending dissemination of divine truth.

The doctrines of the Methodist church in England have already been detailed in chapter V; and the minutes of the British conferences being considered the standard of faith; as such they were determined to be the principles of the Methodists in this country.

The Methodist Creed of faith is contained in 25 articles, most of which are borrowed from the Prayer book of the church of England. The subjects are " the trinity—the son of God—the sufficiency of the scriptures for salvation—the Old Testament—original sin—free grace—justification—good works—works of supererogation—sin after justification—the church—purgatory—speaking in the church in an unknown tongue—the sacraments—baptism—the Lord's supper—both kinds—one oblation of Christ upon the cross—marriage of ministers—rites and ceremonies of churches—rulers of the United States—christian's goods—christian's oath."

The church of England prayer book has been considerably abridged for particular occasions—as for the sacramental service—the baptism of infants and adults—the celebration of matrimony—the burial of the dead—and the ordination of ministers—but these forms are from a variety of causes increasingly disused; and the Methodist societies will soon be divested of the few remains of the English church which yet nominally subsist among them.

The whole body of Methodists in the United States are divided into seven portions under seven conferences.

The New-England conference includes the district of Maine, and the Boston, New-London, and Vermont districts.

The New-York conference comprehends the New-York, Pittsfield, Albany, and Upper Canada districts.

The Philadelphia conference includes the remainder of the state of New-York, all New-Jersey, that part of Pennsylvania which lies on the east of the Susquehannah

METHOD

river, except what belongs to the Susquehanna district, the state of Delaware, the Eastern Shore of Maryland, and all the rest of the Peninsula.

The Baltimore conference includes the remainder of Pennsylvania, the Western Shore of Maryland, the Northern Neck of Virginia, and the Green Briar district.

The Virginia conference includes all that part of Virginia which lies on the south side of the Rappahannock river, and east of the Blue Ridge, and all that part of North-Carolina which lies on the north side of Cape-Fear river, except Wilmington, also the circuits which are situated on the branches of the Yadkin.

The South-Carolina conference includes the remainder of North-Carolina, South-Carolina, and Georgia.

The Western conference includes the states of Tennessee, Kentucky, and Ohio, and that part of Virginia which lies west of the great river Kanawha, with the Illinois, and the Natchez. The bishops have authority, to appoint other yearly conferences in the interval of the general conference, if a sufficiency of new circuits be formed for that purpose.

The following extract from a letter written by Mr. Waters the first American Methodist minister, on the temporal economy of the Methodist societies tends to elucidate the subject of their church government.

" That there should be those who through prejudice, think the Methodists since they have had bishops amongst them, to be quite a different people, is not strange. But is it not strange, that any who know them from the beginning, should admit such a thought? All must know that names do not alter the nature of things. We have from the beginning had one amongst us who has superintended the whole work. At first this person was solely appointed by Mr. Wesley, and called the general assistant; at a time when there was none but European preachers on the continent. But why was the name of general assistant ever changed? The Methodists in England and in America, formerly did not call themselves a particular church; but a religious society in connexion with different churches, but mostly with the Episcopal church. After the revolutionary war, the Episcopal clergy became very scarce, and in far the greatest number of our societies, we had no way of receiving the ordinances of baptism and the Lord's supper. It was this that led many of our preachers, to take upon them the administration of the ordinances. Mr. Rankin, who was our first general assistant, after staying the time in this country he came for, returned home. This was at a time when we had no intercourse with England, and Mr. Asbury, the only old preacher that determined in those perilous times, to give up his parents, country, and all his natural connections, was finally and unanimously chosen by the preachers assembled in conference, our general assistant. He continued such, until the year 1784, when Dr. Coke came over, and not the name only of general assistant was changed to that of superintendent, but we formed ourselves into a separate church. This change was proposed to us by Mr. Wesley, after we had craved his advice on the subject; but it could not take effect till adopted by us: which was done in a deliberate, formal manner, at a conference called for that purpose. After a few years, the name from superintendent was changed to bishop. But from first to last, the business of general assistant, superintendent, or bishop, has been the same; only since we have become a distinct church, he has, with the assistance of two or three elders ordained our ministers; he presides in our conferences, and in case of an equal division on a question, he has the casting vote; but in no instance whatever, has he a negative. He has also the stationing of all the travelling preachers, under

METHODISM.

certain limitations. Which power as it is given him by the general conference, so it can be lessened, or taken from him at any time conference sees fit. But while he superintends the whole work he cannot interfere with the particular charge of any of the preachers in their stations. To see that the preachers fill their places with propriety, and to understand the state of every station, or circuit, that he may the better make the appointments of the preachers, is no doubt, no small part of his duty; but he has nothing to do with receiving, censuring, or excluding members: this belongs wholly to the stationed preacher and members. His power is great, but it intirely respects the travelling preachers. It never can from the nature of things, be put into the hands of any man, but one in whom the whole have the highest confidence, and that no longer than he faithfully executes his trust. I know of no way the preachers can be as well stationed, as by one that goes through the whole work, and is without his local prejudices in favour of, or against any place: as he seldom stays longer in one place than another. The whole body of preachers in conference cannot station themselves; and a committee chosen by them for that purpose, would find many insurmountable difficulties: as they could have but a very superficial knowledge of the particular gifts of many of the preachers, or the state of many of the circuits. The sacrifice that a preacher makes in giving up his choice, and going wherever he is appointed, is not small. But no one is worthy of the name of a travelling preacher, that does not cheerfully go any where he can, for the general good. If he be so circumstanced, that he cannot go any where, and every where that is thought best, he should say so, when he first offers himself to conference: If it so happen, after he has been travelling, he ought to let it be known as soon as possible; and whenever he cannot be accommodated with a circuit that he can fill, he ought to be content to stop till he can. Every station in life has its difficulties. But this cannot be remedied in the present state of things. It is then our duty to do the best we can, under unavoidable difficulties. Better many individuals suffer, than the work at large should. I would rather be in the more general work; yet if circumstances prevent, let me be content, to act in some humble way."

It must be remarked that the doctrines of the Methodist church are stedfastly adhered to by the preachers—whilst the forms in the administration of the gospel ordinances are generally omitted.——The form of prayer is not used at all, and many of the ministers conduct the service altogether extempore—whilst others sometimes use the form of administering the sacrament and the funeral service. But in the act of receiving the Lord's supper—kneeling is not considered indispensable. Indeed there is a probability that these forms would never have been introduced, if Mr. Wesley and Dr. Coke had not been so partial to the English established Church: and the reason for their rejection is obvious, they circumscribe the mind, and destroy the energy of divine worship so much, that the life of religion is lost in "sounding brass and a tinkling cymbal."— But as it respects the admission of members, their rejection, their conduct, their characters, &c. the Methodists adhere to the genuine spirit of their discipline. These remarks will rectify any mistake which might be made by those who judge of the Methodist economy from the volume published by the societies— as that does not notice any departure from the printed regulations.

CONCLUSION.

IF we contemplate the history of the Christian Church since the period of Constantine's accession to the Romish imperial throne, and the public establishment of Christianity as a national religion, a variety of conflicting passions torture the agonized heart. The corruptions which were introduced, the idolatrous worship which was adopted, the infernal doctrines which were admitted instead of the holy truths of the scriptures, the Egyptian obscurity which overwhelmed all Christendom in tangible darkness, and the abominable impieties, blasphemies, cruelties, and impurities of those who dared to call themselves the ministers and disciples of the Saviour of mankind during several centuries, fill the mind with disgust and horror. The Providence of God however brought to a conclusion the dominion of the "Man of Sin;" Luther imbued with the thunder of Boanerges, with great gifts, great grace, and apostolick zeal and fortitude, undauntedly and fearlessly opposed the wrath and cruelty of Popery; and proper instruments being raised up to assist, protect and encourage him, the dawnings of that evangelical light appeared, which has since blazed into perfect day, notwithstanding all the efforts of infidelity, Jesuitism, and hypocrisy to oppose it. But the national church in England, choked the growth of " pure and undefiled religion," and by the heaviest and vilest oppressions, almost destroyed vital Christianity. In France, the " Son of Pertion's" agents, the Jesuits, were so successful as to persuade a silly and haughty monarch to root out of his kingdom, the only industrious, loyal people who lived in his dominions—and the genuine temper and spirit of the lowly Jesus was preserved by very few of those who called themselves by his name. But the prophecies must be fulfilled, the kingdom of God must be extended—three individuals, animated by peculiar talents and grace, possessing much energy and perseverance, have been the instruments of dispersing the gospel throughout Great Britain and America; their example stimulated others; the hand of God co-operated with them; sinners were converted, souls were saved, darkness fled before the sun of righteousness, and idolatry, superstition and infidelity withdraw, as the sweet sounds of redemption approach.

The diffusion of Christianity through the labours of the Messrs. Wesley's and Mr. Whitfield, is almost unprecedented since the primitive ages of the Christian church. Not to mention the additional stimulus which their example gave to all the dissenting churches in England, the two bodies of Christians who boast of these ministers as their spiritual fathers, amount at present to nearly 250,000 professed disciples of Jesus, in the British European dominions; and excepting one doctrinal distinction, are all of one mind, actuated by the same zeal, and striving earnestly to unfold the banner of the gospel of Christ.

Let us rejoice that we live in that period of the world when God has graciously infused into his people a spirit of faith and prayer—when we already see the idolatrous superstitions of the Papists banishing from the earth—when the throne which supports the delusions of Mohammed must fall, amidst the jarring interests of the conflicting European governments—when the ignorance, stupidity and blindness of the Greek church must vanish—and when the Heathens are beginning to sing the songs of Zion, and to hail the name of Jesus, as " a sovereign balm for every wound."

The gospel is now disseminating with great rapidity. The Missionary Society in London have a large and "goodly company" of ministers and others among the Hottentots: they have an establishment of missionaries in the South Sea islands—in France—and in Germany—and application has lately been made to that society for protestant puritanical ministers and the protestant testament, from Naples in Italy and Canton in China. The situation of Germany is completely changed within these two years—the nails of the "Whore of Babylon" have been só clipped—that she can scratch no more; the friends of truth are consequently making increased exertions: and hopes are entertained that no long space of time will elapse, ere the thunders of the gospel shall be sounded in the midst of "Babylon the great."——In the East-Indies, the Baptists have a very large mission—the New Testament is already translated into one of the languages—and the missionaries now possess the means to furnish it in six different tongues—they have extended themselves from Calcutta nearly 500 miles into the interior; and the seed which has been so long sown begins to promise a harvest.——The Moravians have missions in the North of Europe and in the West-Indies—the Methodists have a mission in the West-Indies and in the British American dominions—and the work is advancing in every part of Europe.—The head of the church has kindled a missionary flame in the hearts of his people, which is strengthened and increased, by the success with which he deigns to honour them.

If we advert to the United States, what a powerful instance have we of the success of the gospel! The Congregationalists, Presbyterians and Baptists, are all striving to spread the savour of the Redeemer's religion, and the Lord adds to the church daily such as " shall be saved." Two hundred years ago, the religion of Jesus was not known on the Continent of America. Now in those parts of the states which have been some time settled, the gospel is preached. Fifty years since, it is almost certain that there were not five Methodists, strictly so called, from Maine to Georgia. At this period they pervade every part of the Union, and have extended their labours amongst the Papists both in upper and lower Canada—From Niagara to Penobscot—from Portland to St. Mary's—from New-York to Albany—from Montreal to Pittsburg, and from Baltimore to New-Orleans—few of the inhabited districts are entirely bereft of the gospel—through the labours and self-denial of the Methodist travelling preachers.——Already has a door been opened amongst the benighted multitudes in Louisiana, and great hopes are indulged that the message of the Lord will be productive of fruit.

It may be presumed that the Methodist church at this period includes more members than any other church on the Continent. During the last year 103 travelling preachers were admitted upon trial into the connection—and 14020 additional professors of Christianity joined the church—such a prodigious increase to one church only, augurs well for the United States, and authorises a hope that the mercy of the Lord is still to be continued amongst us.

The following Table has been carefully compiled from the Annual Minutes of the Conferences, it shews the increase of the Methodist church, as nearly as the inaccuracy of the returns in some instances, and the changing of the ministers' stations in others would admit—and I trust will not be deemed the most uninteresting part of the volume.

A TABLE

Exhibiting the number of Itinerant Ministers and Members in the Methodist Societies throughout the United States, from 1773, the year in which the first Conference was held in Philadelphia, until the year 1807.

Year.	Number of Itinerant Preachers.	Total members in Society.
1773	10	1,160

The number of the Preachers was computed by the list of Stations: hence it includes those who were admitted into full connection at the conferences, those who remained upon trial, and those who were admitted upon trial, during the year which is mentioned in the table.

1774	17	2,073
1775	19	3,148
1776	24	4,921
1777	36	6,968
1778	29	6,095
1779	32	8,577

The diminution in the number of the Preachers, during the years 1778 and 1779, was owing to the separation which occurred in consequence of the disputes upon the propriety of the administration of the ordinances of Baptism and the Lord's Supper; to the return to Europe of several ministers who were partizans of the British during the revolutionary contest; to the seclusion from their publick labours, and to the retirement, to which some others were obliged to submit.

1780	44	8,504
1781	54	10,539
1782	59	11,785
1783	82	13,740
1784	83	14,988
1785	104	18,000